THE
GOSPEL
of
INCLUSION

THE GOSPEL of INCLUSION

Reaching Beyond
Religious Fundamentalism
to the True Love
of God and Self

BISHOP
CARLTON PEARSON

ATRIA PAPERBACK

New York   London   Toronto   Sydney

ATRIA PAPERBACK
A Division of Simon & Schuster, Inc.
1230 Avenue of the Americas
New York, NY 10020

First Atria Paperback edition March 2009

ATRIA PAPERBACK and colophon are trademarks of Simon & Schuster, Inc.

For information about special discounts for bulk purchases, please contact Simon & Schuster Special Sales at 1-800-456-6798 or business@simonandschuster.com.

Designed by Nancy Singer

Manufactured in the United States of America

10   9   8   7   6   5   4   3   2   1

The Library of Congress has cataloged the hardcover edition as follows:

Pearson, Carlton.
The gospel of inclusion : reaching beyond religious fundamentalism to the true love of God and self / Carlton Pearson.
p.   cm.
Includes bibliographical references (p. [303]–305).
1. Social conflict—Religious aspects. 2. Peace—Religious aspects. 3. Religious tolerance. I. Title.

BL65.S62 P43   2008
201'.7—dc22   2008271917

ISBN-13: 978-1-4165-8043-0
ISBN-10:   1-4165-8043-3
ISBN-13: 978-1-4165-4793-8 (pbk)
ISBN-10:   1-4165-4793-2 (pbk)

CONTENTS

THE
GOSPEL
of
INCLUSION

INTRODUCTION

> Find out just what any people will quietly submit to, and you have the exact measure of the injustice and wrong which will be imposed upon them. If there is no struggle, there is no progress. Those who profess to favor freedom yet depreciate agitation are men who want the crops without plowing up the ground. They want rain without thunder. They want the ocean without the awful roar of its many waters. . . . This struggle may be a moral one; or it may be a physical one; or it may be both moral and physical; but it must be a struggle.
>
> —*Frederick Douglass*

Carlton, we are concerned about the comment 'The whole world is saved, they just don't know it.' We feel this is misleading and does not reflect the opinion of the university, or of Scriptures."

The speaker was one of the most prominent television pastors in America, with his own television network, millions of faithful followers, and thousands of members in his Texas congregation. I had preached in his church. We both sat on the Board of Regents of Oral Roberts University.

His voice was friendly, but his tone was anxious. At the time, I was heavily involved in working to get George W. Bush in the

White House for his first term as president. Because of my political commitments, I was not able to meet with a group of board members who wanted to challenge my position on Christian doctrine—a position that, according to them, had shaken the very foundations of the Kingdom of God on earth, as it were.

By the time the phone call ended, it was clear that these "friends" had made up their minds: I was wrong and dangerous. I knew I would be either forced to change my position or "encouraged" to resign from the board. It was hard to accept. I was an alumnus of the school, I had served on the Board of Regents for over fifteen years, and I had been close to the founder and his family for over thirty years. I resigned. I wanted to avoid conflict, but it was also important that I be free to pursue this controversial, exciting new direction in my ministry, even if it meant moving away from some of my respected friends and colaborers in Christ.

As I hung up the phone, I knew I was in for one of the roughest rides of my life as a Christian minister. I knew that I was facing the possibility of losing nearly everything I had built over the last thirty years of my life. My crime? I had rediscovered an ancient truth that would forever change my life and my perspective of God. I had begun to preach the Gospel of Inclusion.

A LITTLE CHAT WITH THE CREATOR

In the spring of 1996, while in conversational thought with God (what some would call prayer), I had a profound experience that transformed my worldview—a view that had been steeped in a particular religious mind-set for over forty years. One evening I was watching the nightly news, as I have done religiously for the last twenty-five years. My daughter, Majesté, was less than a year old. I was holding her in one arm and eating my supper with the other. I was watching a news report concerning the return of the

Hutus and Tutsis from Rwanda to Uganda after months of exile, where they had been persecuted and practically starved to death. The news report showed women and children with bellies swollen, collapsing to the ground, and mothers with withered breasts, flies gathered in the corners of their eyes and mouths, and bones protruding through their black, leathery skin.

Feeling guilty and angry, I berated God concerning His "earth project," which appeared to me to be a failure:

"God, I don't know how you can sit on your throne there in heaven and let these poor people drop to the ground hungry, heartbroken, and lost, and just randomly suck them into hell, thinking nothing of it, and be a 'sovereign God,' not to mention a 'God of love.' "

There was an eerie silence before I heard a voice respond within me:

"Is that what you think we're doing, sucking them all into hell?"

"That's what I've been taught," I responded angrily.

"And what would change that?"

"They need to get saved so they can go to heaven," I answered confidently.

"And how would that happen?"

I responded, "Somebody needs to go over there and get them saved by preaching the Gospel to them."

"Well then," the voice resounded, "if you really believe that, why don't you put down your food and your baby, turn off your big-screen TV, and catch the first plane over there and get them saved?"

I burst into an emotional mix of tears of grief, compassion, shame, guilt, and anger. Then I retorted, "Don't put that guilt on me, Lord. I'm doing the best I can! I can't leave this little girl and boy you gave me. If you wanted me to do what you've just suggested, you should have made that clear to me before you gave me this family. I'm doing the best I can, besides, I can't save this whole world!"

"Precisely," the voice responded. "That's what we already did. But these people don't know it, and, regretfully, most of you who claim to be my followers don't believe it. If you would spend your life living and giving this message to people, you wouldn't see such painful and pitiful global pictures."

The voice concluded: "We're not sucking those dear people into hell. Can't you see they're already there? We're bringing them into heaven before they suffer even more in the hell you have created for them and continue to create for yourselves and others all over the planet. We redeemed and reconciled all of humanity at Calvary. That is what the Cross was and is all about."

It had taken God less than five minutes to unravel the truth I had lived by and reshape my understanding of the purpose of my life to come.

WE ARE ALL THE CHOSEN PEOPLE

This experience was the beginning of a total reexamination of everything I had ever believed about God, the universe, and my relationship to it. It challenged what I believed and why I believed it. I began reassessing my worldview and how it was related to my perception of God, creation, Christianity, heaven, and hell.

God does not show partiality when it comes to people, but He does have a distinct purpose for humanity. It is within the circle of that purpose that He unconditionally loves and embraces all people on the planet. As Christians, we are taught that the Jews were chosen for a purpose, that through the Jewish nation, God wanted to present to the world the idea of one God (monotheism) and one ultimate hope for all revealed through a Messiah. This was to address the perception that salvation was necessary, and that the idea of hostility between man and God was false. Messianic consciousness is the expectation of victory over human, spiritual, political, social, and physical conflicts.

The New Testament says, "Understand, then, that those who believe are children of Abraham . . . and heirs according to the promise" (Galatians 3:7 and 3:29). In other words, the blessing of the children of Israel has become a blessing to all. The promise God gave to Abraham, that all nations would be blessed through his seed (Genesis 12:3b), has been actualized in Christ Consciousness and in the Christ Principle.

> The moment we fully and vitally realize who and what we are, we then begin to build our own world even as God builds his.
>
> —*Ralph Waldo Trine,* In Tune with the Infinite

Psst, Everybody IS Saved Already

Christ Consciousness is each person's understanding of the truth that Christ has already achieved what He set out to achieve: total salvation. Nothing else is needed. Our mission in ministry is to awaken people to the extraordinary love and hope of that truth— to become not necessarily Christian but *Christ-like* in bringing humankind together as one in spiritual consciousness. Being Christ-like doesn't necessarily mean being a Christian; after all, neither Christ nor God is. My belief is not only in the Christ Person but in the Christ Principle.

The blasphemy I stand accused of is the simple message of the Gospel of Inclusion: the whole world is saved, but they just don't know it. Saved not only from hell and eternal damnation, but saved from itself—saved from its erroneous perceptions of God and good. Saved from our misperceptions of Self and Savior. God is not our enemy. God is not the antagonist from whom we need protection or salvation. It is my intent to make it clear in this book that what we really need is to be saved from ourselves, from our erroneous perceptions and presumptions. I believe that we need to be saved from the concept that a malicious, capricious God is waiting for us to sin so He can fling us into hell. Such concepts are both superstitious and pagan.

We do not need to be saved from God; we need to be saved from religion. We need to be saved from perceptions of God that portray Him as an angry deity with a customized torture chamber called hell, managed by a malcontent called the devil, where we may be forever consigned because we didn't believe, didn't believe correctly, or didn't obey. If we can get past these preconceived notions, maybe we can start loving each other without prejudice. We can stop worrying about other people's lifestyles and start building our "love style." We have spent a lot of energy over the centuries trying to figure out ways to keep God from killing or persecuting us. All religions assume that role, presuming that God is angry and needs to be appeased. In an effort to placate this angry God, we have created doctrines, dogmas, and disciplines that have contributed to the global conflicts that prevent world peace.

It is time to change. But we cannot change our outer world until we change our inner world. We must change our concepts about the One Intelligence by which this world is created. When we rediscover these truths, they will threaten all that we have ever believed about God. As Robert Farrar Capon declared, "The truth that makes us free is always ticking away like a time bomb in the basement of everybody's church." The truth of the Gospel of Inclusion will blow apart our preconceived ideas about God and His plans for humanity.

Slaves on a Holy Plantation

Religion resists progress. It is a form of witchcraft with which man has become familiar. We know the rites, rituals, doctrines, and disciplines, and we have become dependent on them. They have become a manipulative, fear-based force that holds millions of people hostage. Psychologists call this "addictive codependency."

Religion is the "plantation" on which many people live as slaves or indentured servants. They assume they are better off in the care of the manipulators of their faith than in the freedom and grace God has provided for them. Many religious leaders and denominations act like the old Southern plantation owners, keeping their slaves ignorant, convincing them that they are better off on the plantation. They have created doctrines that persuade them that they are better off living in bondage to an angry God rather than living in spiritual peace with their Emancipator. The emancipator of the American slaves was Abraham Lincoln. The "spiritual emancipator" of slaves to sin, death, and human error is Christ—*not Christianity.*

Christianity seeks to resolve a presumed conflict between a hostile God and His disobedient creation. The Gospel of Inclusion says that the conflict no longer exists, and never really did. Religion manufactured it. This is the message Christ was trying to get across to his disciples and all who would listen. If this premise is true, then maybe the religions of the world, including Christianity, that seek to resolve this age-old conflict are not as necessary as we think. In fact, they may be the cause of perpetual conflict between people who want to get along but are prohibited by the fears cooked up in a pot of religious presuppositions or erroneous man-made assumptions.

If you believe in any God at all, why not believe in One who is great and benevolent enough to preserve everything He (or It) created; One who values His creation enough to redeem it when it

appears lost? The Gospel of Inclusion refutes traditional doctrine and man-made dogmas that reflect human fears, prejudices,
and hatreds. Instead it is about pure faith in a God whom the
eighteenth-century theologian Jonathan Edwards, author of the
sermon "Sinners in the Hands of an Angry God," would not recognize. What if our codependency on religion has replaced any
chance of spiritual intimacy between the soul and God? That is
the chasm Inclusion tries to span.

A NEW, IMPROVED GOD

In writing and studying for this book, I came to the initially stunning conclusion that God is not a Christian, even though I use
Christian Scripture and principles to put forth my premise of Inclusion consciousness. The concepts and principles expressed in
these pages are based upon fundamental theological ideas that lie
at the heart of Christianity. While they are in many ways opposed
to the popular doctrines that many mistake for faith, they are true
to the purest truths of the Christ Consciousness: our faith in a
Creator who loves creation and has an eternal and redemptive purpose for it.

Do we need Jesus to protect us from God? Or is Jesus about
reconnecting us to God in consciousness? If so, has not the Christ
of Christianity already accomplished the work of the "Father God"
he preached? Is it, the work of redemption, finished or isn't it?
While these are shockingly audacious questions to some, the answers lead to the discovery of a "new and improved" image of
God, one more consistent with *agapao* (a Greek word meaning
"unconditional love") and benevolence. The so-called word of
God, referred to as the Bible, is less the true *Logos* (Greek for
"word") of God but rather the word of man about God, as man
perceives Him or Deity.

It is imperative for people to know and recognize this powerful, liberating truth. To those who ask what if I am wrong, I respond that I would rather be wrong in overestimating the love and the grace of God than in underestimating it. I would rather err on the side of the goodness and the greatness of God than on the side of His presumed pettiness and wrath. It is more important to believe what Jesus taught about God than what the churches have taught us about Jesus.

First of all, I could never be as wrong as God is right. Second, I don't necessarily profess to be right as much as I profess to be "real." *Right* is a relative term that means different things to different people in differing cultures and consciences. Being real is more important to me than being right according to someone else's estimation. "To thine own self be true." Many so-called church people insist that I am preaching some new doctrine, and some go so far as to exclaim that it is "doctrines of demons" (1 Timothy 4:1, New King James Version), referring to a passage in the Greek New Testament.

However, the message of Inclusion, also known as Universal Reconciliation, is not new. It was the widely held position and consensus of the most prominent and respected early church fathers and founders throughout the first five hundred years of church history. Therefore I am not presenting a new discovery; I am recovering a lost piece of biblical interpretation and history that should be re-presented to the modern world as the original New Testament or New Covenant plan for world peace (that is, if you believe in the Bible at least in principle as a point of reference). The Gospel of Inclusion has profound global, social, and even political implications.

> The first thing that goes when you begin to think is your theology. If you stick too long to a theological point of view, you become stagnant without vitality.
>
> —Oswald Chambers

GOD'S HERETIC

John Milton, the sixteenth-century British author, observed, "A man may be a heretic in the truth; and if he believes things only because his pastor says so, or the assembly so determines, without knowing other reason, though his belief be true, the very truth he holds becomes his heresy." The doctrine of Inclusion, Universal Reconciliation, is an explosive issue. Many mainstream religious leaders have disagreed with my position, and some have even called it heresy.

So be it. "False doctrine" does not necessarily make one a heretic, but an evil, vengeful, and prejudicial heart can make any doctrine heretical.

The idea that God is not a Christian flies in the face of centuries of traditional thought. It demands not just a leap of faith but of mind. I believe that Christians and all people deserve the freedom not only to think but to ask questions and question answers. Were I not a recognized leader in the born-again Evangelical and charismatic/Pentecostal Christian world, this book and the concepts I preach would not be regarded as such a threat. If I were considered a liberal non-Christian, they would be all but ignored.

What shakes my community so deeply is not just what I am espousing, but *who* I am as an African-American, Evangelical, charismatic/Pentecostal bishop with deep roots in and significant honor and respect for my community. I intend to answer many of the questions my theology has raised, as well as raise questions regarding some of the answers that our age-old traditions have presumed to be true. To many, I am a traitor, shining an unwelcome light on traditions that are more comfortable in shadow. But I agree with the economist John Kenneth Galbraith when he said, "The modern conservative is engaged in one of man's oldest exercises in moral philosophy; that is, the search for a superior moral justification for selfishness."

Many of my colleagues did not want this book published. I am not surprised; revolutions are rarely comfortable. You may believe that I am wrong in my belief, but I hope you will respect that I am being "real." My new path has cost me much, but I feel more liberated than ever before.

As Al Gore said in the film documentary *An Inconvenient Truth,* "It is difficult to get a person to understand something when their salary and, I add, their entire way of life depends on their not understanding it."

The Truth Is Stronger

The writer Ralph Waldo Emerson once said, "The secret of education lies in respecting the pupil." This book is about respecting the disciple who craves a productive, meaningful life that extends beyond the mundane existence so often lived in the shackles of religion. This book acknowledges the value and dignity of inquiry and the pursuit of truth regarding the higher purpose of life, both human and spiritual.

This work is a development of thoughts and reflections I have been contemplating and cultivating for over twenty-five years. It is a work of faith transformed into scholarship and conviction. I write as one to whom the charismatic/Pentecostal community has offered honor, rank, and privilege. These writings come from my perspective as a bishop, pastor, evangelist, and Christian diplomat, whose vows at the time of ordination and consecration included a promise to defend the faith and guard the unity and sanctity of the church. I do not take those vows lightly. My pursuit is a better understanding of the true nature of the Gospel, which has led me to write this book.

A word about my use of passages from Scripture: in an effort to confirm that the Gospel of Inclusion is not heretical or the work of my own mind, I will refer to the Bible often. Some would say that in a book that argues against the evils of mindless doctrine, it is hypocrisy to bulwark one's arguments using the book that many consider a doctrinal work. However, while the Bible may be doctrinal in some ways, it does represent the deepest truths of Christianity, independent of any label or religious order. As my readers and my detractors will see, I will clearly show that the Gospel of Inclusion is consistent with the words of Jesus and other apostolic writings. This would be as impossible without resorting and referring to Scripture, as it would be to tell students about genetics without talking about DNA. I humbly ask your forbearance.

In a sense, I am using the Christian Bible to help prove my thesis that God is not a Christian. I hope you will see God where and as you are—and where and as everyone else is. It is my hope that this realization will dispel the disdain for other religions and other people who do not believe as we do.

As Martin Luther nailed his Ninety-five Theses on the church door in Wittenberg, these are my Theses, nailed to the door of today's religious culture. Like Luther, I declare, "My conscience is captive to the Word [Logos/logic] of God. Here I stand, I can do no other. So help me God."

In July 1890, Andrew Jukes, a clergyman and writer, wrote a letter to one of his dear friends regarding his belief in the concepts of the Gospel of Inclusion. It read, in part:

I need not speak of things like this, I only refer to them to tell you to fear none of these things. The "Truth" is stronger than all lies. If it is misrepresented and condemned and slain, it yet will rise again. Christ is the Truth, and he must go conquering and to conquer, and must reign till all his enemies are subject to him.

Christ will conquer, and that has nothing to do with Christianity. It has only to do with God's grand plan for humankind. It is not the place of religion to conquer or subjugate. Instead, Christ wraps us all in His embrace. Love conquers all in the end.

PART I
TO WHICH CHURCH DOES GOD BELONG?

My daddy is in hell!"

Those were the words of the presiding bishop who had just denounced me as a modern-day heretic, unwelcome in any of the several hundred charismatic/Pentecostal churches represented by the conclave of bishops and pastors who were assembled to try me for doctrinal treason.

He went on to say, "My drug addicted, rebellious son likes all that silly stuff you're preaching. He's on his way to hell too!" I replied, "How do you know your dad is in hell?"

The bishop said, "I know it because he died butt naked with the girl laying on top of him with a pistol in each hand, and he's in hell where he belongs!" The man's rage was burning.

"How long has he been there?" I asked quietly.

"He's been there over ten years."

"You think he's learned his lesson by now?" I asked.

"I don't know!" replied the bishop.

"Did you love your dad?" I pressed.

"I adored him, he was my hero," said the bishop. "But he was abusive to me and to my mother. He was unfaithful and irresponsible, but I loved him."

I asked softly, "Have you forgiven him?"

"Yes, I forgave him then and there on the spot."

I pressed my point: "How about your Heavenly Father? Do you not think He could have forgiven your dad as well?"

The bishop paused a few seconds and blurted out, "I don't know."

I didn't relent. "You say your dad's been in hell weeping, wailing, and gnashing his teeth for some ten years now, eh? You think he's learned his lesson?"

"I don't know, only God knows."

I asked another, tougher question: "Sir, if there was a way you could get your daddy out of hell, would you?"

After an unexpectedly long pause, he answered again, "I don't know."

I queried further: "You said you loved him and forgave him. Are you telling me that even if you could, you wouldn't get your dad out of hell?" Even more astounding to me, he retorted again, "I don't know."

It was at that very moment that I knew without question that the religious system I had embraced all my life—and which had just excommunicated me for basically loving too much and too many—was badly broken and was in no way representative of the God and Christ I had loved and served all my life.

Something had to be done, or that vicious and vindictive spirit displayed by this so-called man of God would continue to blindly lead the blind into a deeper and more destructive ditch. My religion was terminally ill. At first I thought it just needed healing, but I have a feeling it just might die, and perhaps it should. Then we'd be left with just God.

God without religion. Can you imagine the possibilities?

Whose Will Is Master?

At its core, the controversy over the Gospel of Inclusion is about a simple question: whose "will" holds sway over the realm of Ultimate Design, man's or that of God, the Designer? When the two are compared, it begins to seem a laughable question: the infinite wisdom of the subtle, universal Mind beyond Time versus the flawed, distracted human mind that has brought us such religion-fueled atrocities as global jihad, the Crusades, and the Spanish Inquisition and far, far beyond. It's like pitting the New York Yankees against a Little League team in Kansas. God wins.

Man should and does have a crucial role to play in the expression of faith and the fulfillment of God's purpose in creation, but it has become clear to me that man's role should not be as a spiritual guide, but only as a facilitator. The authoritarian dynamics of today's religious sects are an obscene parody of Jesus speaking to and leading his disciples. Such biblical scenes featured the mortal incarnation of Divinity—Christ—delivering lessons of compassion and justice to a chosen band of rough, rugged, streetwise men. Today we have scores of gifted, charismatic individuals, self-anointed and human appointed, as sources of wisdom and perceived truth, begging for money and handing down their narrow interpretation of the *Word of God* on subjects ranging from stem cell research to how to vote—not to mention how the entire world will end—to individuals who are often trained to be ignorant and fearful.

Why has such a pompous, poisonous subculture flourished? Power and self-interest. Religion has no peer as a structure for controlling human activity, without providing any reason why one's orders should be obeyed. The preacher at the pulpit simply claims that the edict in question is "the will of God," settling the issue for most of the sheep in the congregation. Thus have the teachings of Christ and many other enlightened spiritual leaders past and present become perverted into a platform for preaching hatred, intolerance, bigotry, and the destruction of this precious earth God has given us—a breeding ground for "us versus them" dogma.

Inclusion advises that all religions have their place in the culture of human consciousness, but when they insist that all others are evil, they have crossed the line. Most of today's religions have adopted the position "It's not enough that I should succeed. Others must fail."

I find the state of modern Christianity—and modern religion overall—an insult to Divinity and humankind. We who are purportedly created in God's image have a duty to strive for higher consciousness, yet we are led astray by the profoundly flawed teachings of religion, which is a purely human construct. Christ didn't come to create a new religion, nor did He instruct His disciples to. Christ had hoped to reform His own religion, Judaism, expanding it to become more nonjudgmental and inclusive. He taught His disciples and anyone who would listen to live with love, justice, strength, healing, and faith in the Creative Intelligence and fathering Spirit we call God. We cling to religion because it offers us that which we think we need: ritual, a sense of community, explanation of our shortcomings, solace in time of sorrow, and some sense of hope for heaven—or as some view it, "pie-in-the-sky by and by."

But, sadly, religion has become an armed front with two factions facing off: "we," the true believers, and "they," everyone else (who are all *obviously* bound for hell). This lends "we" a sense of superiority, but also populates the world with enemies and casts believers as self-appointed soldiers in the army of the Lord. Under such influence, people will and do slander, attack, abuse, and kill in the name of whatever image of God their particular religion has. They all have their brand of VIP inclusionism and access to their perceived corner on truth.

Institutionalized religion is obsolete. Institutionalized religion is corrupt. It has outlived its usefulness. Inclusion and faith must take its place if we are to fulfill the potential of creation, fully and truly enjoying the peace, beauty, science, and divine order of our planet. It is for this purpose that I have taken up the cause and course of this book.

eryone else (who are all *obviously* bound for hell). This lends "we" a sense of superiority, but also populates the world with enemies and casts believers as self-appointed soldiers in the army of the Lord. Under such influence, people will and do slander, attack, abuse, and kill in the name of whatever image of God their particular religion has. They all have their brand of VIP inclusionism and access to their perceived corner on truth.

Institutionalized religion is obsolete. Institutionalized religion is corrupt. It has outlived its usefulness. Inclusion and faith must take its place if we are to fulfill the potential of creation, fully and truly enjoying the peace, beauty, science, and divine order of our planet. It is for this purpose that I have taken up the cause and course of this book.

CHAPTER ONE

WHAT IS INCLUSION?

We must all learn to live together as brothers, or we will all
perish together as fools.

—Martin Luther King Jr.

This is a trustworthy saying that deserves full acceptance
(and for this we labor and strive), that we have put our hope
in the living God, who is the Savior of all men, and especially
of those who believe.

—1 Timothy 4:9–10

Religion is about the business—and big business it is—of saving or getting people saved from the wrath of God, which
results in banishment to hell. Christianity, the religion I was
brought up in and remain an active member of, teaches that Christ
came to earth to save it by redeeming its inhabitants and reconciling them back to God the Father.

If in fact God through Christ is the Savior of all people, something that most evangelical Christians purportedly believe, is it
not reasonable to assume that He is also the Savior of those who

do not believe and of those who have never heard the Good News?

I remember the late 1960s and early 1970s, when school integration and busing were the new educational standards of the day. As a young African-American who had attended the same elementary, junior high, and high school my older siblings had, I was not excited about attending a predominantly white, rich school in an area of town where my mother, grandmother, and godmother cleaned houses.

In that particular social setting, my sister and I not only felt unwelcome and excluded, we also felt irrelevant to the cultural environment. It was, for both of us, the most unpleasant educational experience of our young lives. What made it unpleasant was our ignorance and unfamiliarity with this social change in American conscience and education. We were familiar enough with racial integration, but this was a change of neighborhood and social mores.

We felt the alienation and dissociation of two young black students from "the ghetto." We never felt included; we felt isolated and even intimidated by the social and economic norms of that community. Needless to say, we didn't last long. Not so much because the education was lacking or that we were unable to learn, but because we didn't fit in, and the people there didn't know how to fit us in, even though they may have wanted to. I have never forgotten that cold, dark, stoic feeling.

DISCOVERING OUR IGNORANCE

Historian Will Durant said, "Education is a progressive discovery of our own ignorance." I am a fourth-generation classical Pentecostal preacher and, oddly enough, none of my predecessors in ministry would have considered himself a scholar, a historian, or even a theologian. Most of them could barely read, some not at all.

This was common among many of the great old preachers of the impoverished social and religious Pentecostal culture in which I was raised.

These preachers were often referred to (in our small culture) as "read-on preachers"; those who couldn't read or didn't read well had their chosen texts publicly read during a church service. They would select a person in the congregation who could read a Scriptural passage aloud. The reader would read a few lines of Scripture, and then the preacher would expound on those passages. When he was finished expounding, he would shout, "Read on!" and the chosen reader would continue. This guarded the inconvenient fact of the preacher's illiteracy.

My great-grandfather (Poppa) was a read-on preacher. In fact, Bishop Charles Harrison Mason, the founder of the denomination in which I was reared, had only a second-grade education. This glamorized a lack of education as something that God used to keep His greatest servants humble and usable by Him. Thus Poppa was (and is to this day) a revered man of God among those who were exposed to his ministry.

My mother was known throughout our religious community as one of the great readers. When Poppa, who lived in East Texas, visited us in the San Diego area, he always expected my mother to be his reader. My uncle would remind my mother that Poppa was the preacher and not her, because she would read as if she were preaching the sermon. Her clear voice would ring out across the small storefront churches until you could hear her about as loudly as the preacher—the only one who had a microphone.

Imagine this environment for a child, with every aspect of life steeped in conservative, evangelical Christian doctrine. In such a setting, terms such as *Universalism, Unitarianism,* and *heresy* were rarely heard, let alone understood. We rarely heard ten-dollar words such as *hermeneutic, homiletic,* or *exegesis,* and when we did, we tuned them out. The terminology and scholasticism didn't relate to us. We weren't scholars; we weren't interested in *theology*. We were blissfully ignorant about the sociological implications of what we believed. A simple message of heaven or hell, reward or punishment, was enough to qualify anyone to preach, and practically everyone in my culture (especially men) gave it a try.

THE DOMINION OF THINKING

I became aware of the doctrine of Universalism back when I was a student at Oral Roberts University in Tulsa, Oklahoma. However, assuming it to be a heretical position and not worthy of serious consideration, I chose not to study it further. I simply ignored it, considering it irrelevant. It was not until people outside of my local assembly heard my sermons, began to accuse me of preaching Universalism, and branded me a heretic that I began to study this doctrine in more depth. You could say that the road to heresy is paved with scholarship.

Dr. Charles Habib Malik, a great philosopher and diplomat born in 1906, understood the dangers of the venomous contempt for intellectual thinking and inquiry that pervaded conservative Christianity even one hundred years ago and continues today. He remarked:

> The greatest danger besetting American Evangelical Christianity is the danger of anti-intellectualism. The mind as to its greatest and deepest reaches is not cared for enough. This cannot take place apart from profound immersion for a period of years in the history of thought and spirit. People are in a hurry to get out of the university and start earning money or serving the church or preaching the gospel. They have no idea of the infinite value of spending years of leisure in conversing with the greatest minds and souls of the past and thereby ripening and sharpening

and enlarging their powers of thinking. The result is that the arena of creative thinking is abdicated and vacated to the enemy.

A study conducted by the Barna Group found that 40 percent of ministers in America have no formal seminary training. Within the charismatic/Pentecostal community, I have no doubt that the figure is considerably higher. We are taught to *feel* more than *think*, guided by Scriptures such as, "For if I pray in a tongue, my spirit prays, but my mind is unfruitful" (1 Corinthians 14:14). Such Scriptures suggest that intellect-driven minds might make errors in spiritual truth. In other words, thinking leads to sin, deception, and error.

Bible schools, especially those sponsored by local churches or denominations, were all right. But seminaries were disdained as "cemeteries"; they were considered dead, lifeless mausoleums where young, aspiring preachers would enter with spiritual zeal but depart with their passion for saving souls bled dry by empty study and uninspiring intellectual thought.

CHRISTIAN INTELLECTUALS: AN ENDANGERED SPECIES?

Institutional Christianity seems fearful of inquiry, fearful of freedom, fearful of knowledge—indeed, fearful of anything except its own repetitious propaganda, which has its origins in a world that none of us any longer inhabit. The church has historically been willing to criticize, marginalize, or even expel its most creative thinkers.

—*John Shelby Spong,* Why Christianity Must Change or Die

One of the greatest commands of the Bible, the one on which Jesus said both the law and the prophets hinge, is: "Love the LORD your God with all your heart and with all your soul and with all your strength, and with all your mind" (Deuteronomy 6:5 and Matthew 22:37). We're pretty good at loving God with our heart, soul, and strength, but loving God with our mind has become a contradiction in terms for many of us. This is a dangerous state to be in. The growth and spread of religion is like the healthy evolution of a species. It cannot rely only on inbreeding from the captive population but must receive an infusion of new blood from new, vital sources—the huge majority of people who would like to be believers but also refuse to relinquish their questioning intellects. With only unquestioning believers, religion stagnates, as is happening now.

Loving God with "all my mind" has not only helped me *see* God but *experience* Him and my own divinity in ways I never imagined. I have become willing to suspend what I *thought I knew* about God in order to know Him in a way I didn't know was possible. The message of Inclusion is anathema to what I was conditioned to believe about God and Satan, heaven and hell, eternal judgment and eternal life. To some people, my theological position is tantamount to "falling from grace." I consider it falling "into" grace.

One of the earliest criticisms I received was from those who insisted that the early church fathers considered Universalism to be heresy. Up to that time, I had not seriously considered the thoughts, teachings, or theology of the early church fathers. Through much contemplation and study, I came to the conclusion that there was not only overwhelming scriptural support for my teachings on Inclusion, but that there was actually *more* scriptural support *for* Inclusion than *against* it. This, as you can imagine, won me no points for popularity among the evangelical community with which I had been associated.

THE EVIDENCE FOR INCLUSION

I began studying more about the church fathers and how they shaped the doctrines and dogmas of early Christianity. I studied profusely, and I learned that I was not the first to preach a Gospel that included all of humankind in the redemptive work of the Cross—the essence of Inclusion. It took me awhile to research the numerous Scriptures that support the ultimate salvation of all, especially in comparison to the few popular Scriptures that suggest that a tiny elect are saved while the rest of humanity is damned. In my research, I was surprised to learn that the early church fathers were strong proponents of Universalism and that it was the prevailing doctrine of the first five hundred years of Christianity.

> In the first five or six centuries of Christianity, there were six theological schools, of which four (Alexandria, Antioch, Caesarea, and Edessa, or Nisibis) were Universalist; one (Ephesus) accepted conditional immortality; one (Carthage or Rome) taught endless punishment of the wicked. Other theological schools are mentioned as founded by Universalists, but their actual doctrine on this subject is not known.
>
> —Schaff-Herzog Encyclopedia of Religious Knowledge

Augustine (354–430), of African descent and one of the four great Latin/Afro church fathers (Augustine, Ambrose, Jerome, and Gregory the Great), admitted, "There are very many in our day, who though not denying the Holy Scriptures, do not believe in endless torments."

Origen, a pupil and successor of Clement of Alexandria, lived from 185 to 254. He founded a school at Caesarea, and is considered by historians to be one of the great theologians and scholars of the Eastern Church. In his book *De Principiis,* he wrote: "We think, indeed, that the goodness of God, through His Christ, may recall all His creatures to one end, even His enemies being conquered and subdued . . . for Christ must reign until He has put all enemies under His feet."

No Christian writer condemned Universalism until the year 394. In that year, a quarrel broke out between the followers of Origen and their opponents. The anti-Origens attacked the tenet of the ultimate salvation of the devil, but did not at first object to the final salvation of all men. But by 553, the Fifth General Council of the church in Constantinople officially condemned Universalism. Promoting it could result in punishment, even death, for heresy.

Here is what some early church fathers had to say on the subject:

> In the end and consummation of the universe, all are to be restored into their original harmonious state, and we all shall be made one body and be united once more into a perfect man, and the prayer of our Savior shall be fulfilled that all may be one.
>
> —St. Jerome, 331–420

> For it is evident that God will in truth be all in all when there shall be no evil in existence, when every created being is at harmony with itself and every tongue shall confess that Jesus Christ is Lord; when every creature shall have been made one body.
>
> —Gregory of Nyssa, 335–390

> We can set no limits to the agency of the Redeemer: to redeem, to rescue, to discipline in his work, and so will he continue to operate after this life. . . . All men are his . . . for either the Lord does not care for all men . . . or he does care for all. For he is savior; not of some and of others not . . . and

how is He savior and Lord, if not the savior and Lord of all? For all things are arranged with a view to the salvation of the universe by the Lord of the universe both generally and particularly.

—*Clement of Alexandria, c. 150–211*

Stronger than all the evils in the soul is the Word, and the healing power that dwells in him, and this healing He applies, according to the will of God, to everyman. The consummation of all things is the destruction of evil . . . to quote Zephaniah 3:8: "My determination to gather the nations, that I am assembling the kings, to pour upon them mine indignation, even say all my fierce anger, for all the earth shall be devoured with the fire of my jealousy. For then will I turn to the people a pure language that they may all call upon the name of the Lord, to serve Him with one consent" . . . Consider carefully the promise, that all shall call upon the Name of the Lord, and serve him with one consent.

—*Origen, 185–254*

The God of Inclusion

Many Christians say, "Jesus is my personal Lord and Savior." I understand what the believer means with that declaration; I have made it all my life. However, in actuality, Scripture never declares that Jesus is the personal Lord and Savior of anyone. It *does* declare that Jesus is Lord and Savior of the universe, the world, and the whole of humankind. There's no ambiguity except what we inject.

God is not a Christian, even though Christianity accurately declares Christ to be divine. God is the one true and Supreme God, and his love and redemption are not exclusive to Christians.

This fact is not simply suggested, it is declared in the Bible in certain terms hundreds of times.

The first and most important Scripture is found in Genesis 22:18 from the King James Version (KJV). God is speaking to Abraham:

> In thy seed shall all the nations of the earth be blessed; because thou hast obeyed my voice.

This promise is written repeatedly throughout the Bible. Psalm 9:7–8 from the New American Standard Bible (NASB) says:

> . . . the LORD abides forever; he has established his throne for judgment. He will judge the world in righteousness; he will execute judgment for [not against] the people with equity.

Psalm 22:27–30, paraphrased from the NIV and NKJV, says:

> All the ends of the earth will remember and turn to the Lord, and all the families of the nations will worship before him. For the kingdom is the Lord's, and he rules over the nations. All the proud of the earth will eat and worship, even he who cannot keep his soul alive. Posterity will serve Him.

There is a primary New Testament passage among many. In it the angels reported to have announced the birth of the Christ Child. They spoke the basic premise of the Gospel, Luke 2:14, paraphrased from the KJV and NIV:

> Glory to God, peace on earth, and good will toward humankind.

WHAT DOES IT MEAN TO BE "SAVED"?

Of course, someone knowledgeable in Scripture will respond, "What about 1 Corinthians 9:22?" There, Paul says "he" became all things to all men in order to save *some,* not all. Doesn't this Scripture clearly indicate exclusion?

But who is the Savior, Jesus or Paul? Does the Apostle, who spent his entire life preaching Jesus Christ as Savior of the world, now assume that he (the Apostle) can actually "save" people? The word *save* is used in many ways in Scripture. For example, the first New Testament reference is to Jesus saving "His people from their sins" (Matthew 1:21). If you take that passage literally, then Jesus came to save only Jews. You'd have to conclude that He is the Messiah only for Israel, not the rest of the world. Even Israel has rejected that concept.

Then in Matthew 8:25, the disciples ask Jesus to save them from the stormy Sea of Galilee. In Matthew 16:25–26, Jesus uses the same word in reference to a person saving his own life or soul: *"For whoever wants to save his life will lose it, but whoever loses his life for me will find it. What good will it be for a man if he gains the whole world, yet forfeits his soul? Or what can a man give in exchange for his soul?"*

Salvation in Jewish consciousness and Scripture is usually a reference to earthly deliverance, not eternal salvation. All of the Old Testament references are to that effect, as are most in the New Testament. In fact, there are only two places in Scripture where Christ is declared to be the "Savior of the world": John 4:42 and 1 John 4:14. However, the concept is implied throughout Scripture and is the generally accepted doctrine of evangelical Christianity worldwide. All religions teach some kind of salvation. That is what religion is about. The word *save* means to preserve, protect, or make safe from (including spiritual) loss or lack. When we spiritualize or "religionize" salvation, we assume it to mean salvation from hell.

Paul never assumed he would be successful at convincing everyone he approached with his gospel. He had already been rejected by Jewish traditionalists and had no illusions. Paul never saw himself as a savior, only as a messenger of the news of salvation in Christ, and he was successful in *saving* some people—bringing them enlightenment, awareness, and the experience of Christ in consciousness.

ARE YOU A PHARISEE?

Most people are familiar with the word *Pharisee.* According to *Strong's Exhaustive Concordance,* in both Hebrew and Greek it means "separatist." The Pharisees were ethnic and religious separatists who, as a rule, did not congregate with anyone who was unlike themselves. In many ways, modern Evangelical Christianity has become extremely Pharisaic. I call this homo-sectarian, or "same sect" relations.

In that context, being accused of being an Inclusionist is a badge I wear proudly. If we believe that God loves and plans to save all of mankind, then we have no choice but to have the same attitude. However, if we believe that God will ultimately cast most of humankind away (what most Evangelical Christians have been taught), we manifest that same spirit here on earth, acting out our caustic judgmentalism. That is why millions dismiss billions of others who do not share their beliefs as subhuman, condemned to burn in hell for eternity and not worth consideration, justice, or compassion here on earth. This perpetuates the adversarial relationships that plague our world to this day. It becomes easier to consign the "unregenerate masses" to damnation than to understand and embrace them. It makes us feel superior, something never reflected or projected in the teaching or actions of Christ. In this way, religion becomes a self-esteem cult.

Two New Testament Scriptures are used prominently to support this perception of exclusion and separatism among my Evangelical detractors:

> And if the righteous scarcely be saved, where shall the ungodly and the sinner appear?
>
> —1 Peter 4:18 (KJV)

> ...Wide is the gate and broad is the road that leads to destruction, and many enter through it. But small is the gate and narrow the road that leads to life, and only a few find it.
>
> —Matthew 7:13–14

These passages do not inspire hope. They inspire hypnotic terror. They imply that redemption is limited to a faithful few. The first is another passage where the word *saved* refers to earthly deliverance rather than to eternal salvation. In 1 Peter 4:17, Peter is attempting to explain to his readers that the terrible persecution being inflicted upon them was a sign that judgment had begun in the "House of God" (the first-century Christian community), and that even the elect were scarcely being saved from the wrath of Nero, the brutal Roman emperor. At this time in history, Christians were being fed to wild animals, sawed in two between planks of wood, and covered in pitch and used as human torches, to name a few ruthless acts of torture. Because most preachers are unaware of the background of Peter's letter, this passage has been interpreted as indicating that even believers would just *barely* be saved, and some not at all. This interpretation paints a picture of a wrathful God eager to send even his children into hell, and has caused a kind of paranoia in Christians for centuries. This mentality makes it much easier to assume the ultimate damnation of non-Christians, since even the righteous are scarcely saved.

This is one of the most frightening Scriptures in the Bible. After all, if Christians can't be sure of making it to heaven, even with the blood of Jesus washing away their sins, how can we ever expect a world of ungodly souls to have a ghost of a chance? Now that you mention it, who are those righteous few who are going to gain salvation? Even if we're Christians, how do we know which group we're in?

Propagating such anxiety, paranoia, and terror is a powerful method of controlling the masses, which is why such fear is world-wide. If there is a devil, it is religion, not some fiend running around in red long johns carrying a pitchfork and sporting horns, hooves, and a pointed tail.

WE CHOOSE WHAT WE SEE

> A great many people think they're thinking when they're merely rearranging their prejudices.
>
> —*William James*

One of the most difficult things to do is to get another person to accept the validity of information that challenges his worldview. The human mind has an amazing faculty for rejecting what it does not wish to see. Many have heard the message of the Gospel and have been taught the glory of accepting it and the peril of rejecting it. However, even many professing Christians remain far from pledging their allegiance to it and molding their lives accordingly. We still accept the parts of the Bible that we like—the ones that seem to forgive our failings, reinforce our bigotries, or damn those whose views do not match our own. It's the "salad bar" approach to belief.

When I first went public with the Gospel of Inclusion, I received thousands of letters and e-mails—some supportive, many outraged. Those who protested Inclusion consistently used the same Scriptures to refute my position; they were shocked when I pointed out scores of references they had never noticed before.

A Chinese proverb says, "Habits are cobwebs at first, cables at last." This applies to cultures, religions, and people. All organized religion is a collection of habits: traditions, customs, rules, doctrines, and dogmas handed down as sacred and untouchable. Because religions generally refuse to adapt to the changes in society and culture, they aggressively seek to make society and culture comply with them. Rather than seeking relevance, religious leaders seek to influence, decree, or dominate. This has been a consistent pattern for millennia.

THE JESUS CARICATURE

The first question many Christians ask concerning Inclusion is: "What if someone rejects Jesus?" The only people who really rejected Jesus as Messiah were the religious leaders of His day, because He was a threat. Instead most people tend to reject the *religion* built around Christ, rather than Jesus Himself. I submit that fewer people would reject Jesus were He presented closer to the way in which He presented Himself as He walked among men. What people continue to reject are the distorted, opportunistic caricatures of Jesus or God at the centers of many Christian denominations.

According to the Old Testament, approximately seven hundred years before Christ's birth, the prophet Isaiah warned that Jesus would be rejected by the dominant people of the time: the Jews, who were led both culturally and theologically by the Pharisees. "He was despised and rejected by men . . ." (Isaiah 53:3). It was the Pharisees who despised and rejected Jesus, not the common Jew or Gentile on the street. The common people loved Him and followed Him by the thousands.

DOES AIR HAVE A DENOMINATION?

It is as impossible to reject God or the Christ Principle as it is to reject the air that we breathe. No one has to preach air or proclaim its existence. Yet every living thing requires it. It is everywhere, invisible and essential. If we began packaging air and branding it culturally, religiously, or ethnically, would some people refuse to breathe a brand of air that wasn't theirs? The prospect seems absurd, yet that is precisely what is occurring in today's Balkanized religious landscape.

The unconditional love of God is as spiritually ubiquitous and necessary as air. But spiritual air and religious air are completely different.

Spiritual air is natural, unable to be rejected or denied. Religious air is a construct of men. It is artificial. Even if religion did not exist, spirituality would.

Religious gods can always be rejected, but the God who is Spirit cannot be, even by the atheist. God is Spirit, *pneuma* in Greek, meaning "air, wind, or breath," and they that worship Him "must worship in spirit and truth" (John 4:24). In other words, worshipping God in Spirit is not optional; it is natural and autonomic, like breathing. We are not just human beings looking for spiritual experiences; we are spirits having an earthly encounter. We do not require religion to worship and love God any more than we require an instruction manual to help us breathe.

GOD IS NOT A RELIGION

Religion seeks to substitute for God, even to replace divinity with its doctrines. This is my point in saying that God is not a Christian. God is neither religion nor religious. God is simply Spirit. (We call God Him, but in reality, He is beyond concepts like gender. We say He simply because it is inconvenient to say He/She/It all the time.) The idea that the secular world is adversarial to faith prevents believers from loving the world enough to approach humankind in the same compassionate spirit with which Christ approached it. As long as we see the world as a sin-racked enemy, we will never be able to appeal to people in the right spirit and with a healthy, hospitable attitude.

John 1:11 says, "He came to that which was his own, but his own did not receive him." It was not the secular world that rejected Jesus, but religious people who despised Him, primarily His Jewish brethren, who were threatened by what He represented. Jesus was a magnet for sinners and those marginalized to the fringes of society. Such people were drawn to Him by His love, as seen in Luke 15:1–7:

> Now the tax collectors and "sinners" were all gathering around to hear him. But the Pharisees and the teachers of the law muttered, "This man welcomes sinners and eats with them." Then Jesus told them this parable. "Suppose one of you has one hundred sheep and loses one of them. Does he not leave the ninety-nine in the open country and go after the lost sheep until he finds it? And when he finds it, he joyfully puts it on his shoulders and goes home. Then he calls his friends and neighbors together and says, 'Rejoice with me; I have found my lost sheep.' I tell you that in the same way there will be more rejoicing in heaven over one sinner who repents than over ninety-nine righteous persons who do not need to repent."

Note that Jesus said that the shepherd had to pick up the lost sheep, hoist it onto his shoulders, and carry it home. Many "lost sheep" will not respond simply to our voice or call, regardless of how elegant or doctrinally accurate we sound. Some people are not only lost but also deaf and wounded. Many are injured and crippled, and need to be picked up emotionally and spiritually and carried back to or reidentified with the fold: God's universal family.

RELIGION NEEDS SALVATION

In Scripture, a reference to "sheep" usually is a reference to Jews. However, in the broadest sense, it is inclusive of the *entire world*. I believe it is right to present God and the Gospel as inclusive in love, tolerance, acceptance, and forgiveness, and as celebrative of the beauty of all diverse peoples—including their glorious salvation in Christ.

Christians, as well as those of other faiths, must attract more and attack less. Religion is too unfriendly; the caustic perception of God intimidates others and cripples religion's ability to be a force for worldwide positive change. Religion is the one in need of salvation. It needs to be delivered from what it has become. It is not the positive force of good it should be.

As relating to "Christian theology," the message of Inclusion maintains that Christ's death accomplished its purpose of reconciling all mankind back to God. The death of Christ made it possible for God to accept humanity, something that has already happened. More important, it demonstrated God's unconditional and redemptive love for His own creative handiwork. I like to call this the Christ Principle. Any separation between mankind and God's grace is an illusion, existing only in man's unenlightened, uninformed, unawakened mind.

CHAPTER TWO

DIVINE ONENESS

Intention is a force in the universe, and everything and everyone is connected to this invisible force.

—*Dr. Wayne W. Dyer*

A s far back as I can remember, we were taught to be like Jesus. I was never really sure what that meant, but I bought it. The confusing part was that we were also taught that we were made in the image and likeness of God, but we were to strive every day to be like Jesus, who we were taught was God in the flesh. Being like God always appeared to me to be out of reach. I never felt that I could relate to God on a personal level. But Jesus was cool and seemed much more relevant.

We were taught that Oneness with God was not a reality, but something to be achieved. It was not a birthright. This, of course, was to be achieved through Christ. Here again, Christianity is the institutional attempt to be like Jesus so that we might someday be like God . . . again. Of course, only a few will ever attain this coveted place, and they would only be Christians, naturally. By this thinking, we were all created in the image and likeness of God, but lost that likeness through no fault of our own. Now we must find our way back to God; something that could only happen by accepting Jesus as personal Lord and Savior. The entire concept is blatantly exclusive and prejudicial, not to mention complex and elusive.

In the Oneness of God, there is room for all. It includes much more than any one religion contains. It is impossible for man to know all things, but I believe as William Blake does: "In the universe, there are things that are known and things that are unknown, and in between, there are doors." If that is the case, then there are doors that remain ajar, through which the curious can peek. The tragedy of traditional theology is that it has closed these doors and robbed us of the "mystery." God is Infinite Spirit, Infinite Reality, and Eternal Design. This means that God is greater than any philosophical or religious concept or construct. Infinity cannot be constrained to religion. However, because we are religious creatures by nature, our approach to God is rarely outside of that context. If God is omnipresent, which we are taught, then He is everywhere at all times, encompassing all things and all beings. Thus it is impossible for all men and women *not* to be one with God.

Even more revelatory is the fact that each of us represents part of the wholeness of the Deity, so we all hold God within ourselves. There is no separation.

FIGURING OUT GOD OR FIGURING INTO GOD

For he [God] has put everything under his [Christ's] feet. Now when it says that "everything" has been put under him, it is clear that this does not include God himself, who put everything under Christ. When he has done this, then the Son himself will be made subject to him who put everything under him, so that God may be all in all.

—1 Corinthians 15:27–28

In Christian theology, Jesus is the mediator between God and man. Jesus did not come to lead us to himself as a substitute for God but to point all men to a new awareness of God—or "Father Consciousness," so to speak. He came to repair the image of God, which had been damaged by religion. God as "all in all" is powerful both prophetically and realistically. The disenfranchisement caused by a sense of alienation from God is the pain of humanity. A view of God as all in all is the hope of humanity.

The religions of this world all seek somehow to figure out what their version of God is. However, in reality, mankind is more likely to figure *into* God rather than figure God out. This is confused and frustrated when we impose our own desires, prejudices, aspirations, and terrors on the scrim of God rather than inquiring into what the true nature of divinity is. We want freedom from the spiritual disconnect caused by our feeling that we are sinful creatures at heart ("sin consciousness"), but we are unwilling to look honestly at what God is and is not because the answer might leave us more afraid than before. It seems far safer to superimpose our own "reality" of God over the eternal, universal reality.

In Deuteronomy 6:4 we read, "Hear, O Israel: the LORD our God is one." The Hebrew word *one* translates as "united, first, alike, alone, or altogether." LORD is translated *Ye'hovah,* meaning "self-existent or eternal," and is derived from the word *hayah,* which means "to exist, be, or become."

So this particular Scripture could be translated, "Our god is one unified existence, being, or becoming." The suggestion is that God *is* and *is becoming.* He is a God of motion and is *in* motion. He is eternal and timeless, and He is evolving and ever-shifting in our time continuum. He becomes by causing others to become. He maintains a spiritual intercourse with intelligent beings; we are His expression in this world. Through us, His creation, He gains expression and evolves in our world.

This is a far cry from the concept of humankind as ants crawling under the wrathful eye of the Almighty, waiting to be cast into the fires of the abyss. Instead we are *important* to God. Anything else is an insult to both creation and the Creator.

WE CRAVE BEING AT ONE

In Neville Goddard's book *Resurrection,* he translates the Deuteronomy passage as follows:

> Hear O man (Human Being), made of the very substance of God: You and God are one and undivided! Man, the world, and all within it are conditioned states of the unconditioned one, God. You are this one; you are God, conditioned as man. All that you believe God to be, you are; but you will never know this to be true until you stop claiming it of another and recognize this seeming other to be yourself. God and man, spirit, matter, the formless and the formed, the creator and the creation, the cause and the effect, your Father and you are one. This one, in whom you live and move and have your being, is your *I am,* your unconditioned consciousness.

Atonement (which can also be read as "at-one-ment") is actually humankind recovering the uniqueness that originated with God, reconnecting to Him in the way He originally created us to be.

We are all pockets of energy moving about in space and time, creating frictions that generate matter. We are all sponsored by divine imagination. Humanity was once an imaginative thought in the mind of God. Through the spoken Word of Creation, that thought took material form, but in our essence we remain spiritual beings of energy. It is this origin that attracts us to one another, and often makes us lonely for each other. Why? We came from a common source. We were all one, and we remain one even if our misaligned perceptions tell us otherwise. We don't necessarily want to go back to Original Thought; we simply want to remain connected to it, and therefore to each other. Being together reminds us of our innate oneness and inextricable tie to the Original Source.

When we encounter one another without prejudice, we recall our common intelligence, knowledge, "beingness," and our common parent. Each of us is a reminder of or monument to the source from which we are all derived. We can forget our unity or choose to ignore it, but that does not change its reality.

DO WE HAVE ANYTHING TO ATONE FOR?

Atonement is a religious term originating in Jewish thought and sacred writings. It has always been a solemn word, reminding us of our innate sinfulness and propensity to offend God. However, the real meaning of the term *atonement* should be cause for jubilation rather than fear or condemnation.

The Hebrew word for atonement is *kaphar,* which means literally "to cover." Its figurative meaning is "to expiate, condone, placate, or cancel." This implies that to atone is to eradicate sin and impute forgiveness. Taken to its logical end, this meaning says that sin has separated us from God, leading to the illusion of a spiritual chasm between Creator and created. This idea is based on the concept of original sin in the Garden of Eden, when Adam and Eve were banished from the garden and the presence of God. This sense of separation and alienation from God has caused dread and fear in humankind for millennia. It suggests that we are uncovered and thus unprotected from either a hostile universe or the hostile God who created it.

The term atonement appears in the New Testament only once, in Romans 5:11: ". . . we also joy in God through our Lord Jesus Christ, by whom we have now received the atonement" (KJV). Other versions of the New Testament use the term *reconciliation.*

But here's the rub: you cannot reconcile a couple that has never been together. The word implies that man and God were once together, and the relationship was damaged.

Since we came from God, we are made of the same substance as Divinity. Therefore we remain intrinsically connected to God and to each other. God created us out of Himself, which means we are innately, internally, and eternally divine. We can experience true peace in this world only when we reconnect to our Original Source. To suggest anything else is to show a profound ignorance for the nature of being, our pre-incarnate selves and souls.

> Every sadness of the human heart, every indignity of the human condition, every tragedy of the human experience, can be attributed to one human decision—the decision to withdraw from each other. The decision to ignore our supreme awareness. The decision to call the natural attraction we have for each other "bad," and our oneness a fiction. In this we have denied our true selves! It is from this self-denial that our negativity has sprung. Our rage, our disappointment, our bitterness has found its birth in the death of our greatest joy—the joy of being one.
>
> —*Neale Donald Walsch,* Friendship with God

THE SCIENCE OF LIFE

I recently read that one of the world's most well-known atheists had changed his mind about the existence of an intelligence behind our world. British philosopher Antony Flew says he now believes that the only explanation for the origin of life and the complexity of nature is a "superintelligence." Flew points to the complex arrangement of DNA necessary to produce life, a view that is similar to that of American intelligent design theorists. He says he still does not believe in a God who is actively involved in the world on a daily basis; however, Flew does think this superintelligence could have personhood, since it is probably intelligent and purposeful.

We are made, in part, of matter, and matter has innate, unavoidable demands that cannot be ignored without causing extreme physical and psychological discomfort. One of man's preoccupations in this material existence is to find and maintain the "creature comforts" that put our material being at ease.

We are naturally inclined to pursue life and living. In Luke 10:25–26, Jesus is asked by a man, "What must I do to inherit eternal life?" In other words, how can I live forever? Jesus's rather profound response was, "What do the laws you live by say, and how do you interpret them?" In other words, what laws or standards validate your life? Jesus implied that a person's quality and continuity of living is based upon the laws or standards that govern his or her life. Whether or not you believe that Jesus is the Son of God, no ethically thinking person can deny that this was one of the most practical, morally sound statements ever uttered.

LOVE AND GOD'S DNA

Jesus taught that two commandments stand above all others:

- Love God with all your heart, soul, mind, and strength.
- Love your neighbor as you love yourself.

Love is the link that knits us together in oneness and makes our lives eternal. We and God have a "love connection." Loving God and one another is the surest path to personal and worldwide peace. We live through each other, by each other, and for each other in God. The physical cessation of life is not true death; true death is disconnection from the source of energy that binds us all together. True death is the illusion of separation from God and each other.

Inclusion is spiritual and scientific. A physicist at the European Organization for Nuclear Research (CERN) in Switzerland actually validated this in 1964: Dr. John S. Bell came up with mathematical proof (now known as Bell's theorem) that showed that the separate parts of the universe all connect in an immediate and inextricable way. His quantum mechanics experiments showed that particles separated by space and time somehow know exactly what the other is doing and react at the precise time a "sister" particle reacts. When one particle is stimulated, the other reacts instantly, which should not be possible. In a way we do not understand, they connect at a deep and profound level.

First Corinthians 12:27 says, "Now ye are the body of Christ, and members in particular" (KJV). We are limbs and ligaments of divine nature. Human beings are sharers in Divinity. The word *nature* (*phusis* in Greek, *physics* in English) means "growth by germination or expansion, or lineal descent." We are germs of Divinity, literally the genes of God. In other words, to get to the awesome point:

We possess the DNA of God.

This is what makes reconciliation such a powerful idea. We can be reconciled because we were *all* originally part of God and still are. We just got disconnected in consciousness, causing the illusion of separation.

LIBELING THE ALMIGHTY

I had always assumed that reconciliation is exclusive to Christians. A fear- and guilt-based reading of Scripture offers ample evidence that that is the case. However, unbiased observation of Christian theology makes it clear that Christ's purpose was to redeem the whole of humanity. Even though it refers to Jews in general, Scripture refers to all of humankind in history—His story. Although this particular letter addressed Christians within the Gentile church of Corinth, it is not exclusive to those readers. Metaphorically and metaphysically, sacred Scripture, in spirit, transcends time and is appropriate and applicable to all seasons, cultures, and peoples:

> To the church of God in Corinth, to those sanctified in Christ Jesus and called to be holy, together with all those everywhere who call on the name of our Lord Jesus Christ— their Lord and ours . . .
>
> —1 Corinthians 1:2

This same writer of the letter to the church of Corinth, the Apostle Paul, wrote a similar missive to the church at Ephesus, another mostly non-Jewish European congregation. It is recorded in Ephesians 2:14–16:

> For he himself [Christ] is our peace, who has made the two [Jew and Gentile] one and has destroyed the barrier, the dividing wall of hostility, by abolishing in his flesh the law with its commandments and regulations. His purpose was to create in himself one new man out of the two, thus making peace, and in this one body to reconcile both of them to God through the cross, by which he put to death their hostility.

Christians hold the writings of Paul and other biblical sources to be their most sacred texts. The same is true of other faiths with regard to their sacred texts. However, the most divisive forces on the planet may be the Bible, Torah, Koran, and similar holy books.

They are separate cultures, countries, and consciousnesses. We have libeled God with our self-serving, divisive interpretations of what were straightforward messages.

For example, according to the text of the letter, God doesn't see us as saved or unsaved, but as Jew or Gentile only. Christ sees all of humanity as one flesh in Himself, "the Body of Christ." The word *body* means a combination of separate parts or particles, each with its own unique function and purpose, but at the same time, uniquely and inseparably knit together. This is the body of Christ. All life is a part of it.

I said earlier that the word *reconciliation* suggests that we were originally one with Divinity. To suggest otherwise is the theological position of those who stubbornly hold on to the idea of hell as most of mankind's final destination. They choose to believe, or perhaps to delude themselves, that the problems of sin cannot be resolved, even by God Himself.

DO WE HAVE THE COURAGE TO BE FREE?

> The wages of sin are death, [Romans 6:23] but by the time taxes are taken out, it's just sort of a tired feeling.
>
> —*Paula Poundstone*

All religions tell a story involving the fall or failure of mankind. This fall necessitates some kind of restitution to put man back into good standing with God. Islam, Judaism, and Christianity all have rules, ways, and rituals based on laws by which man can find atonement for his sins. In each case, unforgiven sin always separates the sinner from God and destines him to some kind of retributive judgment.

In the Genesis account, Satan is said to have come to Eve in the form of a serpent. The serpent questioned the freedom of

Adam and Eve by posing the question "Did God really say, 'You must not eat from any tree in the garden'?" (Genesis 3:1).

As a teenage Christian growing up in a strict Pentecostal religious culture, I interpreted this as Satan taunting us with the question "Is it true you Christians can't do anything fun or appealing to your humanness? Has God put restraints upon you to constrain your freedom of choice and limit your power to control your own soul?" Basically, "Is it true you Christians can't do much of anything without offending your temperamental, intolerant God?"

Eve's response was, in effect, "We have some freedoms, but we are not completely free. We are not free to do just anything we want to do or may be tempted to do. If we take total freedom to do as we please, it will result in our death." Translation: "I am terrified to be free and make my own decisions. I fear the responsibility of freedom of choice. Therefore, give me dogmas, doctrines, and disciplines, or I will die. I cannot live and be totally free. I can't be trusted because I don't trust myself."

We are begging for freedom through bondage. But freedom is not for cowards. We must thrust our lives into the hands of the living God whom we cannot see and trust Him to secure our future. This security must not be built upon our system of ideologies that control, limit, and deceive us. "Walking by faith and not by sight" (2 Corinthians 5:7) literally means walking in unregulated freedom, unhindered by dogma. Can you stand to be free?

BLAME IT ON ADAM

These days hell is inculcated into our consciousness, and remains so profoundly entrenched there that God's original recorded sentence of death seems like a cakewalk in comparison. Remember, the original consequence for sin in Scripture was not hell, but death. Again, in Genesis, God is recorded to have said, "The day you eat of this tree you will surely die." God's punishment for transgression was annihilation, the end of the self. He didn't say anything about eternal damnation.

Have you ever wondered what Adam's and Eve's concept of death could have been, considering that no one is supposed to have lived or died before them? What could the warning "you shall surely die" (Genesis 2:17) have meant to them? It must have been easy for them to eat of the forbidden tree without experiencing a feeling of guilt, since up to that time they had nothing to use as a point of reference for guilt or death. Truly the tree lived up to its name as "the tree of knowledge of good and evil." This is the curse of duality that has plagued the human consciousness for millennia: must something be only all good or all evil? If so, how can we even exist?

". . . But you must not eat from the tree of the knowledge of good and evil [God and devil—the truth of opposing allegiances and loyalties], for when you eat of it you will surely die." Simply said, that means "you will start judging one another based on your human evaluations and estimations of right and wrong, good and bad, black and white, male and female, night and day, and beyond." Once you get the image of two gods, truths, or realities—a good one and a bad one, a God one and a satanic one—you will begin to pursue conflict and kill each other for those perceived transgressions.

Our carnal, unenlightened Adamic nature feels compelled to defend the image we have of God and good. But trying to manage these dichotomies has caused us to systematically destroy ourselves as humankind.

Up to this time in Adam's and Eve's lives, there was only Universalism. We could define Adam as the "God man." There was a direct spiritual connection between God and humankind. In the Genesis scenario, the serpent's response to Eve was, "You will not surely die . . . your eyes will be opened, and you will become like

God, knowing good and evil" (Genesis 3:4–5). In other words, the serpent was suggesting, "You shall become equal to or independent of God. You won't need to depend on Him any longer."

In a real sense, original sin was this act of deliberate disconnection from interdependence on God, which has led us to invent ways to reconnect through religion ever since.

RECONNECTING THE DISCONNECT

The search for security is an illusion. It suggests we are away from safety. In effect, it surmises incorrectly that we are separated from God, something that is impossible, since God is everywhere and everything. Insecurity simply is a form of insanity or amnesia. People who feel insecure have simply forgotten their invisible, invincible, and immutable connection to God.

This brings us to the Christian concept of reconciliation via the Cross of Calvary. The concept is that what was once one, then two, or separated, becomes one again. Reconciliation and atonement are synonyms for the same ultimate end. Jesus prayed it just prior to His death, ". . . that they may be one as we are one" (John 17:11). The four words "as we are one" speak volumes. Jesus was praying that mankind would be reconnected with and to God in oneness and consciousness, as Christ and the Father are unified in Being and Spirit.

I mentioned Dr. John Bell and his scientific assertion that all aspects of the universe are indeed one, at least at the subatomic, quantum level. According to classical physics, communication of information takes time. Information can travel only at the speed of light, so when two bodies are divided in space and time, a message must travel a distance to communicate from one body to another. But at the quantum level, as Dr. Bell discovered, the oneness between the particles that form our essential matter is different. They don't have to communicate. They *know*. They act simultaneously, as if intimately connected in defiance of the concepts of space and time. They behave as if they are one form, making space and time meaningless. Such unity is certainly divinely mysterious, but divine nonetheless.

The message of Inclusion is a miracle in one way, but in another it is not miraculous. It is simply what is, what has always been, and will always be. It is God resolving the problem of separation by introducing His resolution into the inaccurate presumptions of humankind. He reconnects the disconnected particles and makes His body whole once again, by dispelling the erroneous assumption that separation is possible.

CHAPTER THREE

WHAT BRAND OF GOD
DO YOU USE?

To be called an orthodox Christian does not mean that one's point of view is right. It only means that this point of view won out in the ancient debate.

—*John Shelby Spong,* Why Christianity Must Change or Die

When I was growing up, my mother supported a number of missionary organizations. They would send their newsletters, ministry magazines, and other literature to our home, and I would grab them, curl up in a corner, and read every page. I studied the pictures of the huge crowds of people from many cultures and nations, all packed into huge tents or participating in open-air crusades. I read incredible testimonies of salvation, healings, and miracles. Our family supported those organizations because we knew they were helping to carry out the "Great Commission" of preaching the gospel, as we believed Jesus commanded.

All my life, I believed that the Great Commission was each Christian's responsibility "to save the lost at any cost." This is still considered the noblest cause of the Christian Church. The daunting task of converting *everyone* to Christianity has been an aggravating itch for the greater part of my life—a consuming passion motivated by pride, guilt, fear, anxiety, compassion, and, at times, profound depression. At times, it became my obsession, and I am hardly the only one for whom this has been the case. The responsibility of "getting people saved" has taken a severe toll on some of the most benevolent souls I have ever known.

For most of my life, I viewed many of the world religions as deviant, even demonic. I assumed that most of them (including various sects of Christianity) were idolatrous and their followers hell bound. I asked doctrinally unacceptable questions about why God allowed the existence of religions that were presumably leading billions of people into an eternal torture chamber. Why would a loving God eternally torture His children for sins that had a finite existence? The punishment seems to far outweigh the crime and makes as little sense as God's tolerance of religions that were, supposedly, insults to Christ's sacrifice.

Like Atlas, I felt I was bearing the weight of the world's salvation upon my weak shoulders. Ironically, the load was really the weight of self-delusion. The concept of saving others would prove to be completely obsolete.

CATHOLICS DON'T COUNT

When one looks at the number of non-Christians in the world and the reach of even the most determined army of evangelists, the number of "lost souls"—in contrast to those on their way to heaven—is mind-boggling. Of the over six billion people alive today, nearly two billion are Christians. And half of them—nearly one billion—are Roman Catholic. Many of the five hundred million Protestants don't accept Catholics as genuinely saved; they still see the Roman Catholic Church as the deviant, corrupt, idolatrous aberration of Christianity that Martin Luther protested against (hence the name "Protestant"). That reduces our tally of the saved to one billion. That means that out of six billion people, perhaps one billion are saved. That's a .167 batting average, which won't keep anybody in the majors.

The burning question (pardon the pun) Evangelicals ask themselves is, "How will we ever get all of these poor souls saved before Jesus returns and sends them all to hell?" Ah, yes, the Second Coming. There are mixed emotions and many questions concerning the Second Coming, because we are taught that Jesus is coming for a church without defect or blemish (1 Peter 1:19). I find this a scary thought. Forget about saving the world; Christians have never been spotless or perfect. Yet the guilt, grief, and agony of saving the world before Jesus returns gnaws at the gut of every Evangelical Christian.

This mission consumes our lives. Our marriages suffer, our children are often neglected, and our lives are withered by self-doubt. I have known people who lived with a profound sense of futility and depression as they raced against the Second Coming time clock. None of us wants to be caught "with our work undone" (as I've heard all my life). That is a hell many believers experience on a daily basis, and that terror is a great motivator to keep "God's children" (Christians only, of course) under human control.

Under the guise of this supposedly holy mission, are Evangelicals actually committing a greater evil—neglecting families, sparking resentment in the so-called unsaved, and damaging their minds? Would we serve God better if we stopped trying to save others through evangelism and started *saving* them by example? To begin to answer this question, we must first pierce the illusions surrounding Christianity.

WHAT IS CHRISTIANITY?

Christianity is a Jewish religion grafted onto a Latin architecture. In the early fourth century, the Roman emperor Constantine, in an effort to unify his empire, used Christianity as his tool. It was formed initially to promote the message and Gospel of Jesus Christ as Lord, including His death and Resurrection, and the redemption of humankind to God.

The word *Christianity* derives from the Latin word *Christ,* which is a translation of the Hebrew word *Meshiyach*—in English, "messiah." In its original Hebrew expression, *Christ* means "Anointed" or "Anointed One." The word *Christianity* does not appear anywhere in the Bible. The word *Christian* (or Christians) is mentioned in only three places (Acts 11:24, 26:28; 1 Peter 4:16), all but one by non-Christians.

Christianity became a world religion through the influence of the Holy Roman Empire. Many were *forced* to accept the Christian faith under threat of the sword. Gradually Christianity has become the dominant label for the religion built around Christ. Jesus was not a Christian; He was a Jew. His parents, disciples, and nearly all of His followers were Jews. This is what apparently upset the Jewish leadership of His day the most: other Jews, some rather devout, were beginning to believe Jesus as Christ. This "defection" remains a problem for some in the Jewish world.

The dominant religion in Israel during the days when Jesus walked its dusty roads was Judaism. Christianity was an unwelcome invader. It upset the apple cart of over four thousand years of Abrahamic faith. It challenged cherished Jewish customs and hope for a Messiah. Jesus of Nazareth was not the Messiah Jewish leaders were looking for, and still isn't.

Although Jesus was a Jew, Christ was not. Christ, the Logos of God, existed before time. In John 8:58 (KJV) He says, "Before Abraham was, I am." Jesus never intended to start a religion. He seems to have sought to reform his own. He seemed more concerned with a global Kingdom that would include all men and women.

PROPHET OR PROFIT?

In Acts 11:26 we find the first reference to Christians. It says, "The disciples were called Christians first at Antioch." The Greek word for *called* used in this instance is *chrematizo,* which, according to *Vine's Greek Lexicon,* is usually related to conducting business dealings. The term would be equivalent to our English phrase "doing business as," or d/b/a. The disciples were regarded as doing the business of Christianity.

The early disciples had begun to make a living out of following Christ. The *Lexicon* explains, "They were (publicly) called Christians because this was their chief business or occupation." In the most telling etymological evidence, the term *chrematizo* is used in only one other place in the New Testament in this manner, referring to a divorced woman remarrying and making her living as an adulteress, in Romans 7:3. Again, the reference is to generating money, or "doing business" for profit.

Early Christians referred to themselves as "disciples," "saints," or the *ekklesia,* Greek for "the called or called out ones," meaning they were called out of spiritual darkness into light and commitment to Christ. Eventually this became the primary understanding of being called a Christian. But initially the term was used by outsiders about the business dealings of this new sect of reformed Judaism.

Acts 11:26 says, ". . . for a whole year Barnabas and Saul met with the church and taught great numbers of people." Barnabas had been having great success in leading large numbers of people to Christ, especially where miracles were performed. The crowds were great, and the benevolence was commensurate. Money generally follows ministry. Like any well-run business, ministry attracts followers and offerings when it meets the needs of the consumer.

Constantine: First CEO of Christianity Inc.

In Bible School I was taught that Constantine was a born-again Christian who, while at the Battle of Milvian Bridge, converted to Christianity after he miraculously saw the sign of the cross in a cloud formation, with the accompanying words, "By this sign conquer." This is where Christian militarism began, and it remains a huge characteristic of Christian consciousness, especially in the West.

We were taught that Constantine was used by God to stop the horrendous persecution of Christians, and that he ultimately made Christianity the state religion throughout the Roman Empire. However, study shows that Constantine more than likely was baptized on his deathbed rather than undergoing a dramatic conversion. The cross in the sky is just a dramatic bedtime story. He very possibly believed in God and even had faith in Christ. However, it was not necessarily a commitment to Christ that caused him to make Christianity his religion. It was a smart political move. Constantine's objective was to merge Christianity with the "pagan religion" embraced by the Roman culture. In this way he could unify his empire, which seemed destined to split with the growing number of Christians in it.

If the love of money is the root of all evil (1 Timothy 6:10), then that evil was personified in the emerging religion under Constantine. He and Christian leaders manipulated power, money, and sexual repression to control people who depended on all three in subtle and complex ways. Since then, the religions of the world have discovered—and ruthlessly exploited—Constantine's secret to accumulating vast wealth: controlling the minds of numberless masses who are kept in ignorance. Even when the motivation for giving is for benevolent causes, often people's generosity is spurred by guilt or by the desire to avoid hell. Religion/Christianity Inc. often taps people's base emotions for its own ends.

SELLING TICKETS OUT OF HELL

Today we are still doing what Martin Luther protested: selling indulgences. As long as people are willing to buy their way out of hell, someone is going to sell them a ticket. I have no intention of making a vow of poverty; however, greed disguised as ministry is a cancer in the Evangelical community and in organized religion overall.

Religion is a multi-trillion-dollar business. People will pay almost anything to feel better about themselves—to feel that God is pleased with them. Unfortunately this vulnerability has given rise to terrible abuse. The merchandizing of religion threatens the peace and safety of the world. I understand Christians need to generate money to operate their ministries, but all too often, the ability to generate this money requires the spread of ignorance and intolerance that threatens what faith purports to save.

Worship is in our DNA. The discipline of *neurotheology* argues that faith and mystical experience are hardwired into our brains. We all look to a source, force, or power greater than ourselves. If we transcended our religious bigotry, we would be surprised at how similar we really are.

WE BEGAN WITH ONE GOD

According to *Halley's Bible Handbook,* many historians believe that the human race started with a belief in one God, and that polytheistic idolatry developed later. This view has received recent confirmation from archaeologists. Dr. Stephen Langdon of Oxford University found that the earliest Babylonian inscriptions suggested that man's first religion was a belief in one God, and from there the ancient world experienced a gradual decline into polytheism and idolatry.

Egyptologist Sir Flinders Petrie said that the original religion of Egypt was monotheistic. In 1898 Oxford Assyriologist A. H. Sayce announced that he had discovered, on three separate tablets in the British Museum, dating to the time of the Babylonian ruler Hammurabi, the words "Jaw he [Jehovah] is God." Leading anthropologists have recently announced that among all primitive races, there was a belief in one Supreme God.

The great religions of the world all revere sacred writings. The holy books of the non-Christian religions of the world all contain truths essential to the culture they influence, including the Bhagavad Gita of Hinduism, the Dhammapada and Lotus Sutra of Buddhism, the Confucian analects, and the Adi Granth of Sikhism. For thousands of years, religion has developed its deities, demons, and demagoguery based on these texts, and they exert immeasurable influence on global culture and conscience. Christians ignore or devalue them—and the faiths they represent—at our peril.

While unbelievers are considered blinded by the darkness, many believers are blinded by the light. When you make religion your God, you depreciate both. Unfortunately, many Christians appear more interested in Christianity than in Christ. They assume that they own Jesus and have a kind of "all-access pass" to Him. They have locked God within the walls of a religion called Christianity. They defend the religion while ignoring the relationship.

WHAT TO DO ABOUT RELIGION?

From the writings of Dr. Rembert S. Truluck:

> Addiction to abusive religion can destroy your self-esteem, sap your energy, undermine your personal goals and career aspirations, undercut your relationships, make you physically and mentally sick, and leave you gasping for more religion than ever. With this historical context, the importance of religion clearly stems from one simple truth: its potent influence makes it a tool to get what we want: money, power, a sense of superiority, even the suppression of views. Religion saturates our culture, invades our politics, influences business, and reaches into every school and artistic expression. It has exploded beyond the walls of the church.

Religion can be positive. But sick, perverted religion abuses its power to control minds in the name of God. Abusive religion is an illusory trap that snares children before they have the reasoning powers to understand or question it. Childhood religion is usually lifelong religion, guaranteeing that the individual spends decades devoted to doctrine rather than the Original Source, often leading to fanaticism and ever more intolerant doctrine.

The question of what to do about religion is valid but naive. First we must convince people that religion is a problem. As you can imagine, this is a thorny issue. One of the most predictable of human behaviors is irrational anger when one's belief systems are challenged. The scope of the task—reshaping the fundamental worldviews of billions of human beings—is enough to make many enlightened people throw up their hands in despair. Some make an uneasy truce with the misinformation and spiritual violence of religion. Some find new, more open-minded churches. Others abandon belief. These choices mask the larger need: a hunger for spiritual food and fellowship.

The time is ripe for the world's culture to embrace the concept of a new spirituality: self-directed and nontraditional. However, to pursue such journeys, people must learn to let go of the religious baggage that may be holding them back—turn their backs on abusive religious teachings that lead down dark alleys offering no exit. Starting over is difficult. Nothing has a more tenacious grip on our minds than our past. By releasing and reconciling the past, we can free ourselves to discover a new "brand" of God based not on authoritarian doctrine but personal faith.

ADDICTS IN DENIAL

It has taken me nearly fifty years to learn to distinguish the difference between God's creations and my pious illusions—to know truth as God created it and not as we in our religious zeal have invented it. My desire is to know God in His fullness rather than selectively and prejudicially. Even to talk about Inclusion, I had to suspend what I thought I knew about God in order to know Him in a way I had never imagined. I had to replace illusion with intellect and cast aside the anti-intellectual tenor that infects much of modern Christianity and is little less than a kind of pagan superstition.

According to the *American Heritage Dictionary of the English Language,* addiction is defined as a "compulsive physiological and psychological need for a habit-forming substance." It was Karl Marx (a Jewish man) who said, "Religion is the opium of the masses." That statement used to gall me, but I now see what he meant. For many, religion is an addiction that enables them to live in denial that anything is wrong. The familiar, deeply cut paths of religion are difficult to escape.

But as residents of the Kingdom of God on earth, we have a

duty to seek cultural relevance in order to connect with the spiritually uncertain. A crisis in truth is a crisis in trust. The role of Christianity is to create environments conducive to the work of the Holy Spirit in people's minds and hearts. It is desirable that our style and approach change, even though we perceive the truth we preach to be ageless and timeless.

IN-YOUR-FACE SALVATION

> The highest function of the teacher consists not so much in imparting knowledge as in stimulating the pupil in its love and pursuit. . . . To know how to suggest is the art of teaching.
> —*Henri Frédéric Amiel*

All of the world's religions have their disciples, disciplines, masters, and teachers. But there is a profound difference between religion's curriculum and its source. Not only was Jesus not a Christian, but Muhammad was not a Muslim, and the Buddha was not a Buddhist. These religions were established after their deaths. First comes the man, next his message, then a movement, and inevitably the monument to all three—established to preserve the teachings of the teacher. Of course, the teacher is no longer alive to contradict those who reinterpret or misinterpret his teachings any way they choose. How convenient.

Christianity is the only religion associated with aggressive evangelization, coming in second arguably only to Islam in recruiting adherents worldwide. Unfortunately, Evangelical Christians mistakenly interpret *evangelism* as "getting people saved," instead of informing them that they are already saved. This practice is increasingly looked upon with hostility as insulting and condescending to other cultures.

The irony is, Jesus never told us to save anyone. I was won *to* Christ over forty years ago; but as a living spirit, I was won *by*

Christ over two thousand years ago. New Testament writings suggest that the salvation of mankind originated with God and is fulfilled in Christ. "All this is from God, who reconciled us to himself through Christ . . . that God was reconciling the world to himself in Christ, not counting men's sins against them" (2 Corinthians 5:18–19). The world—not just Christians—is reconciled to God.

I have spent the greater part of my life trying to save people from their sins. I now realize that in spite of all that I have been taught, we were never instructed to "save" anyone. Jesus instructed His disciples to "make disciples [students of a higher consciousness and spiritual perceptivity] of all nations" (Matthew 28:19). The more accurate interpretation of Christian theology perceives Christ alone as the Savior, and there is nothing we need do to improve on the finished work of the Cross. Eternal redemption is a done deal. Jesus said, "It is finished" (John 19:30). What say you?

JUST BE LIKE CHRIST

> The great end of education is to discipline rather than to furnish the mind; to train it to use its own powers rather than fill it with the accumulations of others.
>
> —*Tyron Edwards*

The most ghastly irony in Christianity today is the preponderance of leaders who espouse hatred, prejudice, terrorism, arrogance, ignorance, and oppression while claiming all the while to be true followers of Jesus. Other religions that don't profess to follow Christ, but purport to love God, do this as well. Such people are vile hypocrites.

There is a difference between being a follower and being a disciple of Jesus. A follower is a person who accepts the religion built around His teachings. A disciple is a student of Jesus who reflects

His spirit and walks in His teachings in daily life. A true disciple of Christ is like Him in word and deed. He or she will abandon sick, abusive religion and move on, as Jesus did, into more spiritually relevant realities. A disciple recognizes and lets go of the hypocrisy and destruction of religion to embrace a new wholeness.

Religion teaches adherence to particular rules and formulas. But spirituality encompasses union with Divinity by choice. Spirituality is about a higher reality and ethical consciousness—a "God logic" that emphasizes not Christianity but the logic of Christ; what I call the Christ Principle. This spirituality is more than mindless submission to rules and doctrines. It is the life discovered when one ascends into the rarefied air of spiritual thought.

The best each of us can do is to make every attempt to journey toward the highest expression of our consciousness. Once we become aware of the dimension of spirit that exists in parallel with our world, we will go beyond merely surviving life and begin thriving in it. There is much to discover, but first we must free ourselves from the pollution of institutional religious thought. Only then can we begin to explore the essential mystery at the core of every human life.

ACCOUNTABILITY AND JUDGMENT

The greater riches that were promised by the prophets is not the salvation of only some or a few people called by God from the nations, while the vast majority remains doomed, but of all of created humanity exclusive of none and inclusive of all. The promise is for all humanity.

—*Jan Bonda,* The One Purpose of God

The seeds of discovery are constantly floating around us, but they only take root in minds well prepared to receive them.

—*Joseph Henry*

Many people are terrified of death because of the idea of appearing before an angry, vengeful God. Our fear-based theologies teach us that immediately following death, God will judge us by everything we have done in our lives. Talk about terrorism. Few things are more frightening than the notion of standing before an impatient, disappointed supernatural being who has His finger poised over a trapdoor button that will send you sliding into a customized torture chamber forever.

The objections to Inclusion often revolve around this basic question: "But if everyone is saved, how can people be punished for their sins?" The hunger for the punishment of others is one of the most grotesque aspects of human nature, and religion only magnifies this. I believe in accountability, but not as I have been taught as a Christian. Accountability and judgment are completely different.

Accountability suggests that each of us is responsible for answering for how we lived our lives. Judgment suggests verdict and sentence for crimes committed. When Scripture refers to "giving an account of what you did in life," it means that you will offer a record of your life and be rewarded for what you did and how you lived.

Sometimes the reward is immediate, as in Ecclesiastes 12:14, where Solomon says, "For God will bring every deed into judgment, including every hidden thing, whether it is good or evil." At the time, Solomon was in his seventies and facing his own death. He was in a reflective mood and was considering what he had done with his life. He had come to the conclusion that everything was vanity. What a sad way to conclude a life of wealth, wisdom, wine, and women (three hundred wives, seven hundred concubines), all supposedly a blessing from God! He wasn't, at that moment, thinking of future retribution. He was reflecting on his present situation and his years of grief and disappointment based on how he had set his priorities. He saw himself as a public success but a private failure.

Over the years, we have taken Solomon's words (as religions are accustomed to doing) and built a doctrine of fear of the ultimate judgment around them. However, a closer study of Old Testament thought shows that this concept of final judgment was not commonly held. Jews felt judgment for one's life came during life. Eternity was an obscure concept. We find the same idea in the Hindu concept of karma, the idea that what you put into this life will come back to you. There is nothing that supports an interpretation of Solomon's words as evidence of a fearful final judgment.

HOW SHOULD WE THEN LIVE?

Reward and punishment are the basic concepts on which today's major faiths are built. But they are spurious. Any farmer knows that a horse will move if there is a carrot dangling in front of it and a whip to threaten it. But the animal does not believe in the *rightness* of moving forward; he does so to get the treat and to avoid feeling pain.

Religion offers the same carrot and stick and demeans us in the process. Do we honor God and Christ if we live virtuous lives solely because we fear hell, or because we are bribed with the carrot of heaven? By that logic, atheists, who presumably do good not out of hope for an eternal reward but because they feel it is right, are more virtuous than Christians.

The accountants of Christianity who insist on "keeping books" on people's sins are an affront to God. In *The Parables of the Kingdom,* Robert Farrar Capon writes, "The human race is positively addicted to keeping records and remembering scores. What we call our 'life' is, for the most part, simply the juggling of accounts in our heads." He continues, "What the Son will offer the Father at the last day is the silence of his death on the subject of our sins and the power of his resurrection on the subject of our life."

This bookkeeping mentality has destroyed Christianity's reputation. Mahatma Gandhi, a follower of Christ in His purest form, said, "I may have become a Christian were it not for Christians." That is a damning indictment from one of the greatest men of peace of all time.

I remember discussing the Gospel of Inclusion with Bernice King, the youngest daughter of the late civil rights icon Dr. Martin Luther King Jr. Though she didn't necessarily embrace fully my premise, her first response was, "I have always had trouble perceiving or conceiving Mahatma Gandhi in hell when he was such a spiritual and philosophical mentor for my dad and such a powerful man of peace and nonviolence."

I know many people who love the Jesus of Scripture but who keep their distance from his "cult." This saddens me no end, because it is a poor reflection of how Christians have allowed our expression to deteriorate. The consciousness of reward and punishment pervades the Abrahamic faiths—Judaism, Christianity, and Islam. The resulting rage, fear, and reactionary attitudes are responsible for many of the horrors of war, "ethnic cleansing," aggressive religious proselytizing, and self-righteous bigotry and elitism. Our lives should be guided by a higher purpose than avoiding pain and getting goodies. The Apostle Paul got it right when he said that he was compelled, driven, and motivated by God's love (2 Corinthians 5:14).

WHO IS IT THAT NEEDS SAVING AGAIN?

As a Christian minister, I am supposed to be in the business of "saving souls." This means turning people to Jesus Christ, who then points them to God, who then fills them with His Holy Spirit, which convinces them of their wretchedness without Christ and of the advantage of committing to Jesus as Lord and Savior. All of this in turn supposedly gets them a "Get Out of Eternal Damnation Free" card.

Evangelical Christianity teaches that God views the unsaved (or non-Christian) as lost, hell-bound souls from birth whom He, in His merciful benevolence, has provided a means by which they may be saved anyway. The responsibility of getting these poor lost souls saved becomes mine because I am a born-again believer who carries out the Great Commission, as recorded in Matthew 28:19–20 and Mark 16:15.

The torment of every Evangelical is the failure to carry out the Great Commission. We never feel that we are saving enough people; of course, the preachers will never let us forget. I admit that I did that with the rest and best of them. We are taught that God wants everybody saved, and we are told to get out there and save them. Knocking on doors, confronting people in private and public places, passing out tracts, and witnessing on the job or in the classroom are some of the ways in which Christians attempt to carry out the Great Commission.

Some of the larger and more financially secure ministries and churches buy television time to air their messages, get people to call or write in their commitments to Christ, and get them to send money if they are so inclined. Some actually travel overseas to save those they call the "heathens and pagans," risking health and life. They sacrifice the comforts of home life, children, and family, familiar cultural surroundings, and modern conveniences to reach the "unreached" people of the world. My religious tradition has always viewed foreign missions as the highest of callings.

Proclaiming the Really Good News

I contend that the concept of "getting people saved" is wrong. We do not need to go forth and save anyone. In Christ Consciousness, *all* people are already saved! This message must be proclaimed first to those who are assigned to communicate it, Christians, and then to the entire world in a way that appeals to the intellect and respects other cultures and faiths. Evangelism is informing all people, not just those who confess Christ, of their salvation and reconciliation to God. The work is done, regardless of what they believe. Some call this "The Restoration of All Things."

God's will to save is as vast as His will to create. Most Christians do not doubt God's power to create; they will fight fiercely for the doctrine of natural creation. However, these same people denounce just as fiercely the idea that God can and has saved the world He created. The reason? Ego. We are flattered by the concept of an eternal God creating us with His hand, but not so flattered by the notion that we are equal in salvation with a person we regard as a heathen or infidel.

Hans Denck, one of the sixteenth-century Reformers, penned these words as he wrestled with spiritual realities:

> The schism within the Catholic Church that we now call the Reformation was not merely about Luther. It was about many people seeking the freedom to express new ideas. Many of the rebellious groups, the Anabaptists and Quakers, considered the salvation of all as a distinct possibility. Since love in him was perfect, and since love hates or is envious of none, but includes everyone, even though we were all his enemies, surely he would not wish to exclude anyone. And if he had excluded anyone, the love would have been squint-eyed and a respecter of persons. And that, God is not!

The word *repentance* (*metanoe,* in Greek) means "to rethink or reconsider." It doesn't always mean "I'm sorry." It means "I misinterpreted the love of God for mankind and for me." God created us without our choosing, and He can redeem us without our choosing. Believing is important but not essential to eternal salvation. Faith does not save a person. It simply *acknowledges* the reality of salvation. Where believing is essential is in acquiring a consciousness that awakens the broader hopes of life and the life to come.

There are opportunities for redemption in our everyday experiences. If we relegate redemption to eternity, we lose only our ability to make this world the paradise it can be. Redemption is as much a part of our everyday experiences as in the hereafter.

Christians have reduced God from Spirit to religious relics and lifeless rituals. Religion is supposedly in the bridge-building business, but it fails to realize that the bridge has already been constructed—from God's side. Anyone can cross. If they don't, the connection is still made. Oneness—or connection to God—is an immutable reality.

My Catholic Friends

For seven years, my family and I lived in Otay, California, a small, predominantly black and Hispanic community located about five miles north of the Mexican border in Southern California. Many of my closest friends were Mexican-Americans, some undocumented immigrants and nearly all of them devout Roman Catholics. I grew to love them as we worked, played, and studied together. Most of the parents were poor migrant or blue-collar workers. We were together all week, except for Sundays, when we scattered to our different houses of worship. Faith separated us only on Sundays; the rest of the week it wasn't an issue.

Although it was never openly discussed, it was assumed among Evangelical Protestants that Catholics were not born again, were unsaved, and thus hell-bound. This assumption was always a problem for me. I never really believed that God would reject those dear friends with whom I seemed to have so much in common. It seemed unreasonable that all these people were going to end up in hell forever, where they would suffer the infamous "weeping, wailing, and gnashing of teeth," and that they would be sent there by a God who I believed loved them all.

I was especially troubled, since my Catholic friends seemed devout in ways we Pentecostals were not. They made the sign of the cross repeatedly during the day. They didn't eat meat on Fridays, in honor of the day Christ died on the Cross. They often went to Mass during the week, celebrated confirmation, went to catechism weekly, genuflected and dipped their fingers in holy water as they entered the church, placed candles, incense, and icons everywhere, and so on. I especially remember Holy Week, which always began with Ash Wednesday observations. My friends would come to school with ash crosses traced on their foreheads. They seemed proud of their religious expressions and observations.

In contrast, we Pentecostals were ashamed of our religion; it was less popular and was looked upon as weird and even fanatical. We were inhibited publicly when it came to our personal lives, and even more private about our worship. I was sensitive to the fact that our denomination was predominantly African-American, at least in our local church. The Catholics were considerably integrated, with Latinos, Caucasians, Africans, African-Americans, and Asians, all of whom seemed equally devout.

The Shame of Religious Prejudice

Two questions remained with me through junior high and high school. Why were all of these Catholic people, who were friends of mine and whom I loved, going to hell? And were they really going to end up there eternally? Deep within my heart, I hoped that I would someday discover a satisfactory answer that would not leave me perplexed, frustrated, and suspicious. Someday I would resolve the irreconcilable logic of a loving, merciful, and inclusive God, and the angry, bigoted God of my Evangelical upbringing and persuasion.

When I was a little boy growing up in the turbulent 1950s and 1960s, as the civil rights movement and race relations grew from infancy to national firestorm, the only kind of prejudice I was aware of was racial prejudice. I had no concept of anything more vicious or hateful. I certainly did not realize that there was a brand of prejudice more calamitous. However, as I grew older and got more involved in the broader religious world, I discovered that the seductive vices of religious prejudice far outstripped those of racial hatred.

Religious prejudice stands in the way of truth. It arrogantly presupposes that there is nothing more one can learn about God, the Bible, or faith. It insinuates that anyone who suggests otherwise has a hidden agenda, is mentally ill, or is an outright heretic—a dupe of the Antichrist fit only for damnation.

WHAT DID JESUS DO?

As I understand it, the Gospel of Jesus Christ is the *proclamation* of redemption, not the *act* of redemption. It is not a command for righteousness, it is a declaration of righteousness. Jesus at Calvary is the work of salvation. According to Scripture, He is the Beloved Son in whom the Father is well pleased (Matthew 3:17). Why? Because He met all the requirements of the law by which the enemy accuses the entire human race. He paid the price on our behalf.

It has been said, "A true Christian does not necessarily belong to a sect. He realizes he is a child of the universe and of the God who created it. He ceases to wrangle over doctrines, dogmas, and words. He thrives in the midst of sects and religious iconoclasts and keeps above the controversies. He puts his knowing into the life of Christ and in that consciousness. He lives quietly but fully in his awareness of Christ and the finished work of redemption."

There is a popular adage, "What would Jesus do?" The question should be "What *did* Jesus do?" Until we recognize the full revelation of what He finished, we will never really know what He started. If you doubt the ending, you surely must question the beginning!

PART II
THE GOSPELS
OF INCLUSION

One of the few places I was invited to speak (after I was outed as a heretical inclusionist) was a conference in Phoenix, Arizona, that was sponsored and attended by a predominantly gay, Christian fellowship of people and churches headed up by a female bishop I had helped to consecrate to Episcopal office.

Though I had never been an outspoken opponent of homosexuality, I was quietly associated with those who summarily categorized gays as sinners and at least tacitly agreed. Without question, one of the most moving experiences of my ministerial career is what happened to me at this particular conference.

At the close of my sermon, Bishop Yvette Flunder asked me to walk down the center aisle, and allow the people to shake my hand or embrace me as they all gave a rousing, tearful standing ovation. I was deeply touched and moved by the warm reception, but I was even more confounded as I returned to the front to find Bishop Flunder on her knees in front of a vat of warm water and surrounded by a host of celebrants. She asked me to take a seat and remove my socks and shoes, and she, along with other ministers, washed my feet and asked that I become a fathering spirit among them. It was as high an honor for me to accept that spiritual function as it was to accept my initial ordination to full-time ministry over thirty-five years ago.

Yvette Flunder said to me, "Bishop, if you are really an inclusionist, you need to be ready, because we are coming." I wept. The entire experience was profoundly cathartic for me, inspired by a group of which I had never expected to be a part. God used the most marginalized, discriminated-against people in modern culture to embrace me at my lowest, loneliest ebb. You can't teach what you don't know, and you can't lead where you don't go. My life and ministry will never be the same.

YOU SAY YOU WANT A REVOLUTION?

The deconstruction of Christianity and religion is a revolutionary act, since neither institution is fond of scrutiny. However, since doctrinal policies and attitudes fuel the virus that infects so much of the believing community, I must lay down my shovel and begin incising with a scalpel the canons that sicken Christianity around the globe.

Though the words and actions of Christ in the New Testament are generally beneficent and compassionate, the exhortations issuing from the pulpits, Web sites, and press releases of the Christian right are more in line with the image of the Old Testament God: wrath and plagues, fire and brimstone, hate and vengeance. Many of today's self-anointed pulpit prophets would like to take the healing, loving, Redeeming Christ and graft onto Him a visage of God straight from Cotton Mather and Daniel Webster, in which the Lord calls on us to abhor, oppress, and even kill our enemies. Isn't this the crime we Evangelicals accuse the Koran and Islam of?

The motives of small men reflect their minds and spirits. Such dogma is a perversion of the life and death of Jesus, at least as it is supposed to be portrayed in Christian theology. For a faith based on the great hope and light of a resurrected savior, Christianity in the early twenty-first century is obsessed with darkness: the Apocalypse and the appearance of the Antichrist, organized hatred of groups like homosexuals, the suppression of knowledge, and the gleeful damnation of anyone who does not hew to its twisted brand of faith.

Leaving aside that since the fourth century, people have insisted they *knew* they were living in the Last Days (a prescription for absolving oneself of responsibility if I've ever seen one), this path is madness. When love, healing, tolerance, and justice cease to be the cornerstones of the Christian faith, it is not the non-Christians of the world who are damned. It is Christianity itself—damned to resentment in the larger culture, to being marginalized as the domain of "right-wing wackos," to eventual extinction as a relevant force in the world.

Christianity deserves better. Christ deserves better. The faith that sprung from the words of St. Paul of Tarsus (though at times still bigoted himself) has the potential to shape human civilization for the better—to evoke the Divinity that we express all too infrequently. It is my hope that by shining a harsh light onto these credos of the Christian faith, I can not only burn away dead, corrupt tissue, but also stimulate healing and greater self-awareness. As the eighteenth-century English writer Samuel Johnson said, "We are easily shocked by crimes which appear at once in their full magnitude, but the gradual growth of our own wickedness, endeared by interest, and palliated by all the artifices of self-deceit, gives us time to form distinctions in our own favor." I hope to wither some of that self-deceit in the coming chapters.

The next few chapters will deal less with a gospel than with a doctrine considered "gospel truth." Since the term actually means "good news," it will seem inappropriate to call some of the chapters "gospel of," but I do so because the term has evolved to mean not only good news, but presumed truth. I intend to challenge that presumption.

CHAPTER FOUR

THE GOSPEL OF SIN

Since love is all there is, sin in the light of Holy Spirit is a mistake to be corrected rather than an evil to be punished.

—from A Course In Miracles

My ninety-three-year-old aunt, who suffers from severe and crippling arthritis, is the last living daughter of my great-grandfather Poppa Lon's first five children; he had twenty-one others after the death of his first wife. She told me that she believed God's hand had been upon her life since she was a child, and that during a near-death experience angels appeared to her and healed her while her mother sat beside her bed, weeping.

They were extremely poor people living way out in the country, far away from doctors they would not have been able to afford anyway. Insurance wasn't even a concept back then, especially to African-Americans living in the Deep South at the turn of the twentieth century.

She spoke movingly about her assurance that God had something special for her to do, though at age ninety-three, she wasn't sure what it was. After sharing her childhood experience of angelic visitation, she then told me that God was punishing her with her painful and crippling arthritis because she "backslid" during her early teens and went out into the secular world until her forties. She danced, smoked, drank, and did all the things we were taught were horrible sins.

She now considers herself saved, but barely, because she still wrestles with anger, unforgivingness, and other carnal human maladies. God has forgiven her sins, but she hasn't forgiven herself for sinning, and therefore feels tormented with sickness because God is punishing her. I love her deeply and dearly, but I have not been able to convince her how her gospel of sin invites, validates, and emboldens her need for pain and sickness.

In the book *A Course in Miracles,* it says, "Healing involves an understanding of what the illusion of sickness is for. Healing is impossible without this. Healing is accomplished the moment the sufferer no longer sees any value in pain . . ." Our present religious sickness is an election, a decision we've made, a choice of spiritual weakness and lack. Our sickness is a method perceived in madness, placing our religious institutions ahead of the true Spirit of Christ, thus making us victims of doctrines, dogmas, and disciplines that separate us from the broader consciousness of pure Spirit! *A Course in Miracles* emphasizes three basic points: nothing real can be threatened; nothing unreal exists; herein lies the peace of God.

WHAT IS SIN?

I was approached by an elder in my church who complained that I did not preach enough against sin and sinners. He felt my gospel was giving people a license to sin. I responded by saying, "Sir, they are already sinning without a license."

Sin is simply an inappropriate response to a legitimate need. We all have emotional, physical, and spiritual needs that we often feel cannot be met if we are to walk the path laid out for us by religion. But denying the needs that God placed within us by calling them sinful is against the spirit of Christ—anti-Christ.

The word *Antichrist* is one of the most intimidating names in Christian terminology. I began hearing about the Antichrist from infancy. Next to the devil, there is no single entity that triggers more fear and paranoia. Movies, books, and sermons about this subject have traumatized millions, particularly within the Evangelical Christian community, for centuries.

The term *Antichrist* in its original Greek reference means not only "against Christ" but "instead of Christ." It implies someone or something that usurps the name of Christ and His function as Lord. Though most of the Evangelical Christian world views the Antichrist ("man of sin" or "son of perdition") as a literal person, the most pronounced Antichrist spirit is religion itself—even Christianity.

All religions allege that they can achieve something Christian theology teaches that Christ has already done through His substitutionary death on the Cross. In other words, they contend that Christ failed at redeeming the world back to God, as Scripture declares, and that Christianity is essentially finishing what Christ said was already accomplished (John 19:30). This is the spirit of Antichrist, though most Christians don't recognize it as such.

RELIGION USURPS THE WORK OF CHRIST

Religion seeks to resolve a presumed conflict between God and humankind that no longer exists and in reality may really never have, except in the minds of people who have been indoctrinated to believe such. If it did exist, according to Christian theology, it has been resolved in the redemptive, preemptive work of the Cross. When we assume that we are doing something Christ could not, we assume that He fell short and we need to add something to His work. As people of faith, how can we trust ourselves to accomplish something that we evidently don't trust (God in or through) Christ to have been successful at accomplishing?

Religion tends to usurp the role of Christ as the Redeemer, insisting that something more is necessary, and that it has a responsibility to re-create the act of redemption again and again with each succeeding generation, century, and millennium.

Capon, in his book *The Fingerprints of God*, compared the gift of God to man's propensity to prefer a deal over a gift. "Religiosity and moralism go down easier than free forgiveness. Salvation by our own works sells better than the outrageous 'acceptance in the Beloved' that lets disreputable types in for nothing but faith in the Beloved or the faith *of* the Beloved. The human race, faced with the choice between a gift and a deal, will almost invariably prefer the deal."

Christ is the sole remedy for the soul malady. Christ's redemption is comprehensive, all-inclusive, nondiscriminatory, nonsectarian, and unsegregated. It is "one size fits all" salvation. In the Book of Revelation it says, "whosoever will, let him take the water of life freely . . ." (Revelation 22:17, KJV).

Since Jesus manifested as a living man, many Christians have assumed the Antichrist to be a living man who is the opposite of Christ; the would-be destroyer of His legacy. However, the original Greek strongly suggests that many aspects of organized Christianity or the Holy Roman Empire fit the description of a then modern-day Antichrist. To insist that the world is not already redeemed to God by Christ is to suggest that Christ failed in His task. I can understand this position from non-Christians or so-called unbelievers, but it is curious that supposed followers of Jesus don't have more confidence in Him or His "finished work."

JESUS, NOT FAITH, SAVES

I have been accused of teaching that there are other ways to God besides Jesus. That is untrue. I believe unequivocally that Jesus Christ (not Christianity) is the only way to God in redemption. However, His function is not so much to bring us to God but to provide a redemptive consciousness so we won't believe the illusion of separation from God or our own innate divinity. Christian Scripture and theology clearly teach that Jesus is the way to salvation for all, not just some of humankind: "For there is one God, and one mediator between God and men, the man Christ Jesus, who gave himself as a ransom for all men—the testimony given in its proper time" (1 Timothy 2:5–6).

Jesus is not only the way of salvation, He is the *work* of salvation. The Christ Principle provides that Jesus accomplished world reconciliation to God, and those of us who believe in Him should be proclaiming this reality not only through what we say but how we live and how we treat others. All people, no matter their beliefs, are reconciled to God because of a salvation they did not earn—and did not need to. This is faith consciousness at its best, and faith transcends what religion denies.

We are saved by grace through faith; and that not from ourselves, "it is the gift of God—not of works, so that no one can boast" (Ephesians 2:8–9). Read that again. Paul said we *would not be saved through works.* The gift of salvation is not the result of anything we can do, because what needed to be done has already been done. The work of Christ, not Christians, saved the world. If Christ is the lamb that was slain before the foundation of the world (as Scripture declares), then Christ Consciousness and its Principle have been present in every generation since the foundation of the world.

CHRISTIANITY AND SIN

Sin is, we are told, the black mark on our account even from the day we are born. But what does it mean to be a Christian and sin? There are two words prominently used in the Greek New Testament to define the word *sin*. One is *hamartano*, which means "missing the mark." The other is *hamartia*, which means "offense," presumably against God. Christians commit sins, but we are expected not to practice sin or live sinfully. Christians are not "sinless"; we just try to "sin less."

The commission of individual sins will always be present in the lives of human beings, but according to Christian theology, *hamartia* has been washed away by the blood of Jesus. We all miss the mark, but Christ has forever resolved the offense of sin. I like to say it this way: you'll never know you are free *from* sin until you know you are actually free *to* sin and still be loved by God and advocated by Christ (1 John 2:1–2).

The more devout we are, the more sin conscious we are expected to be, and the more effort we are supposed to expend to avoid sin. Devout religious people are expected to live holier, if not *holier than thou,* lives. They supposedly see "the mark" more clearly because of the enlightenment of their Christ Consciousness. Obviously, it's much easier to hit the target when you know it and see it clearly. In Evangelical Christianity, we are expected to live a life of discipline, holiness, and piety. If we fall short, we're expected to fake it till we make it, which is one of a multitude of hypocrisies.

Sin consciousness—the concept that we are inherently delinquent spiritually—is a human invention that inflicts deep psychological wounds on our culture. All of my life I was told that I was "born in sin and shaped in iniquity" (Psalm 51:5, KJV) and that I needed to be born again in order to cancel my contract with my fleshly, sinful nature. This idea leaves us feeling that we are victims of an innate wickedness—"born under a bad sign" and held hostage through no fault of our own. This teaching also suggests and insists we should act out what we have been told we are: sinners.

Subconsciously we presume ourselves to be innately and intrinsically something less than good or godly. Indoctrinated with a sin consciousness, we look for ways to carry out the edict or assignment given us. We invent, create, or develop sins, including handbooks, brands, teachings, and schedules of sin. There are entire cultures and customs based on sin consciousness in America and around the world.

Innocent Until Proven Guilty

Unlike the Napoleonic codes of justice in many other nations, in which the accused is presumed guilty until proven innocent, we are fortunate enough to have a different jurisprudence in the United States. Under it, we are innocent until proven guilty. However, Christianity tells us that we are presumed guilty until proven (by our actions, faith, and obedience) innocent.

We were supposedly rendered innocent by the sacrifice of Christ, weren't we? Yes, but we have allowed our dogmas and disciplines to determine our guilt or innocence instead. This turns us into our own lawyers in the court of Christian expectations, crippled beneath the pressure of trying to prove our innocence.

This mind-set becomes a self-fulfilling prophecy. We say, "If I'm a sinner, I may as well sin!" Here again, we become what we think about. We act out our religiously imposed conscience. Thanks to our religious teachings, we have bought into the lie that we are naked and in need of a covering other than that with which we were originally created (Genesis 3:7). I call this the "fig leaf of deception."

In Genesis 3:11 God is said to have asked the question, "Who told you that you were naked?" when Adam reveals that he was hiding from God out of shame at his nakedness. Here is another way of interpreting God's question: "Who convinced you that you lacked something other than what I have given you when you were created?" Religion amplifies that sense of lack by convincing us that we need the fig leaves of doctrines and dogmas to cover our spiritual nakedness, rather than accepting the grace of God expressed in Christ as all we need.

Contrary to what religion teaches, sin is something we do; it is not who or what we are. I can make mistakes and commit sinful acts—indeed, we all do this daily—yet at my core, I remain unchanged, a person true to the Christ Principle innate within my authentic self; the rest is an impersonation. The sinful nature is the flesh. I have a body, and I have a mind, but I *am* a Spirit.

The Misperception of Original Sin

The infamous concept of original sin is derived from Scriptures like Psalm 51:5: "Behold, I was shapen in iniquity; and in sin did my mother conceive me" (KJV). Based upon that verse of Scripture, I was taught that I was innately sinful from conception. It indicts us from the outset. Thanks to St. Augustine, this idea became doctrine.

However, this was not taught by the earlier church fathers. We can see why such a concept would be popular in the halls of power of the church when we look at religion as what it often has been: a structure for controlling the thoughts and actions of others. The slander that each of us is born carrying a freight of original sin, and that only adherence to ritual will save us from everlasting torment, gives the church a stranglehold on hearts and minds. Even nonbelievers obey church dictates out of fear of sanction by the community.

This indictment has been rooted into our consciousness. It is the curse of all religion. Humans of most religious persuasions are taught that iniquity and criminality are inherent in them. This falsehood has been pounded into us for centuries, to the point where it's now part of the global consciousness: being "human" equals being "fatally flawed."

Religion has done a good job convincing us we were born bad and to *be* bad. But even if original sin were true, it would have been canceled through Christ's atonement. Let's look at the passage of Scripture again. The author writes, "I was shaped in iniquity." The original Hebrew words or even the sentence structure could make the sentence mean many things. It is devilishly ambiguous, scant evidence for damning an entire race.

Who Was the Original Sinner?

There is no original sin. There is only an original sinner. Everything did not begin in sin; it began in God and will climax in Him. According to Genesis, the original state of humankind was Godliness or "God likeness," not sin. Humans were originally created in God's spiritual likeness, not Adam's human frailty. We were Adamic, but more important, we were dynamic. We had the *dunamis,* or power of God, working in and through us. We had God's divine sparkle, zeal, and spontaneity. We had our Father's eyes, and we still do.

Evil, then, is secondary and should never be considered the primary nature of humankind. It is an aberration, a subtle illusion perpetrated by the deceiver to estrange us from our Creator in consciousness. This false consideration warps our self-consciousness, self-worth, and self-esteem. Much of today's religious culture is a low-self-esteem cult: "You're bad, you're evil, you're a sinner, and unless you do what we say, God might throw you into hell right now." It is difficult to feel God *could* love us unconditionally.

You could carpet the world a foot deep with the sermons preached on original sin. However, sin is not original. Only God is original. Sin came later, possibly thousands of years later, and is secondary to the larger reality that is the Divine in all of us. We don't know how long Adam and Eve were in the garden before they ate of the forbidden tree, but we do know that it was not necessarily their initial act. Adam and Eve were created innocent but not necessarily virtuous. Innocence is ignorance of the difference between right and wrong, good and evil. Virtue is coming face-to-face with temptation, and then choosing the good over the evil.

Conceived in Sin, or Just Out of Wedlock?

The Psalmist David in Old Testament Scripture said, "In sin did my mother conceive me" (Psalm 51:5, KJV). Does this mean David was a sinner from conception? Or does it mean that David's mother conceived him outside the Jewish covenant of marriage? David was the youngest of eight brothers, who, according to their portrayal in Scripture, did not have an overwhelming fondness for their spoiled, precocious little brother (1 Samuel 17:28–29). We don't know his mother's name.

The Hebrew word that the KJV interprets as "shapen" is *chul*, which means "to twist or whirl in a circular or spiral manner; to dance or writhe in pain." It is entirely conceivable that David was born to a different mother than his brothers—one who, at the time of conception, was not married to his father, Jesse. David says he was "shaped or fashioned into iniquity." This may mean that he regarded the circumstances of his birth as a path to perversity.

But rather than consider the possible worldly meaning of these words, we have chosen to regard them as an accusation of universal, inborn guilt. This leads to an immediate sense of victimization and alienation from God—the idea that there is an ongoing conflict between God and man that man must resolve. This is the state to which religion has fallen. Rather than enjoying a worshipful and mutually rewarding relationship with the Creator, we have been embroiled in a centuries-old battle with God, which according to the Christ Principle has long been resolved—and, again, may have never really existed.

Actually, the English word *worship* comes from the concept of worth, or *worthship*. As we approach God in adoration, we should feel adored and our self-worth heightened.

Sin, the Devil, and the Angry God

I am not suggesting that there was never a perceived human issue that needed resolution. I am suggesting that these realities do not exist in God's economy as they do in ours. The devil is not an equal rival to God. The devil is something else entirely. The devil is *legalism and stagnation,* the concept that one must seek forgiveness from God through obedience and the practices of the various laws of religion. But if God, as Scripture declares, loves us with an everlasting love, then we don't need forgiveness, because God does not hold grudges and is larger than offense, anger, or hurt.

In 1 John 3:8 we read, "The reason the Son of God appeared was to destroy the devil's work." What is the devil's work? It is described in the first part of the sentence: "He who does what is sinful is of the devil, because the devil has been sinning from the beginning." In 1 John 2:1–2 the writer uses two different Greek words for "sin." In 1 John 3:8, where he says, "He that commits sin is of the devil," he uses the word *hamartia,* which means "to offend." But when he says, ". . . but the devil has been sinning from the beginning," he uses the second word for sin, *hamartano,* which means literally "to miss the mark."

How does one offend an omnipotent being who created the universe? The idea of worshipping God is generally our attempt to absolve ourselves of the sin of *not* worshipping Him. We assume He is going to be angry and even belligerent if we don't flatter His eternal ego—an absurd idea.

In reality, you oppose God by doing that which is in opposition to your own divinity. He who does what is sinful—who does what is opposite to his own divinity—is of the devil, focused on the flesh and not the Spirit. The *devil* represents the duality in religion when he says: "The day you eat of the tree you will not die, you will become like God knowing good and evil" (Genesis 3:4 and 5 paraphrased). That is the duality in us, our obsession with sin and virtue being mutually exclusive.

We use this idea of a devil to personify our sense of right and wrong. We use our doctrines to tell us how to please God. Legalism suggests that God is angry with us and that our disobedience can trigger an emotional outburst from Him, and that the only way to placate Him is to follow religious laws *religiously.* This is an infantile belief common to all religions. All faiths believe man has the capacity to anger God, causing Him to throw a temper tantrum that manifests as an earthquake, volcano, hurricane, or some other natural disaster. This "angry god" syndrome is a holdover from Greek mythology, and it influenced the early church fathers. The Greeks believed that their fate was in the hands of some unstable, psychotic gods. Sound familiar?

Florence Nightingale, considered the pioneer of modern nursing and a radical liberation theologist, had strong, clear views on the love of God versus the angry God of religion:

I can't love because I am ordered—least of all can't I love One who seems only to make me miserable here to torture me hereafter. Show me that He is good, that He is loveable, and I shall love Him without being told. But does any preacher show this? He may say that God is good, but he shows Him to be very bad; he may say that God is "love," but he shows Him to be hate, worse than any hate of man. As the Persian poet says: "If God punishes me for doing evil by doing me evil, how is he better than I?" And it is hard to answer, for certainly the worst man would hardly torture his enemy, if he could, forever. And unless God has a scheme that every man is saved forever, it is hard to say in what He is not worse than man; for all good men would save others if they could. It is of no use saying that God is just, unless we define what justice is. In all Christian times people have said that "God is just" and have credited Him with an injustice such as transcends all human injustice that it is possible to conceive.

The Devil in the Unemployment Line

When I say the "devil," I am talking about legal systems of right and wrong. Paul said that without the law there is no knowledge of sin. Adam and Eve would have attained this knowledge when they ate of the tree of good and evil. The concept was introduced by the subtlety of the serpent. Let's look at John's passage again:

> The one who practices sin is of the devil; for the devil has sinned from the beginning. The Son of God appeared for this purpose, to destroy the works of the devil.
>
> —1 John 3:8 (NASB)

"He who does what is sinful" is of the devil. The first half of the sentence says, "The devil has been sinning from the beginning." Man is not the original sinner. The devil is. Remember, the Greek word that John uses here is *hamartano*, "to miss the mark." The devil's work is "missing the mark." The devil's occupation is to publicize misinformation that is developed into belief systems. Thus we have the destructive doctrine of original sin. Jesus came to destroy this propaganda. The Greek meaning of the word *destroy*, as used in this passage, is *luo*, and it means "to loosen, dissolve, or melt." In the book of Hebrews it is written that not only has the devil's work been defeated, but the devil himself has been destroyed (Hebrews 2:14).

Another interpretation of the word *destroy* is *katargeo*. It comes from two Greek words: *kata*, meaning "down," and *argeo*, which means "to be idle or delayed." The word *argeo* comes from the word *ergon*, which means "to work." The word *katargeo* means "to be out of work or unemployed." The suggestion is that Jesus put the devil (the law) out of work. He is, in effect, in the unemployment line.

In the end, Jesus (embodied in the Christ Principle) is the victor. By atoning for our sins and reestablishing our nature as divine, He has put the devil and his legal system out of work. He takes all of humanity upon His shoulders and brings them home to His Father. All nations and all people will fill the courts of eternity with the sounds of joyous worship and thanksgiving for the great wisdom and passionate love of God.

CHAPTER FIVE

THE GOSPEL OF EVIL

And the LORD God made all kinds of trees grow out of the
ground—trees that were pleasing to the eye and good for
food. In the middle of the garden were the tree of life and
the tree of the knowledge of good and evil.

—Genesis 2:9

In the church I grew up in, we had testimony service nearly every
time we met. One of the statements I heard repeatedly was
a phrase commonly used to close most testimonies: "Pray my
strength in the Lord that I will be faithful to God in these last and
evil days." I was always fascinated by what exactly "these last and
evil days" were.

Evil was a huge part of our religious consciousness. We saw it
everywhere and in everything. It was preached with great fervor
and emotion. There was hardly a sermon that didn't mention evil
somewhere—especially at the close of the sermon, before we were
all invited to come forward to cleanse ourselves of it and pray for
the world to be cleansed of it as well. The concept of evil goes back
as far as our concept of the Garden of Eden, where Adam was
forbidden to indulge in evilness by eating of the tree bearing the

contrasting fruits of what we perceived as "good [God] and evil [devil]."

LOST IN TRANSLATION

We learn much about what the writers of Scripture meant from analyzing the language in which the passages were originally written. English translation is often deceiving. English is a recent language derived mainly from other languages, and many of its words were developed through relative associations with other words. For example, the word *literal* is a derivative of the word *letter.* In 2 Corinthians 3:6 (KJV), when the Apostle Paul says, "the letter killeth," he is implying that a literal interpretation of Jewish writings can be lethal to one's spiritual well-being.

The word *truth* implies an awareness of good and evil. The word *true* in Hebrew is *ken,* and means "properly to set upright or to set up rightly." It is a derivative of the word *kun,* which translates "to be erect or to stand perpendicular, like a tree." Note the similarity in spelling between "tree" and "true."

The English words *cane* and *canon,* which suggest different types of supports to lean on, are drawn from this same meaning. A cane is something upon which one leans, as is the canon of Scripture.

Trees are associated with strength and reliability. They can be leaned upon and climbed. Fruit grows on them, and they can sustain life. They withstand harsh winds and weather. They are deeply rooted. The characteristics of a tree can be associated with the qualities of truth. It is telling that God chose to represent the duality of good and evil with the tree of knowledge, a life form so closely associated with good. This reflects our tendency as human beings—toward good but still afflicted by evils.

THE SPIRIT OF MURDER

Duality is the doctrine that mankind is under the influence of two opposing principles, often perceived as good and evil. Both are woven deeply into our psyche and are central to our beings. Yet people and actions are judged as good or evil, with no gray area in between. This contributes to our intolerance of views and cultures that differ from our own, and impedes our efforts to improve the lot of our fellows. Guilt-ridden over our own capacity for evil, we cripple our ability to love ourselves, much less our brothers and sisters. The inevitable result is a spirit of murder.

We murder people and cultures. We kill our personal relationships, our hopes, and our future. We kill people, religions, or concepts that we see as a threat to our worldview. We judge.

> Do not be like Cain, who belonged to the evil one and murdered his brother. And why did he murder him? Because his own actions were evil and his brother's were righteous.
>
> —1 John 3:12

Notice the distinction that led to the first act of violence: "His actions were evil and his brother's were righteous." This is the first hint as to why God did not want Adam and Eve to eat from the tree of the knowledge of good and evil. Their action ushered into the world the curse of moralism, which has been the primary calamity of human history. Spirituality and grace were replaced by the pursuit of moralism, as man became consumed with the battle between the opposing forces of good and evil within him.

Christian moralism has become the battle cry of the so-called religious right in America, especially in recent years. It has basically polarized the nation, causing a kind of religious cold war.

LIVING IN BLACK AND WHITE

Our obsession with moralism allows us to buttress our self-esteem with the delusion that we are soldiers of God in a fight against evil. So we fight and curse one another based on our perceptions of right and wrong. We evaluate people as black or white, rich or poor, educated or uneducated. James 1:8 (KJV) says, "A double minded man is unstable in all his ways." Double-mindedness degrades diversity. It breeds judgmentalism, prejudice, and distrust as readily as males and females breed children. It tills the ground for the growth of an outlook that encourages us to be at "war" with everything.

But true morality requires *choice.* One cannot be considered obedient if there is no possibility for disobedience. Without heat, we wouldn't recognize cold. Without light, we would not understand darkness. Were it not for death, we could not fully appreciate the miracle of life.

In other words, opposites define who we are and make possible the comprehension of the greatest blessings of our lives. Duality is necessary for us to fully live, and yet when we become fixated on it as a frame for defining the world, we abandon morality for simplistic games of good against evil. As children of God, we are far more complicated.

God and the Devil: The Original Duality

There is only one Supreme God. But to use the term "*one* Supreme God" suggests the possibility of other gods. Some people view religion as different methods used by humankind to find God. But in reality, all religions are something else entirely: they are the account of God's intentions to reveal Himself to humankind.

When viewed in this manner, it becomes clear why different faiths, expressions, and disciplines exist: they put on the mask of their culture in order to speak to the people in a voice they can connect with. Islam, Hinduism, Taoism, and a hundred other faiths all have different doctrines and methods and a Supreme Being. The New Testament has an interesting clarification of the legitimacy of other perceptions of God. First Corinthians 8:4–7 reads:

> . . . We know that an idol is nothing at all in the world and that there is no God but one. For even if there are so called gods, whether in heaven or on earth (as indeed there are many "gods" and many "lords"), yet for us there is but one God, the Father, from whom all things came and for whom we live; and there is but one Lord, Jesus Christ, through whom all things came and through whom we live. But not everyone knows this.

Paul does not denounce other gods. He stresses the supremacy of the one true God. Rather than practice duality, he chooses to recognize other beliefs as what they are: alternative manifestations of a God who is capable of appearing to any people as any type of godhead that will resonate with them.

There is also only one evil, but it is not coequal with God. Many people mistakenly believe the devil is omniscient (all knowing) and omnipresent (everywhere simultaneously). They grant God omnipotence (all-powerful), but that's it. Over the centuries, many have endorsed this eternal rivalry by giving the devil and/or evil nearly the same power and authority as God, leaving him short only in moral goodness—and in some theologies, even that is debatable.

We assume the devil to be everywhere, and we presume him to know what we think and what we want. He is unseen, but we assume he sees and controls all. For centuries we have viewed ourselves as the puppets of God and victims of the devil. In fact, many Christians believe that the devil is the "prince of the powers of the air" (Ephesians 2:2) and thus in charge of the planet, ultimately inheriting as much as 90 percent of its inhabitants, who spend eternity in hell with him.

But when did the devil become Lord, and who made him so? When did we give the world to him? Why do we assume the devil has a hold on most people? Who is the devil, and how did he gain such prominence among Christians who supposedly believe in a triumphant Christ? For the most part, the devil many of us were taught to believe in is a man-made invention. We have given it substance by our entrenched false and deluded perceptions.

THE GOOD, THE BAD, AND THE UGLY

We placed the devil on a lofty, religion-based pedestal. We did so by subscribing to that simplistic, venomous duality that compels us to name everything as part of the team of Good (which wins the World Series every year) or the team of Evil (which cheats but cannot help but finish last). Such thinking must be banished to the same cellar of ignorance as the concept of red devils on our shoulders telling us to be naughty. When we label all things as sacred or profane based on our limited perceptions, we place ourselves above God. Only He can determine the nature of His creations, and according to Scripture, He determined all He created to be good. This means that anything impersonating evil is an imposter.

In reality, all things have a good purpose in God's eyes, even though we cannot always perceive it. Rich, black soil on a fine Persian rug can be revolting, yet wonderful on a farm or in a potted plant. The soil itself is not intrinsically bad; it just seems bad when it is not in a role that fits our preconceptions. There are beneficial bacteria that protect our bodies from disease, and there are harmful bacteria that can cause fatal disease. We have both in our bodies. They complement each other in ways only the Creator could have designed. In the ultimate realizations, there are probably no good or bad bacteria; there are only complex microscopic organisms carrying out their appointed roles. The substances we eliminate from our bodies daily—sweat, tears, urine, dead skin, and so on—all have purpose. What comes out of us had to come into us, and it served a meaningful purpose until it could do so no longer. The good, the bad, and the ugly all have their places in the ultimate cause.

BEAUTY AND THE BEAST

> And God said, Let the earth bring forth the living creature after his kind, cattle, and creeping thing. . . . And God made the beast of the earth after his kind, and cattle after their kind, and every thing that creepeth upon the earth after his kind.
>
> —*Genesis 1:24–25 (KJV)*

I have always been fascinated with the movie *Beauty and the Beast* (either the modern Disney version or the Jean Cocteau classic version will serve). From the beginning, God ordained that we humans would have the ability to manage the beasts of the earth; both the animals around us *and the beastly nature within us.* The creepy-crawly creatures of mind and body are ultimately subject to us and have been from the beginning.

We are all managing conversations in our conscious and subconscious minds that have been there since we became conscious of our selves. This internal dialogue between the angelic, spiritual aspects of our nature and our base, fleshly characteristics makes us unique in God's creation.

What makes *Beauty and the Beast* such a classic is that it acknowledges that our untamed, amoral, dangerous side is undeniably attracted to our beautiful, sacred self—and our higher self feels just as strong an attraction to the darkness within us. More frightening, in order for beauty and beast to be together—for us to be whole—each must become more like the other!

There is a beauty and a beast inside each of us. We have been taught that they are enemies. They are not. They complement each other. While we think the phrase is "beauty and the beast," it should actually be "the beauty in the beast" or "the beast in the beauty." Both sides of our nature come from God, and are thus good. We are attracted to our chaotic, fleshly nature, or to someone in our lives who is a little dangerous. We just want to make sure that the beast does not overrule us and consume us. At the same time, we must also be careful that we do not deny our earthly nature and live according to some impotent, purely spiritual mantra that denies the joys of the physical world God has given us.

Living according to God's design does not mean inhibiting either the beast or beauty within, but acknowledging them, managing them, and being self-aware enough to give them both fair and balanced expression. We do this by allowing coexistence. Denying either side of the self could be said to be the true source of all evil!

Where There Is Balance, There Is No Evil

The beast is often beautiful, while beauty is often beastly. Both of these realities within us engage mind and spirit in a conversation that at times becomes a violent argument. We argue not because the two disagree but because they often *do* agree, and we presume they're not supposed to. We insist they remain in opposition to each other; this makes us feel more comfortable. This is like households in racist communities where parents notice that children who do not learn to discriminate based on ethnicity enjoy playing with everyone—until they are taught that people of different skin colors are not supposed to get along. Hatred does not come naturally. Only love does. Hatred is a taught and learned response.

The so-called argument between our spiritual and earthy selves (our "good" and "evil" sides) is equally manufactured. It did not originate in God. It is re-created in each new generation that makes the same errors as the Puritans: rejecting one side of the natural human duality as evil and thereby stunting the essential meaning of humanity.

We were created as one. All things work together. The music of all life is harmony, albeit one that we may not be able to hear entirely. The beauty and the beast are soul mates with a covenant to coexist. They don't compete; they complete each other. What God calls upon us to do is balance the two. That's atonement or "at-one-ment." Balance of beast and beauty means that rather than suppressing some aspect of yourself, you celebrate it as part of the complete person you are. The belief that something about us needs to be exterminated leads to repression and then depression, and then often to the truly violent, terrible acts some humans commit as a way of fulfilling the belief that they are inherently evil.

The Mystery of the Good and the Bad

The ultimate truth is that there is neither good nor bad, not as we perceive them with our limited minds. There are only choices with consequences. The beast is not bad. You merely took something that was godly and judged it to be evil. God calls on us to manage the beast and beauty by integrating them into the whole and allowing them to subsist side by side, just as God made light and darkness, so that neither could be without the other.

The word *manage* comes from the Latin *manus,* which means "hand." To manage means not only "to maintain control or influence over" but to handle with care! It means to confront yourself with the truth of *who you are.* Once you get a precise perception of who you are—both the beast and the beauty you are created to be—then you will value and appreciate the beauty and beast in all other human beings. We spend a lot of time trying to tame the beast in others, while the real challenge begins and ends with managing the beauty and the beast within ourselves.

The Apostle Paul said, in Romans 7:19–21:

> When I want to do good, evil is right there or present with me.
> In my inner being I desire to do what is right, but I find another
> law at work in the members of my body, waging war against the
> law of my mind and making me a prisoner to the law of sin at
> work within my members.

In this passage, which I have paraphrased, Paul uses the word *hamartia* for sin, meaning, as we have seen, alienation from godly growth. The word *members* is the Greek word *melos,* translated "limb or part of the body." Sin is never of the whole. It is never comprehensive. It is always partial and impermanent. It is not eternal; only God is eternal. When you sin, you sin against part of you, but not your whole being. Neither does your entire being sin.

Paul goes on to say, "O wretched man that I am, who shall deliver or rescue me from the body of this deadly nature?" (Romans 7:24; also paraphrased). In other words, how can I stop harboring this sin consciousness about the beast inside me? Religion constantly reminds us that we are not good enough. It impedes the human psyche. Religion always seeks to put the beast in a zoo, detaining and caging it for the public to gawk at, provided they pay to gain entrance. Paul is asking for a path to be free to be all of who he is—literally, to run free.

Throughout our history, religion has taken ordinary, blameless human acts—ranging from drinking alcohol and playing dice, to eating pork or drawing representations of prophets—declared them evil, made us ashamed, and driven the activities underground. Yes, there are human acts of violence and theft that are vile and deserve condemnation. But even these are not evil; they are the results of a soul sickness that leads to destructive choices and terrible consequences. They are a symptom of a spirit out of balance.

Knowing Good and Evil

> And the LORD God said, "The man has now become like one of us, knowing good and evil."
>
> —Genesis 3:22

There is a fascinating truth to this statement. There are aspects of God we have never dared imagine, facets that we would consider dualistic in nature but are part of God's completeness. Our perception of evil differs from God's. God knows evil as well as good. After all, we draw our wholeness from God in total; there is nothing in us that does not exist in Him. We were made in His image and likeness. This is a glimpse into the vastness of God that we have rarely dared to investigate.

Interestingly, the first mention of evil in Scripture is its association with God. But isn't evil supposed to be the realm of Satan? The devil is supposed to be the lord and master of it; how then can Scripture associate God with evil? God is infinite; His good and evil aspects are part of His totality. As He states, evil is part of who He is.

Our concept of sin is also different from God's in this post-Calvary era. In light of the Cross, God is uninterested in sin. Sin implies judgment, and in Christ Consciousness, God has laid down his judgment of man. Human beings, on the other hand, have a major preoccupation with sin. Judging one another based on our own egocentric criteria may be our favorite global pastime. In doing so, we pile catastrophe upon catastrophe on one another in the name of what we presume to be "righteous judgment."

In the Christ-like view, the idea of evil has lost its original significance. If we want to stop committing evil, we must learn to lose interest in it, just as God has lost interest. We have so glamorized evil that it dominates our world culture. It has become difficult, if not impossible, for the person with strong religious beliefs to perceive God outside of a self-reviling consciousness of personal evil and sinfulness. Yet evil would not exist were it not part of God. And since God is by definition good . . .

evil can be only a mere misunderstood aspect of good and of God in ourselves.

EVIL IS JUST GOOD MISUNDERSTOOD

Astronomers estimate that the Milky Way, the galaxy to which our earth and solar system belong, contains over 30,000,000,000 suns, many of them immensely larger than the earth's sun, which is a million and a half times larger than earth. The Milky Way is shaped like a thin watch. Its diameter from rim to rim is 200,000 light-years. (A light-year is the distance light can travel in a year, traveling at 186,000 miles per second.) There are at least 100,000 galaxies like the Milky Way, some of them millions of light-years apart. However, this may only be a tiny speck of what is beyond in the infinite, endless reaches of space. God is that reach and that space, whatever and wherever it leads to.

—Halley's Bible Handbook

God is not religious. His vastness is beyond our ability to understand or contain. He can be all things, and He is beyond the simplistic nature that we ascribe to Him. In Robert Heinlein's novel *Time Enough for Love,* the character Lazarus Long says, "Men rarely (if ever) manage to dream up a god superior to themselves. Most gods have the manners and morals of a spoiled child." In assuming a black-and-white, good-and-evil stance toward the world, we turn God into that spoiled child.

He cannot be limited to any single perception. He can be a Christian and anything else that is consistent with His moral character, but he can't be limited to that. He is not a Christian God. He just happens to be the God of Christianity. There is a difference. Therefore, in light of Genesis 3:22, it is safe enough to say that God, in His infinite nature and essence, is both good and evil. A reference in Isaiah 45:7 (KJV) indicates that God actually created evil: "I form the light, and create darkness, I make peace and create evil. I the LORD do all these things."

If evil is in God, and God is all good, does it not follow that evil in God's nature is different than in man's perception? There could only be a benign evil in God, rather than the malevolent one in our earthly consciousness. God's concept of evil must be benevolent, since everything He created is good. In God's evil there is always good. There is no separation. God sees the bigger picture, in which evil has a larger purpose that serves the ultimate good. Perhaps evil is a form of good. Evil may just be good . . . misunderstood.

EVERYTHING IS RELATIVE

Evil, then, is good distorted. According to this concept, it is entirely reasonable to consider the possibility that evil could be a complementary rather than an opposing presentation of good. Evil may *complete* good, rather than *compete* with it. We might say that evil is good in a different form, mode, or mood. This is, to say the least, an explosive idea.

In the New Testament, Peter's well-intentioned resistance to Jesus was deemed satanic when Jesus said, "Get behind me, Satan" (Matthew 16:23) to Peter's denunciation of the possibility of the crucifixion. And yet to Judas, who was the betrayer, Jesus said with compassion, "Go do what you have to do." In our minds, Judas left the meal, and what he did was evil. Yet according to biblical prophecy, that supposed "evil deed" was ordained by God from Judas's birth. There had to be a betrayer. It was a fulfillment of prophecy. If Judas had not betrayed Jesus, he would have been violating his prophetic purpose. How then could what he did be evil if it was part of the purpose of God?

There are many who will despise this view as relativism, which states that good or evil are matters of one's own point of view. According to the absolutists who loathe relativism, there are stark, moral, black-and-white goods and evils that are good or evil no matter where or when they are carried out. And yet this defies the nature of God. God is inclusive of all knowledge. God sees human actions from all perspectives at all times. Is it really possible that God being without limits is Himself limited to a single perspective on an act or thought, so that anyone's single idea of what is good or evil is alone valid? Of course not. For God, all things are relative.

The Moral Majority, then, subscribe to a failed religious policy. Moralism takes the focus off God and places it on good and evil. You cannot impose your own form of morality upon others.

Doing so does nothing but create divisions within the culture, creating armed camps where believers compete to see which is more self-righteous. It clothes religious people in judges' robes woven of their prejudiced, limited, fearful human consciousnesses. This is why religion as a basis for political power has always led to horrific abuse in any culture.

God did not create us to judge one another. That is not our role. We are not here to force our own values of good and evil on others. Our role as people living in Christ Consciousness is simply to announce that sin is no longer the issue. It has been made irrelevant by the work of Christ. We should turn our attention to the development of our own minds and our own righteous actions. When we do, the world will be a far better, more tolerant, and understanding place.

CHAPTER SIX

THE GOSPEL OF SALVATION

I do not just want the peace which passeth understanding, I want the understanding which bringeth about peace.

—*Helen Keller*

Life is an unanswered question, but the question is important. In high school, as I was witnessing about Jesus Christ to a group of students (something we were taught to do at every opportunity; never mind its corrosive effect on our social lives), a fellow student asked, "If Jesus is the answer, what is the question?"

I quickly retorted, "The question is, why don't you accept Him as your personal Savior and get born again?" He responded, "I have, but I still have questions, and lots of them." I knew he was onto something, but I didn't know how to answer the question. I wasn't even willing, at the time, to acknowledge its validity. There is a terror of questions in today's religious community. Asking them is discouraged, which is a colossal error.

Ever since that day, I have tried not only to answer questions but to question my answers. In his book *Journey into the Self*, Leo Stein writes, "To be intelligent is to be open minded, activememoried, and persistently experimental." I have found that sometimes it is easier to speak what you wish to be true than to speak truths that may be disturbingly complex. One question pondered by much of humankind is "Will my sins keep me out of heaven and condemn me to an eternal hell?"

In other words, can innate sinfulness overrule innate "sonship"? Can the sins of a child of God make that person stop being loved as God's child or cease to be God's offspring?

THE LOVE OF A PARENT

Parents of murderers, rapists, and terrorists profess that they still love their children. Perhaps nothing is more unbreakable than the love of parent for child. This concept was driven home for me when my first child, Julian, was barely two years old. He had just learned how to walk, and I was watching him toddle around the family room. I heard an inner voice ask me, "What could that boy do to make you banish him to an eternity of torture?" My answer was instant, unequivocal, and without a moment's hesitation: "Absolutely nothing." Then it dawned on me that the goodness of God was truly that of a parent, based on love more than just grace or good will.

Grace is defined by most as unmerited favor. But your kids don't earn your love. They simply receive love from the core of your being, and they always will. They are loved before they know or recognize it as such. They don't have to ask for it, confess, or intentionally acknowledge it. It is simply there for them, and they receive it automatically. The love of God is as unconditional and immutable. To put it clearly:

There is nothing you can do to make God love or stop loving you.

John 1:29 says: "The next day John saw Jesus coming toward him and said, 'Look, the Lamb of God, who takes away the sin of the world!' " This passage of Scripture is often erroneously quoted as "*sins* of the world." Jesus did not take away our individual transgressions and failings, our tendency to "miss the mark," as we discussed earlier. Rather, He took away the offense those acts would cause without His divine expiation. Again, you will never really know that you are free *from* sin until you know that you are actually free *to* sin and still be loved by God, and advocated by Christ.

CAN YOU OFFEND GOD?

Decades later, John wrote in 1 John 2:1–2: "My dear children, I write this to you so that you will not sin.

"But if anybody does sin, we have one who speaks to the Father in our defense—Jesus Christ the Righteous One. He is the atoning sacrifice for our sins, and not only for ours but also for the sins of the whole world."

In the first verse, John uses the Greek word *hamartano* (to miss the mark for sin); in the second verse, he uses *hamartia* (offense). This is a point that is rarely noted. Many assume that if people knew they could sin without going to hell, the world would spin out of control with no moral restraint.

According to Christian doctrine, since the Cross, it is impossible to *hamartia* (sin or offend God); you can only *hamartano* (miss the mark). Nothing you do can offend God to the point that you lose His love and salvation. The final result is always grace, forgiveness, and restoration. Those who try to avoid sin supposedly do so because of their commitment to God—"If you love Me, Keep my commandments" (John 14:15, NKJV). However, most religious obedience is more out of fear than love. If "perfect love drives out fear" (1 John 4:18), would that not include fear of hell or a God who can send you there? The verse goes on to say, "Fear has to do with punishment." Fear of the tortures of hell has become one the strongest motivators (and manipulators) in convincing people to confess their sins and commit their lives to Christ. But has someone terrorized into accepting Christ had a true spiritual encounter, or has he simply had the hell scared out of him? Therein beats the manipulative heart of institutionalized religion.

There are plenty of Christians asking some hard questions about this equation: *Who should we be more suspicious of, the devil, or God, who allows and created him? Who should we fear, hell, or the God who can banish us there? Which is hotter, the fire, the kettle, or the boiling water in the kettle?* This fear-based theology is corrosive to the psyche. Fear does have its place in theology. However, it should not be prominent under the new and better covenant begun with Christ.

We have been taught to fear the angry, vengeful God of the Old Testament. But while we should stand in awe and reverence of God, fear and the slavery it creates have no place in the grace of the New Covenant, which is based on love, not law.

CAN I DO ANYTHING I WANT AND STILL GO TO HEAVEN?

To want what you want, is to want what your want leads to.
—*French proverb*

This is the single biggest question I hear when I talk about Inclusion: "Are you telling me that I can do anything I want and still go to heaven?" This idea profoundly disturbs people, not only because of what it means for themselves but for others. As is so common in today's religious community, we spend more time worrying about what others are doing than commandeering our own souls.

The implication of Inclusion seems to be that even murderers and traitors ultimately get off scot-free. For most people, their sense of what is right and fair cannot allow this to be the case. Understandably, we want evil to be punished.

Ironically, this question is asked almost exclusively by Evangelical Christians, who seem to struggle most with the Inclusion message. My first response to their question is, "What do you want to do?" This leaves most people at a loss and compels me to ask even more provocative questions:

- What are some of the things that Christians really want to do yet don't do?
- Why don't they do them?
- Do Christians avoid doing certain things because they love God or because they are afraid of hell, or both?
- Are many Christians really sinful people restrained only by the fear of the abyss, waiting to commit heinous acts as soon as someone removes the threat of damnation?

For the third question, I find the answer is usually "both," and for the fourth, "of course not." Augustine said, "Love is the beauty of the soul. Love, and do what you like." The modern-day Christian, obsessed with sin consciousness, would recoil from such a statement. But such people do not understand the power of love. Religion has taught them to live in a world fixated on fear and sin.

When a person becomes, according to Evangelical theology, born again and a committed Christian, do his natural desires change, or does he simply keep those desires in check until he goes to heaven? For example, many Christians assume that drinking, smoking, illegal drug consumption, and sex outside of marriage are things that only non-Christians or backsliding Christians do. Wrong. People do what they want to do. If they don't do something, it is because they either lack the desire or have the desire but are disciplined enough to resist the temptation. A married person may be sexually attracted to another person not his or her spouse but have the willpower to resist violating the vows of marriage. The Apostle Paul said, "When I want to do good, evil is right there with me" (Romans 7:21). It appears from his comment that good will always have evil for company. Perhaps that's what helps define it as good.

There are millions of nonreligious and non-Christian people who never consider doing some of the things forbidden by Christian biblical or denominational laws. As a young Christian growing up, I assumed that everybody who was not "saved" spent their lives drinking, drugging, and committing illicit acts. I indicted the entire human race as hell-bound infidels. Of course, that's utterly absurd. Most people, regardless of culture and faith, are decent souls with a conscience, who go to work, pay their taxes, and want the best for themselves, their family, and others.

Being a Christian does not make a person virtuous.
Being a non-Christian does not make a person villainous.

We have a long way to go before we begin to judge our fellow human beings by their actions and their hearts rather than by their brand of faith—or the lack thereof. Who but God knows the heart anyway?

RESISTING THE DEVIL

James 4:7 instructs Christians to "submit yourselves, then, to God. Resist the devil and he will flee from you." Christians, in general, and Evangelicals in particular, are obsessed with "resisting the devil." However, resisting the devil can be emotionally depleting to the point of causing mental, emotional, and physical illness.

Interestingly enough, the instruction to resist the devil is preceded by the instruction to submit to God. Which is easier, to submit to God or resist the devil? Does one automatically lead to the other? If a person submits to God, does it mean that he or she is simultaneously resisting the devil? Who is easier to resist, God or the devil? If you are not resisting the devil, does it mean that you are submitting to him—or it? If you are not submitting to God, does it mean you're resisting Him?

There are no hard, fast rules for this cosmic tug-of-war; this makes the conflict a cause of anxiety and emotional distress for people of deep religious convictions. I have seen the destructive results that this kind of religious frame of mind produces in people's lives.

Most people don't want to commit sinful acts. They simply fantasize about what it would be like if they did. There are many non-Christians who do not go to church, pay tithes, or witness to people on the street, yet they do acts of benevolence, show compassion, and give to various charitable and philanthropic causes. Many are more generous and cheerful about it than some Christians who grudgingly, ritualistically pay their tithes. Somehow Christians have convinced themselves that the only reason they are not out whoring, drinking, and fornicating is their dedication to Jesus Christ and their fear of God. That's that fatal, legalistic point of view at work again: follow God's law or be cast into hell forever!

Committing a Sin, or a Committed Sinner?

Jesus infers that to *want* to do something is, in effect, to do it in your heart (Matthew 5:21–28). He speaks specifically of murder and adultery. He suggests that if in your subconscious you want to do something, then in your heart you have actually committed that act. But let's turn this around: if in your heart you want to do something good, like more acts of kindness, give to more charitable causes, or even go to church more, yet you don't, does God say, "Well, in your heart you really wanted to do those things, so you've done them"?

After being asked "Can I do anything I want and still go to heaven?" so many times, I believe the primary reason that Christians (and fundamentalists of other faiths) try not to sin is not really because of their commitment to God but because of their fear of the custom-made, eternal torture chamber called hell.

However, there is a difference between committing sin and being a committed sinner. Christians commit sins, but, theoretically, they don't practice sin. Again, Christians are not sinless, they just *supposedly* sin less; I assume the same about other fundamentalist faithful. King Solomon says in Proverbs 23:7, "As a man thinks in his heart, so is he." We are all guilty of thinking, wanting, or coveting something sinful for which we would supposedly be judged if we actually carried it out.

But what if this also applies to the good we think and feel but don't act upon? Paul says that the good he wants to do, he doesn't do. In Romans 7:22 he says that in his inner being, he "delights" in the law of God, even though he favors another law at work within his humanness. If wanting to do something sinful means that you have done it, then why would that principle not apply the other way around? If in my heart I want to do right, even though I fail repeatedly, why wouldn't God consider my intentions as equivalent to the act?

WHAT IS HATE?

In Romans 7:15 Paul says, ". . . what I want to do, I do not do, but what I hate I do." The Greek word Paul uses for hate is *miseo,* meaning "to detest." At its root, the word *detest* means literally "to curse while calling a deity to witness." Essentially, Paul is saying, "I want God to know that what I am strongly tempted to do—

disobey Him—is something I detest." In other words, "I am not denying that I have strong natural inclinations to do what may be destructive, but I am not in covenant with these inclinations. I am just tempted by them. They are at work in me, but they do not define me." We are originally good and pure like the God who created us in His image.

In its biblical context, *hate* means "to love less or differently." In Matthew 6:24 Jesus says you can't love both God and money simultaneously; that you will love the one and hate the other. I know many Christians (myself included), who love both God and money. What is actually implied is that you should love money differently (or less) than you love God.

In Luke 14:26 Jesus says, "If anyone comes to me and does not hate his father and mother, his wife and children, his brothers and sisters—yes, even his own life—he cannot be my disciple." No one would suggest that Christ is encouraging His disciples to literally hate their families in order to follow Him. He is, however, suggesting that your love for God should be on a different level from your love for your family. God is not competing with the family He gave you; why would He need to?

We must not misconstrue our natural inclination to sin as part of our "résumé" that determines whether or not we can be with God or even be like Him. Likewise, we should not assume that our actions affect God's attitude toward His creation. Submitting to God does not mean never making a misstep or a mistake. It means submitting to the fuller expression of God as lovingly willing and capable of redeeming all of humankind *in spite of* our sinful nature. Sin or no sin, God is love, and He loves all people without their permission—and often without their knowledge.

What We Do Versus What We Ought to Do

A man's heart is right when he wants what God wants.

—*St. Thomas Aquinas*

Because the Apostle Paul was indoctrinated in legalistic Jewish religious tradition, he hated his sinful tendencies, which were undeniable. He really wanted to do what he felt was right, but he was consistently unable to follow through with his desires. He struggled constantly with feelings of condemnation. He recognized this battle in his new religion, called the Way. He begins the eighth chapter of Romans: "Therefore, there is now no condemnation for those who are in Christ Jesus [more recent manuscripts add ". . . who do not live according to the sinful nature but according to the Spirit"], because through Christ Jesus the law of the Spirit of life set me free from the law of sin and death" (Romans 8:1–2).

It is important to note that all we have of Scriptures are copies of copies of copies. There are no originals available. There are also, according to many scholars, several additions in the more recent manuscripts that are not present in the oldest, most reliable manuscripts. I accept and love the Bible in principle, but I do not see it as infallible, despite what I've been taught all my life. In fact, any true biblical scholar must admit that there are many fallacies, errors, and contradictions in the text. We must be careful about taking *all* Scripture as literal, or as an instruction manual for modern life. There is much practical wisdom in Scripture, but much of it relates only to the ancient cultures to and in which it was written.

Philippians 2:13 says: ". . . for it is God who works in you to will and act according to his good pleasure." What a person knows he should do and what he wants to do are often in conflict. Conscience is what we *know;* subconscious is what or who we *are.*

Oswald Chambers's commentary on this passage in *My Utmost for His Highest* is profound. He writes: "Your spirit will agree with God. But in your flesh there is an inclination that renders you powerless to do what you ought to do. When the Holy Spirit initially makes contact with your conscience, your will is immediately awakened. What causes a person to say 'no' to God is something less deep and penetrating, something much shallower than his will. It is his perversity and stubbornness which never agree with God. Sin is not the biggest problem in a person's life. The most profound issue in a person is his will."

The Sun of God?

> The Lord is not slow in keeping his promise, as some understand slowness. He is patient with you, not wanting anyone to perish, but everyone to come to repentance.
>
> —*2 Peter 3:9*

If there were in fact such a thing as "the will of God," it would be His will for all of humankind to be loved and equally redeemed. Christian theology teaches that this was accomplished through the substitutionary death of Jesus on the Cross. I am amazed at the number of Christians who don't believe or accept unconditional love that overrules and overrides the conditions of law.

My detractors often say that God does not force His will on people. I agree. He no more has to force His will on people than He has to force the sun to shine. Think about it. The sun shines automatically, without anybody's vote for or against its light. No one needs to acknowledge or even believe that it is ninety-three million miles away from the earth. The sun is no respecter of persons; it just shines. There is a reason that so many cultures have worshipped the sun. It shines because God designed it to shine. By the same token, the *Son* (of God) shines spiritually and metaphysically as evenly, whether you ask Him to or not, whether you acknowledge Him or not. According to John 1:9, true light gives light to every man. John goes on to say in John 3:19, "This is the verdict: Light has come into the world, but men love darkness instead of light because their deeds were evil."

Who actually belongs to Christ and to God? Would that be only all the Christians or Jews in the world, or would that include everybody? Most Christians quickly proclaim that Jesus is Lord. However, they really mean that He is Lord only if you believe and confess He is. That is patently ridiculous. Do you stop being you because someone doesn't believe you exist? The sun shines whether you believe in it or not. When we say Jesus is Lord, we are proclaiming Him the supreme authority of all souls on earth. We are not saying that the religion bearing his name is supreme. Christ in consciousness, as Lord, has nothing to do with religion—it is entirely a spiritual concept enhancing the wholeness of life.

Jesus said in Matthew 28:18, "All authority ["power," in the King James Version] in heaven and on earth has been given to me." This particular use of the word *power* in the Greek is *exousia,* and means "privileged or delegated influence, authority." If Jesus is Lord, and He has all legal jurisdiction and delegated authority, then He is not subject to earthly powers or influences. He can do what He wants to do. He cannot be interrupted or interfered with. His divine purpose is unalterable.

In fact, according to Scripture, He has already done what He intended to do and is seated at the right hand of the Father. His purpose was to redeem the world to God. Mission accomplished! Who are we to dispute His claims? Unless we think He lied or is incapable of rescuing humanity from eternal horror, we should all be easily persuaded that the world is saved.

You don't have to subscribe to this concept, but from a Christian point of view, it is quite reasonable and theologically sound.

DOES GOD NEED ANYTHING?

Does God need our help in being God? In Acts 17:25, Paul, speaking to non-Christian Greek mythologists and philosophers, says that God "is not served by human hands, as if he needed anything, because he himself gives all men life and breath and everything else." The Greek word he uses for "needed" is *prosdeomai,* meaning "to require additionally or to want further." This Scripture can be both insulting and liberating to people who, like me, grew up believing that God was depending on them to help save the world.

God doesn't need you or me to save the world, except perhaps from itself. We are not called to save a world that has already been reconciled to God by Christ. We are simply called to make the world's people aware of their salvation so they can enjoy it consciously and live with joy and hope instead of worrying about an angry, grieving, inconsolable God and His hell.

Questions remain. What actually saves us? When are we saved? Did Christ finish the work of redemption, or is there something else we must do? The Abrahamic faiths tend to require more than a deity who guarantees eternal life for us. Jews have a plethora of rules and religious dos and don'ts, as do Muslims. Neither religion emphasizes the redemptive work of a Savior, though Jews anticipate a Messiah, and Muslims revere Muhammad as their chief prophet and earthly representative of deity and look forward to a Second Coming of Christ.

Christianity emphasizes a God who saves and redeems the world He created, a world that fell to satanic seduction through the first Adam. Christ is believed to be the last Adam, sent to the planet to correct the errors of the first one and redeem the universe from the curses of death, defeat, and decay. Is this miracle a present fact, or is it something to be realized in an unforeseeable future?

The English word *salvation* has in it the root *salve,* which is a soothing ointment or balm applied to a wound, or in a larger meaning, a soothing application, influence, or agency. The loving parent we imagine God to be could not view His children as diseased with a terminal illness called sin and not apply a healing salve to all of them. Even if He were as selective as Calvinists insist, why would He apply the salve (salvation) to such a small number of sick, supposedly hell-bound souls? It makes far more sense that He would be the savior of the vast majority of His children, if not absolutely all of them, as opposed to a few who walk a narrow doctrinal path. To suggest otherwise is a theological oxymoron.

GOD: ETERNALLY IN A BAD MOOD?

In the film *Troy,* the Greek warrior Achilles says that the gods, rather than desiring us to become like them, would prefer to become like *us,* because we are mortals, and they are eternal. Our misery ends; theirs is infinite. If God is as jealous for constant flattery and as aggrieved over man as our religious leaders claim He is, then not only has He been in this miserable state of mind since the creation of humankind, but He will remain bitter and vengeful for all time. The concept of an eternal hell requires that God not be benevolent and loving but eternally spiteful, sorrowful, and utterly bereft of mercy forever. He would have to be a monstrous, amoral God without conscience or compassion.

According to religious traditions, God is unhappy, melancholy, neurotic, and even paranoid. He's a character in a Woody Allen movie. Nothing is further from the truth. If you believe in God at all, you should believe in one who is the benevolent Savior of all humankind, even if He has a special regard for those who believe (1 Timothy 4:9–10). To believe otherwise is to perpetuate an angry, judgmental caricature.

What's worse, when we perceive God to dislike something or

someone, we tend to act out that dislike and claim it to be on His behalf. What a convenient excuse for wars, oppression, suppression of knowledge, theft of human rights, and neglect of social justice! The perception of a loving, lenient, and forgiving God would rob the fearmongers of their motivational whips and change much about our world that needs changing.

YOU ARE ALREADY BORN AGAIN

No subject in Evangelical thought is more sensitive than being born again. It is the crux of our faith, the number one prerequisite to salvation.

This conversation, in John 3:3–8, is also the most-cited Scripture supporting the erroneous concept of exclusivity with regard to salvation:

> In reply Jesus declared, "I tell you the truth, no one can see the kingdom of God unless he is born again."

> "How can a man be born when he is old?" Nicodemus asked. "Surely he cannot enter a second time into his mother's womb to be born!"

> Jesus answered, "I tell you the truth, no one can enter the kingdom of God unless he is born of water and the Spirit. Flesh gives birth to flesh, but the Spirit gives birth to spirit. You should not be surprised at my saying, 'You must be born again.' The wind blows wherever it pleases. You hear its sound, but you cannot tell where it comes from or where it is going. So it is with everyone born of the Spirit."

When I was a kid growing up in the black Pentecostal tradition, we rarely used the term *born again*. We'd ask the question, Are you saved? Born again was more of a white non-Pentecostal terminology. To us, you were either saved and on your way to heaven or unsaved and on your way to hell; there were no in-betweens.

The Gospel of Inclusion suggests that humankind is already saved. However, most people just don't, can't, and won't know it until they are "born again" or awakened in their thinking. Again, in Christian theology, there is a spiritual rebirth associated directly with the Resurrection of Christ from the dead, and there is a psychological rebirth that is the result of simply waking up to its reality. This is Christ Consciousness—the connection to God that humans have always sensed and sought long before Jesus walked the earth. Jesus came to emphasize that consciousness, not to create it. The consciousness itself has existed since Adam, as the story is told, walked with God in the cool of the day (Genesis 3:8).

Evangelical Christians teach that unless a person has a personal experience with Christ wherein they recognize Him as Savior, they are not saved and will not go to heaven. This encounter is considered the born-again experience and constitutes their initial rite of passage into that special remnant of persons who are privileged to know God and live forever with Him in heaven. According to this doctrine, everyone else will go to hell forever. This belief lends itself to a sense of superiority over those bound for eternal fire; indeed, that is one of its purposes. For many readers, this concept is a bunch of pagan superstition, but for billions it is an unavoidable truth and thus part of the debate. After all, denial of hell is what cost me my ministry.

As important as being born again is thought to be, the term itself has very little mention in Scripture. It is mentioned once by Jesus, at night, to one person, in a private conversation—never to the masses and never by the apostles who succeeded Christ in the ministry of the Gospel. There is a reason for this.

Scripture states in 1 Corinthians 15:22 that all die because of Adam; and in Christ all will be made alive. If that is true, then the same principle has to be connected to being born again. Jesus is referred to as the "first born of all creation" in Colossians 1:15 (NASB). The use of the word *first* suggests there must be others following. I (and most others) have always assumed those followers to be Christians. However, if all of humankind dies because of the first Adam then does it not follow that in the last Adam— Christ—all of humankind is resurrected, or born anew (Romans 6:3–8)? Why would death and destruction be automatic and indiscriminate, while life and resurrection are prejudiced and selective?

EVERYONE TO COME IS ALSO SAVED

According to the New Testament, when Christ died on the Cross, was buried in the tomb, and then resurrected, all of humanity was in Him crucified, buried, and resurrected. In other words, Christ's death was the seed that went into the womb of the earth, took root, grew, and came out three days later having birthed a new human race free from the curse of sin and death. Is this not Christian theology? In the economics of creation, the Resurrection of Christ is when we as a human race were born again. This was the purpose of the Cross in the first place. Why would any other result be considered reasonable? If it was the purpose of Christ to save the world, then the world is saved. Period.

God is not limited to time and space. God's consciousness is unlimited. He is omnipotent, omniscient, and omnipresent. He is not bound by time as we are, but is present everywhere past, present, and future. Whatever this Infinite Spirit does has been accomplished and realized in eternity, not time. The salvation of the entire human race is a fait accompli, including those who have yet to be born. Only our theologies insist there is conflict, one that they manufacture and sustain.

JUMPING THE FENCE INTO HEAVEN?

I have always been proud of being an American citizen. However, one of the things that I am most ashamed of about America is how we have, over the years, plucked so many "illegal immigrants" out of the ocean and returned them to their impoverished and often oppressive nations, where many had been persecuted. All because they were not born here, had not obtained legal citizenship, or had not entered the country by accepted means.

This practice reminds me of the attitude of far too many Christians who insist that non-Christian people can gain entrance to the Kingdom of God only by the traditionally accepted, approved path. Take the oath of citizenship rather than swim the spiritual Rio Grande, as it were.

Many illegal immigrants live, work, play, and pray on American soil, and do quite well until they are discovered to be here illegally or without documentation. They live as free a life as they can, even though they don't have the legal right to vote, drive, or own real estate. They function, survive, and sometimes thrive in America, and often show a deeper love of this nation than many who were born here. I know many American citizens who are a greater threat to our country than many of the aliens we feel so threatened by.

Romans 2:11 says that God is no respecter of persons. The NIV says, "God does not show favoritism." Christians like to quote this Scripture, but few believe or practice it. Instead they act as if they are God's favorites, and all others are inferior to them. People calling themselves Christians have often judged non-Christians as illegal immigrants of Christianity. We pluck them out of their rickety, non-Christian boats and mercilessly ship them back to wherever they came from, demanding that they stay there or get their freedom from sin based on our denominational rules and regulations.

As a believer in the redemptive plan of God, I submit that Christ is the way to God, but not just for Christians! This is where Christians fall into the idolatry of religion. Christ, not the religion that bears his name, has opened the door for all of humanity. He is the agent who has made it possible for all of us, even if we do not toe a particular doctrinal line, to become citizens of the ultimate Kingdom.

DOES FAITH ALTER FACT?

Believing something and *knowing* it are very different. I believe the sun is ninety-three million miles away from the earth, but I lack the scientific skills to prove it. I also don't doubt it. If I discovered that the sun was not ninety-three million miles away, I doubt such information would change my world much. Unless my awareness of the error would cause the sun to cease shining, it would be completely irrelevant to me.

Believing in Jesus and God—or not believing in them—will not cause them to cease to be or change how they function. God is inviolate, and His plan will ultimately overrule any and every other reality. The Truth of Christ as person and principle is immutable. Your faith may make it more real to you in a personal way, but it can't change who Christ is and what He accomplished. Redemption is a done deal with or without your help, approval, acceptance, or belief.

Job said, "I know that my Redeemer lives" (Job 19:25). Yet he had no concept of Jesus. Are we to assume that he went to hell because he didn't know Christ? The Hebrew prophets Moses and Elijah didn't know Jesus Christ as we imagine Him, yet they are reported to have appeared with Him on the Mount of Transfiguration (Matthew 17:2), several thousand years after they disappeared from the planet.

God's plan works (and is working) with or without our awareness or deliberate cooperation. God's plan works by His rules, not ours. This is good news. God is in control. God's will, word, and work stand secure. All we need to do is realize this truth and enjoy its liberating knowledge.

WHAT DOES JESUS SAVE US FROM?

Salvation, in Christian doctrine, can be viewed in three separate but simultaneous states of being: *instantaneous, evolutionary,* and *ultimate.* Through the redemptive work of the Cross, we *are* saved, we are *being* saved, and we ultimately *will be* saved. That begs the question "From what are we saved?" New Testament Scripture uses the word *salvation* in reference to deliverance from wrath, judgment, sin, hell, the curse of the law—the list goes on.

According to the way that many Evangelical Christians think, Christians are being saved from God *by* God. In traditional religious thinking, mankind seeks protection from an irate God whose constant threat of punishment keeps us in a state of insecurity, guilt, and fear. Therefore it has become our primary objective to avoid the "wrath of God." Religious people are not much different from children growing up in a home with an abusive father.

If we are being saved from God's punishment, and if God's punishment is hell, then both God and hell are one and the same. Who should we fear: the devil and hell, or the God who created both? In light of the Christian concept that Jesus took the punishment for the sins of the world (Isaiah 53:5–6 and 1 Peter 2:24), it's reasonable to assume that hell is basically irrelevant. For if there is a hell where people go for everlasting punishment for sin, then the doctrine of atonement may need to be altered. Or worse, maybe Jesus misrepresented His intentions when He said the work of redemption was finished—unless we are being saved from something else entirely.

TWO KINDS OF SALVATION

Again, as we said earlier, do we need Jesus to protect us from God? Does Jesus represent the mother who protects her children from an angry and abusive father, God? In 370, Gregory of Nyssa, one of the most respected early church fathers, said, "God would not have permitted the experience of hell unless He had foreseen through redemption that all rational beings would in the end attain to the same blessed fellowship with Himself."

After studying the Apostle Paul's doctrine of salvation, it appears that there is a salvation that the whole world has received, called *redemption,* and a salvation that the whole world needs, called *sanctification* (separation to higher consciousness) or *identification* (recognition of the new side of mind). Redemption cannot be done or undone by man's belief or unbelief. Redemption basically means to be bought and brought back to Authentic Self at soul-bed. Belief does not bring salvation. However, belief does *recognize* salvation, enhance its reality in a person's life, and lead to conversion and personal reform. This kind of salvation is an evolving process, intended to inspire the recipient to become a better, nobler, more compassionate child of God.

Redemption is not a process. Redemption is instantaneous and immediate, the result of the finished work of the Cross. It requires neither action nor belief. However, identification does require action. It requires the recipient to recognize and embrace the truth of redemption through Christ, leading to a personal conversion and the reform of that person's life, values, and lifestyle. Teaching this truth to others is the work that Christians are duty bound to perform.

In Proverbs 23:7 Solomon says, "As a man thinks in his heart, so is he." If we think we are saved, then in our reality we are saved. If we think we are not saved, then in our reality we are not. Perception is the ultimate reality but not necessarily the ultimate truth. We are (or we become) what we think. Life is a self-fulfilling prophecy. The Apostle John writes: ". . . now we are children of God, and what we will be has not yet been made known. But we know that when he appears, we shall be like him, for we shall see him as he is" (1 John 3:2). Most people have limited vision. Our desire should be to continually improve in vision, insight, perception, and consciousness.

The word *soul* in Greek is *psuche,* from which we get the English *psyche* and *psychology.* Salvation is an awareness and attitude of the mind. It is the illumination of a person's thinking life. Or as it is written in *A Course in Miracles* by the Foundation for Inner Peace: "Miracles are examples of right thinking. Miracles occur as the result of people aligning their lives with Truth, as God created it, not as man has invented it. We should pray, 'Lord, heal our perceptions until the knowledge of the Divine is possible.' " In the most practical sense, this is salvation.

WHAT ABOUT PRAYING TO JESUS?

One of my very close, longtime friends is Kathie Lee Gifford, the television personality. Kathie and I sang with the Oral Roberts University World Action Singers nearly thirty years ago. One night, after she and I had dinner in Los Angeles, where we were recording the weekly *Oral Roberts and You* telecasts, Kathie offered to close our evening with a prayer (a common practice for us in those days, and remains so to this day in my family, as well as in hers).

Kathie closed her eyes and began her prayer with words typical to most born-again Christians. She said, "Dear Jesus, we just thank you for your son Jesus." Realizing the redundancy, she paused to collect her thoughts, trying not to break the solemnity of the spirit of prayer. Instead we both burst into uncontrollable laughter for several minutes, as we realized the absurdity of her reference to Jesus and His Son, Jesus. Neither of us thought the prayer should have been corrected by saying, "Dear Jesus, we just thank you for your Father, God," as if God was something Jesus gave us as a gift, rather than the other way around.

In Philippians 2:6 Paul says, in reference to Christ, "who, being in very nature God, did not consider equality with God something to be grasped." Many Christians have made an idol out of the mediator who God sent to re-present Him in consciousness but not replace Him. We have built an entire religion around Christ Jesus, and many Christians actually prefer Christ to God; he's more user friendly.

I love Jesus Christ with all my heart. However, I believe that Christians have become cult followers of Him in a way quite different from what God or Jesus may have intended. Let's look at a conversation in Matthew 19:16–17 (paraphrased) between Jesus and the rich, young ruler. The question was posed to Jesus, "Good Master, what good thing shall I do, that I may have eternal life?" Jesus responded, "Why do you call me good? There is none good but one, that is God."

Maybe It's Not about Accepting Jesus . . .

Jesus didn't use that opportunity to say, "Accept me as your personal Savior, get born again and convert to Christianity, and you will have eternal life." Instead Jesus turned the man's attention away from Him and directed it to God.

Jesus did encourage His disciples to take up their Cross and follow Him, but He never suggested that to the masses of people who came to hear Him speak or receive His miracles. He always pointed the people to God, not to Himself. I'm not negating or neglecting Christ as good or godly. I am simply drawing attention to the importance of Christ's purpose, which was to reconnect us to the Father in awareness. He was careful to say things like "not mine but Thy will be done" (Matthew 26:39), "I must work the works of Him who sent me" (John 5:30 and 6:38 [KJV]), and so on.

Could Christians be mistaken in trying to get people to accept Christ? Should we instead be trying to convince people that they are already accepted by God *through* Christ? What exactly *is* our mission? Jesus did instruct His disciples to make disciples of all nations or nationalities, but He never really instructed us to convert people to our religion or disregard theirs. Instead of encouraging people to become disciples of Christ, we have resorted to recruiting people to become disciples of Christianity, and there is a difference.

I am walking a tightrope here, but it's a walk too vital not to make. Christ was about reconnecting people to their destiny in Deity and Divinity, not to religion built around a Deity. God is not religious; we are. We must become more like Him without insisting that He become more like us, or that He fit Himself into the mold we prescribe. Jesus said that "God is Spirit, and they that worship him must do so in spirit and do it truthfully" (John 4:24). I submit that such worship when compelled by the greed for salvation and the fear of hell is not pure. It is a perversion of the intent of God and the mission of the Christ.

GOD IS A MYSTICAL EXPERIENCE

Romans 8:28 (NKJV) says: "All things work together for good to those who love God, to those who are called according to *His* purpose." The English word *God* is derived from the English concept of good, and vice versa. Who doesn't love what is good? But good, like beauty, is in the eye of the beholder. Everyone residing on earth loves his or her idea of what good is, meaning that we all love our idea of what God is.

The human psyche struggles with loving God because our mind perceives God and good differently from the way our spirit perceives them. In our spirit, we all know God because we all *are* God. We originated in God and came forth out of Divinity. When God saves us, He saves that which is part of Himself, as a parent would do anything, even give up his life, to save his child. We are taught in Christian theology that God gave up the life of His Son in order to conquer it for the rest of His children.

To slave owners, slavery seemed good, even scriptural. Their justification was, "Those heathen, pagan slaves are better off with us, their oppressors, than they would have been back in Africa with their uncivilized ways and backward forms of worship." Ironically, some slaveholders actually thought they were saving their slaves from hell in the next life—while subjecting them to it in this life.

Christianity does the same thing today in trying to "save" people in Third World countries. I believe most missionaries are sincere, but their perceptions are mistaken. The most "uncivilized" native in the deepest jungles of the Amazon is no more or less far from the Father's grace than the most devoted born-again Christian in America. Physics teaches us that in an infinite universe, any single point is just as far from the outer edge of the universe as any other point. With an infinite, timeless God, each of us is exactly as close to His heart or to Spirit as all the others. For Christians, the challenge is to put aside ego, stop attaching such self-importance to the notion of being *born again,* and work to inspire others to reach their God-ordained potential, regardless of their particular faith or tradition.

Salvation is not a matter of religious mechanics. It is spiritual and even mystical. We must move beyond the superficial and superstitious as we ponder God's nature. Jesus described the mystery of being born again like this: "You should not be surprised at my saying, 'You must be born again.' The wind blows wherever it pleases. You hear its sound, but you cannot tell where it comes from or where it is going. So it is with everyone born of the Spirit" (John 3:7–8).

CHAPTER SEVEN

THE GOSPEL OF HATE

The world is full of beauty, as other worlds above,
And if we did our duty, it might be as full of love.

—Gerald Massey, 1828–1907

The earth is the Lord's and everything in it, the world and all
who live in it.

—King David (Psalm 24:1)

God loves you unconditionally and wants you to spend eternity with Him in heaven. Do you believe this?" I said to the uninterested young man who stood there stoically with a half-filled beer can.

"And what if I don't?" he replied.

"You will die and spend eternity in hell," I retorted.

"Get the hell out of my face, you stupid religious faggot!" he exclaimed.

I was hurt, insulted, and angered by his response. As I walked away, I said, "You will burn in hell!" as I moved on to my next hell-bound victim.

I didn't recognize it at the time, but I was saying, in effect, that

God loves you unconditionally—unless you don't believe He does, in which case He will torture you forever. How quickly God's love is turned to God's hatred of the ones He is said to have just loved!

HATING THE UNBELIEVER

Before I awakened to this broader hope, I would look at non-Christian "unbelievers" as hell-bound, anti-Christ, rejects hated by God—and, by association, hated by me. But this feeling did not sit well with me. I despised the way I was expected to regard my fellow human beings, all of them children of God, who did not necessarily share my particular religion. I was not always conscious of this bitterness, but I felt its inner harassments. My notions of an angry, hateful God disturbed me profoundly. It was forcing me to impersonate something: someone inauthentic.

Until I discovered my fresh understanding of God's inclusive, redemptive love, like most Evangelical Christians I willingly but not eagerly viewed the world as an evil, sinister, and secular adversary, worthy of being burned in an eternal inferno. It is a great irony that Christians generally interpret Scripture as instructing us to despise the world, yet we are expected to reach that same world lovingly with the "Good News." This has always been a huge conflict for me. I have always loved the complex, beautiful world outside the church, and always wanted to travel and experience it in ways that were not encouraged when I was growing up in the church. However, I always feared this world—saw it as a kind of contagion that would infect my soul and cause me to end up in hell with most of its other inhabitants.

My family was fortunate to have a pastor who was much broader in his concept of the world. He traveled, watched television (a no-no in our tradition), read books (even secular ones), and encouraged education. His influence made me love the world even more. Hating the world was always a nuisance for me, because I've always loved it and been fascinated by it. In the context of Inclusion, willful ignorance of the world of men (and the preoccupation with hating that world based on doctrine, not knowledge) seems to undermine the true mission of Christianity: to unite a global society that has come to regard the faith with suspicion—a lot of it justified.

LOVE NOT THE WORLD?

Scriptures such as 1 John 2:15 (KJV) ("Love not the world, neither the things that are in the world. If any man love the world, the love of the Father is not in him") send a confusing message. We are taught from childhood that we are to shun worldly things, yet we are expected to reach that world for Jesus. The contradiction gives many Evangelical Christians an attitude problem in interpreting God's love for humanity.

One of the most popular Scriptures in the Bible is John 3:16 (NASB), which declares, "God so loved the world, that He gave His only begotten Son, that whosoever believeth in him should not perish, but have eternal life." And in 2 Corinthians 5:18–19, Paul writes: "All this is from God, who reconciled us to himself through Christ and gave us the ministry [*not* doctrine] of reconciliation: that God was reconciling the world to himself in Christ, not counting men's sins against them. And he has committed to us the message of reconciliation."

If, in fact, God loved the world so much, why then are we instructed in Scripture *not* to love it? How can we think unkindly of that part of God's creation that Christ died to save? If the world is valuable enough for God to love and Christ to die for, then is it not probable that Christians have misinterpreted scriptural instruction to do otherwise?

Since 1611 most Western Evangelical Christians have viewed

non-believers, or so-called heathens, as in need of being saved. Such condescending ideas make it difficult to reach out to the world in a positive, respectful, Christ-like way. Many Evangelicals find themselves "preaching down to" people they consider less intelligent or enlightened than themselves, resulting in a negative backlash. Christian arrogance is largely responsible for the hostility that persists between Christianity and other cultures.

It's nearly impossible for Christians to act with benevolence and charity toward those that our religious tradition portrays as evil and bound for hell. I have found attitudes such as "What's the use? Most of them are going to hell anyway" to be quite common. We display the same attitude toward the environment, since we believe God will ultimately destroy it with fire anyway. Why preserve it?

Christian missionaries of centuries past committed terrible acts of disrespect and violence against native cultures that "needed saving," often wiping out indigenous traditions. But this is not always the case; there have been many who transcended these disturbing attitudes. Yet for the most part, we buy into the propaganda: the world is a hateful place that we must save but otherwise avoid being tainted by, leaving it for God to punish and destroy.

It's OK to Love the World

It is impossible to help and heal a world we hold in contempt. But the world is not going to change. If we want to better it in any meaningful way, we must change our perception of it. Our prayer must become "Lord, help us by your Holiness to recognize your universal mark on all of your children and remove our faulty perceptions of lack, isolation, and deterioration!" If we are to spread the Good News in this world, we must learn to *love* it.

The Italian playwright Carlo Goloni (1707–1798) said: "The world is a beautiful book, but is of no use to him who cannot read it." Reading and reverencing the world is the duty of all its inhabitants. If God loved it enough to create it, then it seems reasonable—even spiritual—to cherish it as holy to both Creator and created.

Christianity has rarely maintained such a charitable stance toward God's handiwork. According to popular Evangelical Christian thought, God does not accept all of mankind as redeemed, and the majority of the earth's populace will never accept Christ as the Savior of all mankind. This may explain why there is a conspicuous discrepancy between the *efforts* of nearly twenty centuries of Christian evangelism and its *effects.* It alleges a selective gospel while demanding global acceptance. We expect everyone to accept Jesus, but we believe that most to whom we preach are not *worthy* of salvation and will not be accepted by God. That is the deepest hypocrisy.

"IT IS FINISHED"

Evangelical Christians are very good at preaching Christianity but not so hot at preaching Christ. It's as if we think we "own" Jesus and have control over who does or does not go to heaven. We base the efficacy of the Cross on a person's knowledge, belief, and acceptance of Jesus—in other words, we believe "if the person will not, God cannot," even though Jesus said, "It is finished" (John 19:30). It couldn't be finished if there was still a world alienated from God's love. Just because the world seems unaware of God's love for it doesn't mean the love isn't there. If there is a purpose for the Church, it is to share and communicate this love.

In Christian theology, Jesus, with the statement, "It is finished," was saying figuratively, "Mission accomplished!" He is believed to have redeemed all humankind from the Adamic curse of sin and death. End of story. As Paul told the church at Colossae, Christ had reconciled all things back to God, the Original Source and Intention: where there was no peace, he had brought peace to the world. "And, having made peace through the blood of his cross, by him to reconcile all things unto himself; by him, I say, whether they be things in earth, or things in Heaven" (Colossians 1:20, KJV).

A passage in Paul's letter to the church at Philippi reflects the love inherent in Christ's coming into our world: "Therefore God exalted him to the highest place and gave him the name that is above every name, that at the name of Jesus every knee should bow, in heaven and on earth and under the earth, and every tongue confess that Jesus Christ is Lord, to the glory of God the Father" (Philippians 2:9–11).

This passage seems to indicate that Jesus did something that earned Him a promotion to the "highest place." What could that act have been but the completed redemption of all God's creation? Unfortunately, most Christians interpret Christ's elevation to mean that Christianity has been elevated to the highest place among religions. They can't separate Christ from the religion that bears His name. This inspires an ugly, unhealthy sense of superiority and religious elitism.

WHO'S GOT THE POWER?

> Far from turning us away from the world, Christ directs us to it. He awakens in us an altogether new concern for it.
>
> —Paul Tournier, 1898–1986

Growing up in my strong spiritual tradition as a Bible-toting, pew-jumping, devil-thumping Pentecostal, I heard the statement "That ain't nothing but the devil" as much or more than I heard "Praise the Lord!"

The subtle concept of duality and the worship of two Gods, one good, the other evil, leaves us as supposed people of faith in an ongoing tug-of-war as to which one of these supernatural entities really has the ultimate power.

In Matthew 7:13–14 Jesus is recorded to have said, "Enter through the narrow gate. For wide is the gate and broad is the road that leads to destruction, and many enter through it. But small is the gate and narrow the road that leads to life, and only a few find it." This has always left me wondering who the winner really was in this supposed battle for the souls of the universe.

We were taught that we followed a triumphant Christ, and yet we glorify the devil as if he would have the final victory over the souls of men, with only a few faithful souls making it to heaven. This always left me with a feeling of defeat and discouragement with the religion that we were taught was a religion of world peace.

A loving and merciful God who is wise, moral, benevolent, and ultimately triumphant is the only concept of a Savior that makes sense—any other concept would make God weak, immoral, malevolent, even vulgar. Consider the illogic of many Christians' conclusion that God's work through Christ is incomplete. This logic leads one to conclude that Satan, not God, is more powerful, and that God's love and wisdom could not compete with the web of evil that Satan had woven into the soul of man.

Philippians 2:5–8 describes what Christ did in order to win His special distinction as Lord: His crucifixion on the Cross. It is a kind of coronation that Jesus earned through His sacrificial death. Elevation to the highest position in eternity was Christ's reward for making such a powerful sacrifice. There would be no coronation if the job were unfinished.

This payment was *not* to become head of any Christian church. It was lordship over the universe and all of the spirits reconciled to the consciousness of God. The eternal sweepstakes won by Christ was not just for Christians, it was an inclusive plan of global redemption. This is why it is recorded in Hebrews 12:2 that "for the joy set before him, Jesus endured the cross, scorning its shame, and sat down at the right hand of the throne of God." The joy Jesus was expecting was the reception of all His brethren (humankind) and the exhilaration that would come when He presented us all to the Father in the oneness of God's original intent. He restored the eternal family!

The nineteenth-century British preacher Charles Spurgeon had a good take on this: "The world is just the materializing of God's thoughts; for the world is a thought in God's eye. He made it first from a thought that came from his own mighty mind, and everything in the majestic temple he has made has a meaning."

WHAT WORLD HATED CHRIST?

> I suspect that worse dishonesty, and greater injustice, are to be found among the champions, lay and cleric, of religious opinion than in any other class.
>
> —George MacDonald (1824–1905)

The only world I ever really knew for my first eighteen to twenty-five years was the small, sequestered world of the Pentecostal denomination in which my family had been immersed for four generations. We were aware of the other, secular world; we just never saw it as relevant to us except to get it saved. It simply wasn't our world. Our world was the world of God's righteous people. We didn't dip (use snuff), sip (drink alcoholic beverages), or tip (step out on our spouses). We presumed that everyone in the outside world did all of the above. We were proud of being the true citizens of the Kingdom of God.

In John 15:18 Jesus says, "If the world hates you, keep in mind that it hated me first." This statement has been misunderstood and misinterpreted over the centuries. As a result, Christianity has had a profound, unmerited victim consciousness. Based on this passage (and several others like it), I was taught from my childhood that because I was a Christian, the secular world would always hate me, and possibly persecute and torture me, even to death. Well-meaning church elders felt that while they were proud of being a part of the "world's despised few," they should also be wary of this evil world, and warned us likewise.

This adversarial, contemptuous perception of the world fits well into our perception of Christ being a victim of it. We are profoundly influenced by the heroic spirit of Christ's suffering and death and can't relate to Him fully without a victim consciousness. We basically expect—and often invite—the world to hate and victimize us. We don't even realize that the idea of a faith with more than one billion adherents—the most influential creed in the world's most powerful nation—being seen as victimized is completely absurd. In some ways it is the victimizer.

If nonbelievers do not hate us, we perceive that as a sign we aren't fully representing Christ or that we are not following His example. We base this martyr complex on Scriptures like these:

> You adulterous people, don't you know that friendship with the world is hatred toward God? Anyone who chooses to be a friend of the world becomes an enemy of God.
>
> —James 4:4

> If we suffer, we will also reign with him.
>
> —2 Timothy 2:12 (KJV)

> . . . all that will live godly in Christ Jesus shall suffer persecution.
>
> —2 Timothy 3:12 (KJV)

This is insanity! Are we to believe that we should *invite* people to *hate* Christians in order to fulfill our mission of awakening them to God's *love*? One does not sow dragon's teeth and expect to reap daisies.

Like Gandhi, people of other religions often love and understand Christ's message; they just don't get along with His followers. Muslims, for example, revere Jesus as a prophet, but not as divine. Of course, the important point of the Gospel is not that Muslims consider Christ, but that Christ considers Muslims as loved by God and precious enough to redeem along with all other human beings. A careful study of the words and works of Christ reveals that the secular, non-Jewish world, along with the Jewish laity, loved Christ and was eager to receive His message and ministry. It was the religious leaders of His day who hated and opposed Christ.

The same is the case today. Those in control of certain denominations tend to despise those who are beyond their control—namely, those who live for and by God but do so outside the traditional bounds of a familiar religious dogma.

WHAT'S WRONG WITH THIS PICTURE?

The United States is the most religiously diverse nation in the world. Christianity is the greatest single force in the midst of this religious diversity. According to recent statistics, 70 percent of Americans belong to some form of Christian religion. Even more distinctive, in terms of its tolerance for the free expression of many kinds of faith, America is the most tolerant nation that has ever existed.

In light of this, it is interesting to note that in spite of the Christian influence in this country, we have not had a more positive effect on the nation's morals. In fact, the evidence suggests quite the contrary. Consider these facts:

- The United States has the largest prison population in the developed world.
- Tulsa County in Oklahoma, where I live, known to some as the "buckle of the Bible Belt," has the second highest divorce rate in the country, surpassed only by Las Vegas.
- In addition, we have one of the nation's largest recorded out-of-wedlock teenage pregnancy rates, and a higher-than-average per capita homosexual population, many of whom profess to be born-again Christians. I'm told that we also have one of the highest mental illness rates per capita in the nation.
- A 2005 study showed that the nation's highest rates of divorce, spousal abuse, and murder are in so-called red states—states that tend to vote conservative in part because of their large fundamentalist Christian populations. The state with the lowest divorce rate? Massachusetts, bastion of university education, gay marriage, and supposed liberalism.

Such astonishing statistics should cause any critically thinking person to ask, "What's wrong with this picture?" The facts don't lie. We Christians are not inspiring greater kindness and nobility in our fellows because we are not *practicing* them ourselves.

Morality cannot be educated or legislated. It can only be demonstrated, and we Christians don't demonstrate it very well. Atheists have a lower divorce rate than we do. It seems to me that the more laws we make, the more we break. We seem to think it is enough to say that we're Christian, as if that makes us virtuous. It does not. Actions determine virtue.

After nearly forty years of preaching holiness and its twin message of eternal damnation, I have been arrested by the Holy Spirit and convinced that I have not been preaching an accurate Gospel message. I am embarrassed that the Christian Evangelical Church has become more *indicting* than *inviting*. We should do less *attacking,* and more *attracting*. We should talk *less* and act *more*. Extremist preachers of the Christian doctrine are just as incendiary as extremist preachers of Islam. Both provoke rage, rebellion, and warmongering.

WHAT IS A MATURE CHRISTIAN?

Most Christians struggle with spiritual maturity, no matter how long they've been confessing Christ. An admonition in Hebrews 6:1–2 insists that we "... leave the elementary teachings about Christ [Christian fundamentalism] and go on to perfection (NKJV), [maturity] not laying again the foundation of repentance from acts that lead to death, and of faith in God, instruction about baptisms, the laying on of hands, the resurrection of the dead, and eternal judgment."

In talking about "perfection," the passage is saying we should become mature followers of Christ. What does that mean? The idea of "going on to maturity" intimidates many in the Evangelical Christian and charismatic/Pentecostal communities. Why? Because mature Christianity insists on removing the fear tactics that have become, as it were, the bread and wine of the Evangelical movement. Maturity requires that Christians stop using fear tactics to force others into salvation.

Mature Christianity insists that we go from religion to relationship—from simply liking Christ to becoming Christ-like. It demands "perfect love" that casts out the fear that torments the seeker and cripples his trust in God's ability to love unconditionally. In 1 John 4:17, John suggests that love is the one thing that gives us confidence on the "day of judgment," which in many ways seems to be the greatest fear of those who oppose the Gospel of Inclusion.

The question etched in the minds of most believers is, "What will happen on Judgment Day, and will I make it to heaven?" We all say we love God because He first loved us (1 John 4:19). But many are fearful that His love will not last. My response to that suspicion is found in Romans 8:38–39, where Paul says that nothing shall be able to separate us from God's love; neither death nor demons. And I would like to add doctrines and dogmas to that. If God indeed loved us once in Christ, He will love us always in Him and because of Him. Indeed, this should be the core belief of all bona fide Christians, and that is the message we should be striving to convey to everyone else. Those who cannot are what I would call "immature" Christians—bullies who bludgeon nonbelievers with horror stories of everlasting hellfire.

THE GODS MUST BE ANGRY

The Greek New Testament uses three primary words for religion: *Ioudaios,* which means Judaism; *threskeia,* which means ceremonial observance or piety, and *deisidaimonia,* the most disturbing, which the KJV translates as "superstition" and means *deos* or *deilia*—fear of demons. In Greek mythology, demons or Furies were pagan deities that the people feared greatly. Fear of the gods is the basis of more world religions than is faith.

A careful study of Greek mythology reveals how much it spilled over into Christianity. Christianity was birthed during the Roman Empire, which was preceded by the Greek Empire and was significantly influenced by both. The Greek Empire was dominated by its religion, which revolved around the kingdom of the gods believed to be living on Mount Olympus. This polytheistic Greek religion began about 750 BC and lasted more than one thousand years, extending its influence throughout the Mediterranean world and beyond.

In the Greek religion, numerous gods controlled various natural forces: Poseidon (the sea), Demeter (agriculture), Hera (marriage), and so on. The myths of the Greek religion deal with the creation of the world of the gods; the struggle among them for supremacy, and the triumph of Zeus; the love affairs and quarrels of the gods; and the effects of their adventures on the mortal world. The Greek gods were petulant, short-tempered, and quick to strike at mortals for the smallest infractions. In this religion, death was a hateful state, and the dead lived in Hades. Great wrongdoers suffered in Tartarus after death. Mystery religions, including Christianity, emerged to satisfy the desire for personal guidance, salvation, and immortality.

Gods, Demons, and the Religious World

As the Greeks gave way to the Romans, so their gods became the Roman gods, albeit with different names. With Christianity being born in Roman times, it doesn't take much research to prove Greek mythology's influence upon the early scholars of this newly formed spinoff of first-century Judaism.

Greek believers spent their lives and fortunes attempting to please the temperamental gods. The Roman religion, which was in full swing during the days of Christ's ministry in Israel, had similar gods who also affected early Christian thought and religious concepts. Roman gods were mollified or appeased through the development of the *jus divinum,* or divine law, prescribing what should and should not be done to please the gods. This was the religious climate in which Christianity was born and shaped. Judaism's monotheism was all but ignored by the dominant religions of the world. Demons and demon-gods, each directing a different aspect of the visible world, were the fashion of the day and had been for centuries.

I've always thought of demons as ugly, hairy creatures with fangs, claws, and pointy tails. However, if demons exist, I suspect they are fragmented spirits. In metaphysical consciousness, they would be indistinct, and thus perverted and twisted energies. They hover between two realities, and thus are both confused and confusing. They are vagabond spirits seeking residence anywhere they can find embodiment in this reality. The religions of the world have feared them for centuries. Many worship them. Yet demons are drawn, as a negative charge is drawn to a positive, to the light of God within each of us.

As I was listening to a minister teaching on the importance of demonstrating God in our lives, I noticed a play on the word *demonstrate* as "demon straight." The idea is to straighten out the demon—that misunderstood and distorted spirit or consciousness in you—and you will neutralize any negative effect it has on your life.

FEAR IS FAITH IN REVERSE

As stated earlier, one of the Greek translations of the word *religion* is *deisidaimonia,* or "fear of demons." As I heard evangelist Kenneth Copeland say at a conference I was conducting years ago, "Fear is faith in reverse. Fear of a serpent is faith in the serpent's power to harm or destroy you."

Fear is simply a perversion of faith. It is faith distorted, twisted, abused, and misused. If fear simply neutralized faith, that would be less threatening, but to reverse it is to bring about injury in a way that neutralizing it cannot. It is like the difference between not making more money and losing all the money you have. One is nonproductive; the other is destructive. Fear corrodes reality to the point that it ceases to resemble the beauty of faith in a perfect divinity.

Fear of God creates more harm than good for the human race. God isn't angry with mankind. But because of erroneous concepts of God, most human beings are secretly angry with God. Let's go back to the Old Testament roots of "fear of God" in Judeo-Christian thought.

In Exodus 20:18–19 and Deuteronomy 5:22–33, Moses and

the children of Israel were standing before Mount Sinai, where God is said to have spoken the Ten Commandments to the Israelites. This was such a dramatic, frightening experience that the people decided Moses should speak to them instead of God. "Moses said to the people, 'Do not be afraid. God has come to test you, so that the fear of God will be with you to keep you from sinning.' The people remained at a distance, while Moses approached the thick darkness where God was" (Exodus 20:20–21). Notice that the passage said where, not *what*, God was. God is not darkness. ". . . God is light; in him there is no darkness at all" (1 John 1:5).

This same deadly fear experienced by the children of Israel continues to torment many Christians and other believers, keeping them alienated from the conscious presence of God. The fear causes an existential dread that they will displease God and thus incur His unbearable wrath. It also causes people (including Christians) to remain at a distance, ignorant of what God really is, while others like Moses press into the thick darkness to see the truth. This is why religious people can be some of the most hateful people on earth. They hate because they are angry at their own fear, and it becomes easier to inflict that fear upon others than to rise above it.

The Angry God Concept Is a Mental Illness

So we come to the most grotesque of all ironies: war in the name of a God whose Son, Christians believe, died professing peace and love. In this way, immature, toxic Christianity has been a more virulent curse on humankind than all the plagues ever unleashed.

If you perceive God to hate someone enough to execute and torture him in hell forever, then in your subconscious you will devalue and hate that person as well. Given the opportunity or provocation, you will act out that hatred. Thus we have wars where we kill those who do not do what we think our God wants. For example, as a Christian, if I assume that all Muslims or Hindus hate God or Jesus and are hated by them, I will view them as enemies of the truth I live by and will be willing to kill them. This prejudice has inflamed ignorant Christians (and those of other religions) for centuries and driven the most horrid and barbaric wars, killing, and bloodshed in history, from the Crusades to the genocides in the Balkans and Rwanda. After all, we are taught that the first murder in history took place between two brothers, Cain and Abel, who were unable to agree on how to worship (Genesis 4).

To perceive any deity as angry at everyone who does not believe in the same way that you do is a form of mental illness that produces psychotic behavior. Trying to appease an angry God is a debilitating cancer of our religious sensibilities.

As a leader in the Evangelical and charismatic Christian community, I have observed an inexplicable, almost gleeful support for military aggression by conservative Christians. This propensity to support war—including use of weapons of mass destruction—against any country or culture we perceive as opposed to Judeo-Christian beliefs is an abject betrayal of the teachings of Jesus. It is the greatest evil we can commit. The proliferation of "Who Would Jesus Bomb?" bumper stickers says much about how many conservative Christians' support for war is poisoning our mission and our perception in a culture we should be striving to inspire.

The Devaluation of Human Life

The famous 1741 sermon by Jonathan Edwards, "Sinners in the Hands of an Angry God," is said to have caused grown men to clutch the backs of the pews until their knuckles turned white. They literally trembled in fear and rushed to the altar to repent of their sins as they heard these words:

The use may be of *awakening* to unconverted persons in this congregation. This that you have heard is the case of every one of you that are out of Christ. That world of misery, that lake of burning brimstone, is extended abroad under you. *There* is the dreadful pit of the glowing flames of the wrath of God; there is hell's wide gaping mouth open; and you have nothing to stand upon, nor any thing to take hold of: there is nothing between you and hell but the air; 'tis only the power and mere pleasure of God that holds you up.

Congregants literally *wanted* to be terrified, in part because they felt that appeasing their angry Deity made them soldiers in an eternal fight against the unrighteous, which is to say, everyone else. This dangerous narcissism persists and even flourishes today.

Christians refer to this American reformation as a great revival, but the element of fear that pervades such conversions is more like the Old Testament Israel's terrorizing experiences on the mountain (Exodus 20:18–21) than the goodness of the God of the New Testament expressed in Jesus Christ. This preaching as terrorism has woven into the fabric of Christianity a cheapening, or devaluing of human life.

As a young evangelist, I was fascinated by the possibility of emotional, dramatic responses among the people in our audiences. There is effectiveness in the fear of God coming upon a person and creating in him a great remorse for his sinfulness. But even if it is a reverential fear, fear it remains, not faith born of love for God.

Until a person grows in God and in his relationship with Christ in consciousness, he will be obedient to the commands of God only out of fear, rather than love. That is no different than the dread of the gods felt by ancient pagans. Galatians 5:6 says, "The only thing that counts is faith expressing itself through love." Our greatest challenge of these times is to rise above the religion of fear until we rediscover the God of all love.

What's Love Got to Do with It?

> If faith can't believe without sensation, it isn't faith at all, but doubt looking for proof and looking in the wrong place.
>
> —*Unknown Author*

"This is going to hurt me more than it hurts you." It's an oldie but goodie, spoken by parents down through the generations just before a child was to receive a sound whipping. My parents never said this to me or to my siblings. We just got the whipping. No one ever apologized for it, but we never doubted that the punishment came from the need for discipline that stems from love. Love was the justification for some pretty painful acts of corrective discipline delivered by parents, pastors, even teachers. "He who spares the rod hates his son" (Proverbs 13:24) is a scriptural relic of an earlier era.

The second shortest sentence in the Bible—second only to "Jesus wept" (John 11:35)—is 1 John 4:16, "God is love." Yet this scripture is a contradiction. How can we reconcile eternal damnation and unconditional love? Both are blockbuster hits in religions and seem to have support in Scripture. But there are probably more people who believe in hell than who believe in God's unconditional love. What does that say about how Christians have been taught about their worthiness to *receive* that love?

I never doubted my parents' love for us, despite some fairly severe whippings as we were growing up. I did, however, wonder about the unceasing torture that God's anger would supposedly sentence us to, especially when I was told that His anger was a result of our refusing His love.

My older (and only) brother, for whom I've always had unconditional love, never fit the image of "saved." I could never reconcile the fact that while I would always forgive him for his crimes,
God would not. This makes no sense. How many parents have
heard their adolescent children shout the painful words "I hate
you!"? Do those parents really think their children hate them and
lock their beloved offspring in a basement to starve? Of course
not. That would be both illegal and immoral. In the same manner,
it has always been difficult for me to reconcile God's love *and* His
purported unspeakable wrath.

According to many people, love is the "impossible" dream,
while hell is the "probable" dread. Love is the hope; hell is the
promise. We must earn God's love, but if we don't, hell is an automatic sentence. However, according to 1 Corinthians 13:1–8, love
never fails, is patient, kind, doesn't envy or boast, isn't proud, rude,
or self-seeking, is not easily angered, and keeps no record of
wrongs. So where do hell, judgment, and damnation fit into the
picture? We must choose a hateful God or a loving God; we cannot have both.

The love of God is different and deeper than I have learned or
taught in my fifty-plus years as an Evangelical Christian. Christians like to say that nothing is impossible for God, but I disagree.
I would like to offer one more heretical notion and suggest something that is impossible for the Creator:

God cannot be love and also be hate.
God cannot be what God is not.

The meaning of the Cross and the Resurrection is not only that
God loves us but that He has the power and the will to overcome
evil, including eternal damnation. To believe that a loving God
would permit a single soul He had created to be destroyed or eternally separated from Him is an oxymoron. It would be a defeat for

God, who most believe is all-powerful. It is impossible that God would have created millions of people only to cast them into hell. It would mean that creation is essentially a failure. Eternal damnation is a lie fabricated to keep people terrified and obedient to the religion that seeks to control its adherents.

SOLDIERS OF THE LORD, FALL OUT!

The message inherent in this truth is this: God does not need us to do anything to earn His love; we already have it. Tragically, many of us delude ourselves into the belief that we must perform God's will on earth, even though we have already established the belief that the Father is omniscient, and omnipresent, and omnipotent. Taken to its extremes, this performance-oriented dogmatism leads to death and horror.

I have noticed many placards waved by Islamic protesters that have slogans such as, "Praise to Allah and death to Americans." The same hateful stupidity is at work in those who proclaim "God hates fags," or in those who bomb abortion clinics and assassinate abortion doctors in the name of the Lord. Remember the Houston mother who drowned her five children, using the excuse that she was protecting them from hell and washing them clean from the demons that inhabited them? Slaveholders supported the practice of slavery by quoting Scriptures that say "Slaves obey your masters." You couldn't join the Ku Klux Klan without confessing Jesus as Lord. The earth is drenched with the blood of those butchered and tortured with God's supposed approbation. Look hard enough, and you can find something in the Bible to support any atrocity.

The concept of Crusades is literally a mission to aid the *cruz,* the Latin word for "cross." Man has always felt that he was obligated to aid God in being God, and has conveniently justified endless atrocities in the name of this "holy" calling. But God does not need our help. He does not want it. We are the saved, not the saviors. Christians believe the man named Christ Jesus filled that role and achieved ultimate victory, so why do we attempt to improve on it? This is how we view taking up our Cross daily and following Christ (Luke 9:23). Our religion has given us a martyr consciousness. We expect to be abused, and thus *we* abuse.

Long before Islamic extremists flew jets into the World Trade Center towers, the Pentagon, and a field in Pennsylvania, Christian religious extremists set out to protect the Holy Land from Muslims, and in doing so destroyed towers and buildings in Jerusalem, filling the streets with rivers of blood. Popes have sanctioned witch burning, and wars over which brand of Christianity was the right one have riddled Europe and the world. Merciless violence and vicious hatred have been the result of men justifying the expression of their deepest personal hatreds, fears, and lusts for power by claiming to be acting out God's will. Could any of them really have believed they were honoring God with such brutality? That remains a mystery.

GOD HAS A WONDERFUL PLAN FOR YOUR LIFE: ETERNAL HELLFIRE!

Many well-meaning Christian evangelists follow a similar, albeit less violent, path when they violate people's privacy and insult their faith by cramming Jesus down their throats and calling it "witnessing for the Lord." They then dismiss those who reject or resent their obnoxious behavior by informing them of their "death sentence" to hell.

One moment it's, "Jesus loves you and gave His life for you," and in the next, "You'd better love Him back and give Him your life, or enjoy your stay in hell, buddy." Is it any wonder we get doors slammed in our faces? For centuries, Christians have been directly or indirectly projecting condescension, intolerance, and condemnation to those who do not follow them in lockstep, and we wonder why we aren't received with love, enthusiasm, and understanding in return?

In this theology, hell has been elevated to equal status with heaven. Many Christians believe that hell is the ultimate home of far more souls than heaven. "Accept God's love and love Him back or go to hell" is not mature love; it is fear and torment. *It is a lie.* If you believe something only out of fear, you will never know what it means to believe it by faith. First John 4:10 says, "This is love: not that we loved God, but that he [God] loved us and sent his Son as an atoning sacrifice for our sins." First John 2:2 completes the thought: ". . . and not only ours, but also for the sins of the whole world." That is Inclusion. Evangelism is not getting people saved; it is informing people of God's redemptive love toward them. Faith doesn't save you; faith just recognizes that you are saved.

The Parable of the Loving Father

The story of the prodigal son (Luke 15:11–32) is more of a story about a father's unconditional love toward a wasteful, extravagant son than it is a story of two sons with different temperaments. Note how the father anxiously awaited the return of his lost son, and noticed him from a "long way off" (Luke 15:20). The fifteenth chapter of Luke runs over with parables describing the recovery of lost possessions, including money, sheep, and, of course, sons. Jesus shared these parables to indicate God's willingness to recover anyone who was lost or felt lost. In fact, the Gospels of Jesus are filled with aphorisms about God's love for the least, the last, and the lost. He told us that He came so that the least would become the greatest, the last would be first, and the lost would be found. This applies not only to Jews or Christians, but to anyone lost or languishing. Is it not ironic that those whom the Church considers to be the least and last should become greatest and the first in Father's kingdom? This is the outrageous, scandalous love of God.

In the parable of the prodigal son, we see an encounter between the father and his eldest son. This son had no patience with or compassion for his younger brother. The younger sibling was a screwup who demanded and then wasted his inheritance and had dishonored the family. He needed to pay for his actions. Watching his father's exhibition of joy over his brother's homecoming infuriated the elder son. Was his father out of his mind? How could he just take that little traitor back without requiring one single thing from him? This was crazy! After all, the elder brother was the one who had worked hard his whole life on his father's behalf. He had never sinned against the family name. He had always been a good son, always faithfully working for his father.

Henri Nouwen, in his book *The Return of the Prodigal Son,* wrote of the older brother, "There is so much frozen anger among the people who are so concerned about avoiding 'sin.' " There are too many "older brothers" in the Body of Christ who are judgmental and filled with anger and jealousy. This attitude reminds me of the manner that most of my detractors have displayed regarding Inclusion. They protest the unconditional inclusion of others outside the Christian faith or a specific denomination. They don't consider those outside Christianity to be included in the master plan of universal reconciliation. In their minds, Christianity qualifies you, not Christ.

The son who never left home was jealous of the one who did, and he felt his father's acceptance of the prodigal son was unfair. He was judging based on his brother's error, not on the father's love. He didn't understand Paul's admonishment in Romans 5:20 (KJV) that where sin abounds grace abounds the more.

Granted, the prodigal son was repentant, but his father did not require repentance of him. He described his son as having been lost but now found, dead but now alive. Even though the son had fled, he was never out of his father's mind or heart. He was always welcome at home, and his place as a son had not changed.

CHRISTIANS ARE FAILING IN THE MISSION

Such is the case with all of God's lost sheep. None of us is lost to God. We can only be lost *from* Him, and that only in our minds, not His. Colossians 1:21–22 says: "Once you were alienated from God and were enemies in your minds because of your evil behavior. But now he has reconciled you by Christ's physical body through death to present you holy in his sight, without blemish and free from accusation."

Imagine if the son who stayed home had gone out searching for his prodigal brother to assure him of his father's unconditional love. This would have been a wonderful example of Christian evangelism. We are the older brothers, assigned to go forth to tell others of our Father's unending welcome and eagerness for all to return to His home. But Jesus was a realist; He knew that religious people usually prefer the bludgeon of judgment to the gentle persuasion of love.

This is what Christians are supposed to be doing—not telling people how evil and wrong they are, but how loved they are by God. A forgiving, redemptive message has infinitely more power than damnation. Emphasizing judgment and hellfire negates the Cross, the place of God's ultimate judgment upon sin. God is not angry and has no issue with humankind that has not already been resolved by Christ Jesus our Lord. In failing to deliver that hopeful message, we are failing to fulfill God's faith in us.

WE HAVE THE POWER TO CREATE A BETTER GOD

Albert Einstein said, "We can't solve problems by using the same kind of thinking we used when we created them." If we can create the negative concepts of death, hell, and judgment, we can create and sow ideas of love, peace, cohabitation, and tolerance.

We believe what we choose to believe. We blame God for allowing nature to malfunction and kill innocent millions. Pernicious religious leaders announce that a storm, a tsunami, or terrorist attack is really God's wrath against us for not praying enough, tolerating homosexuality, or some other perceived transgression— a cosmic wagging finger saying, "I warned you." Do we buy that fraudulent message? Do we forgive God, or do we act on our fear by oppressing and killing others in a desperate attempt to appease Him, a return to the days when maidens were sacrificed to stem the lightning? Do we assume that punishing others is something God plans to do anyway, so we're actually helping Him mete out His ultimate judgment on the world?

When earthquakes spawn tsunamis that kill hundreds of thousands in South Asia, how do we deal with these disasters without holding grudges against the Deity who was supposed to protect us from such horrors, especially when we presume the Deity actually sent the disaster upon us? The only way we can justify such misfortunes is to tell ourselves that somehow we deserved it—that something we did or didn't do brought the wrath of God down on us.

Recently in America a convicted rapist and murderer was taken off death row because a jury had used the Old Testament principle of "an eye for an eye, a tooth for a tooth" to justify the death penalty. This act was viewed as a violation of the separation of church and state, and the death sentence was invalidated. The juror in question was unsure whether his position as a Christian would allow him to decide for the death penalty, and another juror actually brought her Bible into the jury room to support her opinion that Scripture validated the death penalty.

We have two warring perceptions of God: Old Testament anger and fire against New Testament kindness and approachability. These conflicting perceptions battle for preeminence in our consciousnesses. Which do we choose to believe? Which do we act upon? As Einstein also said, we can harness the power of our thoughts to create a better future by changing our perception of the God who created our past, present, and future.

Ralph Waldo Emerson knew the power of a thought surging through the spirit of man, writing "The soul of God is poured into the world through the thoughts of men." If that thought originates in God, it is pure. Thoughts drive our actions. Solomon put it this way: "As in water face reflects face, so the heart of man reflects man" (Proverbs 27:19, NASB). My hope is to challenge and change the thinking of all who see God as anything but light, love, and logic. If these thoughts become entrenched in the thinking of all people, especially Christians, they will influence the way we respond to all of God's creation. Perhaps then, the older brother in all of us might go in search of our lost brothers to remind them that their Father loves them and is waiting to wrap them in His loving arms.

CHAPTER EIGHT

THE GOSPEL OF HELL

> Oh, my Jesus, forgive us our sins. Save us from the fires of hell. Lead all souls to heaven, especially those who are most in need of thy mercy. Amen.
>
> —*Catholic prayer*

My brother-in-law, who suffers from paranoid schizophrenia, alcoholism, and substance abuse, quoted this prayer one night in my hearing as I was visiting the home where he, though an adult, lived much of the time with his mother, now deceased, in a small Catholic parish in Louisiana.

He had stepped outside to smoke a cigarette and quoted this prayer passionately and from memory on his way out the front door. It struck me as strange that he would recite this prayer. I asked him to repeat it so I could write it down. He did so proudly, as if he were showing off. I was both impressed and amused, as he doesn't talk much, and I was not aware of that religious side of his personality.

It is a prayer that hundreds of millions of Catholics know by heart and recite daily. The prayer has two parts; the first asks for forgiveness and salvation from hell, but it is the second part that appeals to my Inclusion consciousness: "Lead all souls to heaven, *especially those who are most in need of thy mercy.*"

God is mostly a human idea more than a spiritual one. We have created varying concepts of God for at least the last three thousand years. God has not been perceived outside a concept of a devil, and heaven has not been perceived outside a concept of hell. It is as if one is incomplete or unacceptable without the other.

BLAME DANTE

Dante Alighieri, an Italian poet of the thirteenth and fourteenth centuries, created the common rendering of hell in his epic poem *Inferno,* part of *The Divine Comedy.* He was backed up by John Milton, who in seventeenth-century England reinforced the popular image of hell with *Paradise Lost.* Ever since, hell has been a place regarded by Christians with a horrified fascination—an everlasting car wreck that we pass, unable to look away. As the supposed place of punishment for those who defy the edicts of God, disbelieve, or simply refuse to repent their sins, hell has become far more intriguing to us than heaven, just as bad behavior is always more interesting than good. We can't help but wonder: What is hell like? Will my friends go there? Will I go there?

A commonsense analysis of the sovereignty, moral character, and omniscience of God renders it impossible that He would have created mankind if He saw hell as our ultimate, eternal destiny. A God who would allow eternal torment would not be godly, but demonic. If atonement means the reconciliation of humankind to God, then it must result in the ultimate, universal salvation of all humankind. That means hell cannot be the place of eternal torment that so many of our religious leaders gleefully claim most of us are destined for. Hell must be something else entirely.

THE DEVIL MADE ME DO IT?

Picture a dapper man in a red suit, with horns and a goatee, sidling up to you offering untold riches in return for your soul. This melodramatic image of the devil is deeply embedded in the consciousness of billions. The denial of the concept of a personal devil with the same level of influence as Jesus Christ is one of the most controversial aspects of Inclusion. Yet while this image of the devil is far from the truth, for centuries it has psychologically, emotionally, and spiritually crippled people's hopes for the future.

Many people assume God to be fallible. They believe He suffered a mutiny in heaven and lost a third of His angels. He banished them all to hell (though they don't explain where hell came from), (or earth), which the devil ruined. Subsequently, God created humankind, supposedly through Adam and Eve, and then allowed this same devil to get into the Garden of Eden, where he corrupted them. Shortly thereafter, Cain murdered Abel and was sent off like a vagabond to continue the cycle of sin, destruction, and death.

So by this accounting, we have three major deific failures: Satan's mutiny in heaven, the serpent on earth, and Adam, the floundering earthling. Not to mention the continuation of Satan's influence on earth, where hundreds of generations have assumed the Evil One to be lurking behind every tree and in every heart, waiting to trip up anyone he can, especially Christians, and shish-kebab their souls on his pitchfork as he herds them into hell.

THE DIVINE DO-OVER

Later, according to Genesis 6:5–7, God realizes that He has made another mistake, repents of His creation of man, and decides to use His "eraser" again—getting a divine do-over, as if He had hit a golf ball into the rough. He sends a great flood to wash away everything and nearly everybody, leaving only eight human beings on the planet and a variety of animals to restart the ecosystem. However, no sooner than the earth is dry again, Noah overdoes the celebration, gets drunk, and things once again start going downhill.

No wonder we can't trust God to be as good as we hoped! Scripture portrays God to be a real screwup, like an inexperienced carpenter. His "earth project" appears to have crooked walls, peeling paint, and a cracked foundation, yet we are taught to "walk before me [Him] and be thou perfect" (Genesis 17:1, KJV). How can we expect perfection when we subconsciously believe that God made glaring mistakes that make our lives on earth impossibly difficult? It's not much of a leap to think that humans are a mistake as well.

This kind of thinking assumes that all of Creation was the result of God's irresponsible playing with His own power, and that He really didn't know what He was doing. Under this logic, Creation is damned. This obscene notion of God as a malicious child with a set of Legos, creating structures and then stamping them flat out of pique, creates hell on earth between God and man as well as brother and brother. These misconceptions create tension in human society that will not disappear until the concepts that support them change.

The more I consider all these legends, myths, and mysteries, the more childishly superstitious these concepts of God and history sound. My faith in the ultimate reality called God is as strong as ever, but the haphazard and fumbling cosmic puppeteer to which religion has reduced Him is becoming increasingly ridiculous.

WHY DOES A PERFECT GOD ALLOW EVIL?

If God is so careless or awkward in his dealings as Scripture portrays Him, then we have a real cosmic dilemma before us. Would such an accident-prone God trust Himself to play with the fires of creation? If God is in fact as omniscient and infallible as we believe, we have to find a better explanation for His "mistakes." They had to be foreseen and allowed to unfold by Him for a reason. That reason, I believe, lies in the concept of what I call the Law of Opposites.

There seem to be laws and sciences beyond our knowledge that govern the eternal design, and creation itself is bound by them. Thus, in creating us as creatures of duality, God defined an entire fabric of opposites in our existence. For example, we live in a world filled with microorganisms. Some are beneficial, while others inflict deadly pathogens on us. Yet we continue to exist in balance between these opposites—until we tip the balance, and the killer organisms overwhelm the benign.

In the same way, there are positives and negatives in life that have their necessary and legitimate functions. The law of physics teaches that two positives will repel each other. The creation of energy, the tension in drama, the beat of a heart—all require the interaction between the positive and the negative. As long as a patient's heartbeat is displayed on the heart monitor as moving up and down, the patient is still alive. When there is no movement between positive and negative, death is imminent.

The law of opposites not only makes life exciting, it makes life possible. Jesus emphasized this point when He said to let the wheat and the tares grow together (Matthew 13:27–30, KJV). "Wheat and tares" represent the positives and negatives of life, good and evil, right and wrong, truth and deception. In this passage of Scripture, Jesus is indicating that the positive and the negative each has its purpose in life. Because we don't understand the essential nature of opposites, we have developed a negative duality that maddens us. Again, this may be why Adam and Eve were forbidden to eat from the tree of dualities.

Self-hatred is born out of misunderstood duality. It is the result of living in constant opposition to our essential natures as creatures of both good and evil—of perceiving only good as worthy and evil as something that must be suppressed at all costs. But evil comes from God as much as good—only God may not necessarily call it evil. I don't know what He calls it, but it has something to do with balance. Everything and everyone ultimately comes back to God, so what we see as evil in us must ultimately serve God's purpose and *not* be evil, but divine.

ENJOY YOUR STAY AT CLUB DEAD!

> I form the light and create darkness: I make peace and create evil: I the LORD do all these things.
>
> —*Isaiah 45:7 (KJV)*

The terrifying mystery of hell is the number one tactic Christians have used to bring people to their knees. During the first five centuries of New Testament church history, there were many different views of hell. Each supported a belief in hell, but differed in terms of what happened in hell, how long a person stayed there, and why a person was sentenced to hell. This is the difference between *primary* and *secondary* doctrine, and it circles back to my original Inclusion point: *doctrine is the problem.*

Primary doctrine teaches a basic belief: that there is a hell, or that Jesus is coming again. Secondary doctrine teaches the interpretation of that belief: what happens in hell, or when Jesus is due to arrive. Secondary doctrine is open to question and interpretation; primary doctrine, in most cases, is not. As believers (and theologians), we are not supposed to disagree on primary issues, even though we do, but we can disagree on secondary, doctrinal distinctions. In these discussions, many possibilities of hell play out. Hell is everlasting, but not endless. It can be ageless without being endless. Hell will last, perhaps eternally, but those who go there may not necessarily be there forever, and so on.

Psalm 139:8 says, "If I go up to the heavens, you are there; if I make my bed in the depths [KJV uses the word *hell*], you are there." This Scripture indicates that God Himself will be in hell as well as heaven. Psalm 16:10–11 (KJV) says, "For thou wilt not leave my soul in hell; neither wilt thou suffer thine Holy One to see corruption. Thou wilt show me the path of life: in thy presence is fullness of joy. . . ." The Psalmist uses the Hebrew word *Sheol*, which refers to the grave, but the King James Version mistranslates it as hell. The more accurate modern translations redefine it as Hades, which is usually a reference to the grave. The word *hell*, or *sh'eol*, was sometimes used to refer to God's judgment upon a foreign nation, as punishment for their crimes against His people or their attempts to thwart His plan. In no case was it a reference to eternal judgment and fire.

The concept of a God who systematically and eternally tortures His enemies is one of the great errors in religious thinking. The conflict stems from this fact: the God of Christianity and a God who is Christian are two different concepts. The God of Christianity is a God of eternal love, grace, and mercy. However, the Christian God has become something else entirely: frighteningly cruel, unforgiving, legalistic, and draconian. He is lord, but not the Lord. He is the one who uses hell to intimidate masses of ignorant, innocent people.

HADES AND GREEK MYTHOLOGY

We have already seen how Greek religion, and its continuation in the Roman culture, influenced early Christian doctrine. So it is with the concept of hell and existence after death. In Roman mythology, Hades is called Pluto and represents both the god of the underworld and the underworld itself. To the Romans, Pluto was the god to whom all men must eventually go. They believed him to be the god of the dead and the dark, misty regions of the afterlife.

According to the *Encyclopædia Britannica,* Hades was a Greek god or celestial being. In Greek, Hades means "unseen," similar to the Hebrew word *sh'eol,* which means "pit, grave, or out of sight." The implication is something unknown, hidden by shadow, and unknowable. The KJV translates the Old Testament word *sh'eol* as *hell* thirty-one times, *grave* thirty-one times, and *pit* three times. The New Testament equivalent of *sh'eol* is Hades, and it appears only thirteen times. It usually means "grave" rather than the fiery inferno modern Christianity perceives it to be.

The parallels between Christian theology and Greek and Roman mysticism are understandable, but they are no excuse for confusion or ignorance. They should be identified for what they are, and Christians should be aware of how inappropriate they are in influencing some of our doctrinal teachings.

According to Edward Fudge, author of *The Fire That Consumes,* in Hades, Charon ferried the souls of the dead across the rivers of Styx or Acheron into an abode where the three-headed watchdog Cerberus guarded the gate so that none might escape. This pagan mythos contained all the elements for medieval eschatology (the study of the end times or afterlife). There was the pleasant Elysium, the gloomy Tartarus, and even the Plain of Asphodel, where the ghosts, who were suited for none of the above, wandered. The word *Hades* came into biblical usage when the Septuagint translators chose it to represent the Hebrew *sh'eol,* a vastly different Old Testament concept. *Sh'eol,* too, received all the dead, but the Old Testament says nothing about punishment or reward.

HELL ON EARTH—REALLY?

So what we have with hell is a confused stew of belief systems. The reality of hell is far more complex. It is not my intention to deny the existence of hell but to define it biblically rather than according to Greek mythology. We've always seen hell as God's answer to sin. This perception is only partially true, if at all.

In many ways, the Church seems to hate evil more than it loves good or even God. Christians have made evil and the devil equal rivals to God, glamorizing both into a form of idolatrous theology. We are obsessed with evil, sin, and with figuring out (according to our own bigotries and preoccupations) which behaviors will send their perpetrators into eternal fire.

In our obsession with hell, the devil, and evil, we have become spiritual warmongers of the first order. I have received scores of letters from Evangelical Christians insisting that by teaching there is no literal hell, I am simply leading millions there—and will end up there myself. This is a response I sent to one of those correspondents:

> *Your commitment and devotion to hell, devils, the first Adam, and death is cultish and dangerous. I'm sure you mean well and have interpreted the Bible to support your fear-based theologies, but they are inaccurate and anti-Christ in nature. Hell is a place we unwittingly create and/or invent for ourselves, not a place God created or would have created for anyone. God is not that vulgar and hateful.*
>
> *I believe in an eternal God who judges, but not in a God who judges eternally. According to Christian theology, all of the judgment of God against sin was in Christ at Calvary. Any other judgment of sin is temporary and immediate, never eternal. Only Mercy endures forever, as Scripture says, mercy will triumph over judgment (James 2:13).*

Heaven and hell are states of consciousness. Hell begins and ends here in our earth consciousness. It is something we have invented out of fear, and we continue to re-create it simply because we've been taught to. Only degenerate minds dream up such profane delusions as eternal torture and then blame them on God.

People without sound minds, who don't know the transcendent nature of God's love, invent such horrifying experiences. Hell exists, but we create many versions of it ourselves. Prison is one of the hells we create. There's plenty of weeping, wailing, and gnashing of teeth there. I have a brother who spent three and a half years in federal prison. It was hell for him and for us, too—especially our parents. He called prison the front door to hell; hospitals were the back door.

The concepts of Hades, Sheol, and other synonyms for a place of eternal torment have no relevance here. Hell is not a Christian concept taught by the apostles or Christ. Jesus spoke of Gehenna (the Valley of Hinnom), which was the city dump on the southeast side of Jerusalem. The term is used allegorically as a reference to separation in consciousness, from the truth and hope that exists in God. Jesus declared that hell's gates would not prevail.

The original biblical consequence for sin was death, not hell. The concept of hell was brought into the picture some 4,500 years after Adam and Eve's misstep in the garden. Jesus died once for all (2 Corinthians 5:14) and removed the sting from death, making it simply a transition into another consciousness rather than the annihilation it probably was before the Resurrection. Jesus opened the way to heaven. Hell was never part of the equation.

JESUS ON HELL

In his book *Conversations with God,* Neale Donald Walsch gives one of the best descriptions of hell I have ever read: "Hell is the experience of the worst possible outcome of our choices, decisions, and creations; the natural consequences of any thought which denies God or says no to who you are in relationship to Him and your purpose in Him. It is the pain we suffer through inaccurate thinking. Hell is the opposite of joy; it is unfulfillment. It is, perhaps, to know who you are and fail to experience that. It is being less, lack, or incomplete. It is nonrealization!"

I believe hell is a form of insanity. It is mental and spiritual illness, indefinitely incurable, until rescued and healed by truth. Jesus described it lucidly, though metaphorically, as a place where one can see, hear, think, speak, desire, reason, and be totally aware, but is unable to realize the most basic desires. There is no reference to the literal "weeping, wailing, and gnashing of teeth" that we usually associate with the experience of hell and which can be found in other references. It all seems to be metaphorical as opposed to literal.

The Scripture with the greatest detail on hell was spoken by Jesus Himself, in Luke 16:23–31:

In hell, where he was in torment, he [the rich man] looked up and saw Abraham far away, with Lazarus by his side. So he called to him, "Father Abraham, have pity on me and send Lazarus to dip the tip of his finger in water and cool my tongue, because I am in agony in this fire."

But Abraham replied, "Son, remember that in your lifetime you received your good things, while Lazarus received bad things, but now he is comforted here and you are in agony. And besides all this, between us and you a great chasm has been fixed, so that those who want to go from here to you cannot, nor can anyone cross over from there to us."

He answered, "Then I beg you, father, send Lazarus to my father's house, for I have five brothers. Let him warn them, so that they will not also come to this place of torment."

Abraham replied, "They have Moses and the prophets; let them listen to them." "No father Abraham," he said, "but if someone from the dead goes to them, they will repent."

He said to him, "If they do not listen to Moses and the prophets, they will not be convinced even if someone rises from the dead."

Let me make an important observation about the concept of torment used in the above passage. The Greek word used is *basanos,* which has as its root *basis*—in English, "base" or "bottom." The insertion of the concept of torture is curious but suspicious. According to *Strong's Exhaustive Concordance, basanos* has to do with walking or pacing oneself. It suggests footing or foundation. The references to the dark abyss and the rest are all the influences of the mythology we've already discussed. God has been the victim of millennia of misinformation.

It is evident that the rich man is a Jew, and that he is acutely aware of his situation. He feels compassion, as well as compunction. He is somewhat repentant and desirous of a second chance. He sees water, but cannot drink. He is able to request only a tiny portion of it, almost as if he knows that in hell he won't be able to experience the fulfillment of any desire. In other words, he cannot enjoy a full cup of water, life, joy, food, or any normal human desire, even though he obviously had them. He lovingly remembers his family and desires to communicate with them; however, this is not possible. He can see the rest and comfort of heaven but is unable to go there. He is dwelling in the place of unfulfillment.

The "gnashing of teeth" is a metaphor for anger and resentment. Many people experience hell daily in their homes, their unhappy marriages, and their unfulfilling jobs. Adolf Hitler was a prime example of unmitigated gnashing of teeth. Anybody who hates millions of people to the point that he attempts genocide is in hell. Such people, even if they seem victorious in this life, are in reality the most miserable, tormented people on the planet.

People filled with hatred, fear, and hopelessness to the point where they inflict their pain on others—the Osama bin Ladens, Saddam Husseins, Josef Stalins, Vladimir Lenins, slave traders of the world, and a host of other human violators, some in pulpits—are souls in hell. They represent what Jesus must have meant with regard to weeping, wailing, and gnashing of teeth. Millions of people who feel alienated from the peace and presence of God in consciousness also experience the same kind of agony.

Jesus's discussion of hell took place prior to His death. Perhaps He was describing the pitiful plight of a world without a Savior, a world filled only with lifeless, powerless religious laws. In the story of Lazarus and the rich man, there is no reference to God or Christ, only Abraham as the one being prayed to for help. Perhaps Jesus was suggesting to His Jewish brethren that Abrahamic ancestry would provide no answer to the question of how those hearing His parable would spend eternity.

THE GOOD NEWS ABOUT HELL

Abraham could not help those on their way to hell or living in it while on earth. In Christian theology, the way out or through hell is Christ Jesus. It always has been, and always will be. But unlike what the world's religions tell us, we don't have to know it, believe it, or accept it. Jesus accomplished world redemption without our permission, before any of us was present on the planet. According to the Christian Bible, Jesus is the "Lamb that was slain [before] the creation of the world" (Revelation 13:8).

The gospel (or "Good News") about hell is that there isn't one. There is no horrible eternal inferno. If you feel defenseless without one, remember that hell is easily created by any of us. We create hell all the time—in Darfur, in inner-city gang territories, in communities divided by prejudice and bigotry. But the literal hell stuff stops here. It is a human idea based on human ignorance and fear of the unknown. Hell is a man-made concept, as are some of our concepts of heaven. If that unbalances you, ask yourself this: Why or how is the knowledge that others are suffering in hell part of the bliss of heaven for many people? Is that a Christ-like belief? Or is it a vindictive human need for power and superiority?

We damn ourselves here, now. Or we can save ourselves here and now with choices based on love, hope, and justice. God has taken care of our eternal salvation already. The rest is up to us.

CHAPTER NINE

THE GOSPEL OF FAITH

Faith in faith is faith gone astray.

—A. W. Tozer

To travel hopefully is a better thing than to arrive.

—Robert Louis Stevenson

Christians believe that Christ died for all sin—except the sin of not believing He died for all sin. This is such a gross fallacy that it begs to be confronted.

I had the privilege of knowing the popular healing evangelist Ms. Kathryn Kuhlman personally. She had long-running television and radio shows titled *I Believe in Miracles* and was a friend of Oral Roberts. I met her on the ORU campus in the spring of 1972, when she was the baccalaureate speaker. We became fairly close friends over the next four years until she passed away. She was known and loved by millions for her huge "miracle" services, where tens of thousands jammed the venues, expecting to be miraculously healed.

In one of my private times with her, she told me she didn't like being called a faith healer because she wasn't sure exactly what faith was, but that she believed more in the sovereignty of God. She was constantly astounded as to how often the people who seemed to receive healing in her crusades were those who came out of doubt and cynicism, while many others who claimed to have *all the faith in the world* left her services with no apparent change in their condition. She insisted that her faith was in God, not in faith. I've never forgotten the conversation.

THE TABLOID-IZATION OF FAITH

I once heard a preacher say, "If faith cannot believe without sensation, it is not faith at all, but doubt is looking for proof and looking in the wrong place." Religion sensationalizes faith by embellishing it with a gaudy, ambiguous cloak of doctrines, dogmas, and rituals created by men. Belief and trust in God become difficult because they have been freighted with the fear-based theologies that sustain modern religion.

The New Testament says that we are saved by *hope* (Romans 8:24). It also says, "Now faith is the substance of things *hoped* for" (Hebrews 11:1, KJV). Because no one in our modern age has died and come back to tell us about it (except on all the major talk shows, followed by a best-selling memoir and then a movie), we cannot say for certain what awaits on the other side of death. Most religions believe in an afterlife, but these beliefs are as diverse as the number of religions in the world. Faith requires us to regard the unknowable with hope—and trust in our Deity.

THE SPIRITUAL TWINS: FAITH AND DOUBT

Some wise men speak about faith:

> Doubt is not the opposite of faith; it is one element of faith.
>
> —Paul Tillich

There lives more faith in honest doubt...than in half the creeds.

—*Alfred Lord Tennyson*

Doubt is a pain too lonely to know that faith is his twin brother.

—*Kahlil Gibran*

Doubt is not always a sign that a man is wrong; it may be a sign that he is thinking.

—*Oswald Chambers,* My Utmost for His Highest

Chambers also said, "If God were to remove from us the possibility of disobedience, there would be no value in our obedience; it would be a mechanical business." This same principle holds true with faith and doubt. If God were to remove from us the possibility of doubt and fear, there would be no value in our faith; it would be a reflexive exercise. Therefore it is reasonable for me to say, "I hope I'm saved, and that I will spend eternity with God in absolute fulfillment and that others will join me in similar bliss."

I find it curious that in the Old Testament, the word *faith* only occurs twice, and yet faith is presumed throughout the history of Judaic culture. This is probably because as far back as history can recall, faith in God or the gods was universal. From the earliest civilizations, humankind has looked to a higher power to explain the natural occurrences of the world, affirm our values, and make us feel less fearful about our place in the cosmos. In early pre-agrarian societies, these expressions of faith in an invisible god were primal and simple, without religious doctrine. Unlike religion, faith is not taught; it simply *is.* Faith is the anticipation of the existence of God and His blessing. Religion is the quest to systematize that feeling, to organize it under rules and laws. Religion could, not unreasonably, be called "industrial faith."

The only two mentions of faith in the Old Testament, Deuteronomy 32:20 and Habakkuk 2:4, are both references to stability and reliability rather than spirituality. In neither case are they used as a reference to the eternal salvation or heaven that Western Evangelicals and modern-day Christians preach. Faith was presumed, but obedience was optional, based on one's level of faith and experience (Romans 14:1). In other words, everybody believed in spirits and disembodied entities, but not everyone had the same devotion to the *religion* built around them.

Faith is personal. It requires no structures, organizations, or permission. It requires no one to be baptized, confirmed, or to take Jesus as his or her personal Savior. It simply exists. Religion is a choice to adhere to structures and strictures, to accept the pronouncements of men who presume to speak for God. They are *not* the same.

GOD'S OWNER'S MANUAL

The Irish author C. S. Lewis, in anguish over the death of his beloved wife, Joy, only a few years after the remission of her cancer, which he attributed to prayer and faith, wrote:

> Talk to me about the truth of religion and I will listen gladly; talk to me about the duty of religion and I will listen submissively. But don't come talking to me about the consolation of religion or I shall suspect that you don't understand. The conclusion is not that there is no God at all, it is instead, so this is what God is really like, a cosmic sadist, a spiteful imbecile?

Many so-called believers believe in a God in whom they are profoundly disappointed, as well as being in profound terror of. They have faith, but is their faith positive and redemptive? Or is it a kind of doomed resignation—a faith that anticipates a cruel, unreasonable, and arbitrary God?

The most famous reference to faith in modern times is the Old Testament verse in Habakkuk 2:4 (KJV), "The just shall live by his faith." Protestant Christianity is built on the bulwark of that single verse. Martin Luther, the great reformer, was transformed by the revelation that came to him while reading this verse quoted by Paul in Romans 1:17. It became the basis for the Reformation in the sixteenth century, the greatest schism in the history of Christianity. It is interesting that the single most divisive incident in Western theology was based around a question of faith, incited by a single verse from the Bible (and fanned by centuries of Catholic corruption such as simony, the selling of church offices, and paid indulgences to "buy" one's way out of purgatory).

Billions of people of faith do not regard the Bible as the authentic, inerrant word of God. Many Christians regard the book as a collection of allegories that are also fraught with contradictions, not as a document to be taken literally. In the past I would have simply written off such people as secular humanists who needed to be saved. No longer. As Evangelical Christians, our faith is tied to our Bible, but in proclaiming gospel truths to others, we fail to acknowledge that the vast majority of those to whom we preach, particularly those outside the Western world of religious thought, do not regard the Bible as anything more than pulped trees between cardboard covers. In reaching out to others, Christians make the error of assuming that the superiority of our doctrine is self-evident—a mentality that is disrespectful and counterproductive as well as extremely naive.

We should not assume that everybody, including many Christian and Jewish believers, accepts the Bible as the absolute rule of faith. Many people have faith in God but don't put stock in what some have called "God's owner's manual" or our concepts of divinity. I had a rather rude awakening to this when as a college student I was confronted with the question "What makes you think your Bible is the *only* true word of God and the only rule of faith in Him?" I was stunned and even offended, but since then, I have accepted this as a legitimate question that cannot and should not be ignored.

The Bible Is *a* Source, Not *the* Source

In American jurisprudence, witnesses swear on the Bible to tell "the truth, the whole truth, and nothing but the truth, so help you God." There was a time when this was as American as apple pie, the Pledge of Allegiance, and hot dogs at a baseball game. However, because of the spirit of e pluribus unum ("from many, one") that underlies American culture, we must look not only at how we use the Bible, but at how relevant it can be if our interpretations of it do not evolve and change as human society changes.

I am not suggesting that the Bible is not important or that it doesn't play an important role in our religious life. Without question, it is central to our faith. However, to rely solely on its literal interpretation for direction on everything from how to raise our children to whom we regard as sinners is to ignore two millennia of social, scientific, technological, civil, sexual mores, morality, and political change. The Bible may be inspired by the Word (*Logos* in Greek) of God, but it was written down by men—men who were children of their times and therefore colored by the fears, knowledge, and societal mores of their era. They were as flawed and prejudicial as any among us today. I don't view the Bible as so much the inspired Word of God as the inspired word of men *about* God. And some of the so-called inspired Word is now "expired" and irrelevant.

Perhaps more than any other aspect of Inclusion, this view of the Bible angers the Evangelical leadership and laity. That is understandable but it's also shortsighted. Some hard-line religious leaders, chained by absolute adherence to doctrine, ask, "Why should we change? Why should we adapt to a pluralistic society? Why should we not command that the members of that society recognize the eternal truths that we preach?"

This is a sentiment admirable for its passion, but not for its realism. The truths of God may be unchanging, but human society and culture are not. The world of humankind is the stage on which God's drama plays out, and that stage is always shifting. One of the reasons religion finds itself increasingly obsolete on that stage is that it refuses to change or evolve with the fabric of human progress, expecting society to change instead. These are truths we can't afford to ignore if we expect Christianity to remain relevant in contemporary society.

I do take the Bible seriously, but I *do not* take all of it literally. The Bible is essential to the shaping and expression of our faith, and to our ability to connect with the truths that lie at the heart of what many perceive as God's logic, the history of Judeo-Christian faith, and the deeds of Jesus Christ. But I don't constrain God (or good) to a single interpretation. I respect the Bible more for its historical allegory than for its factual authenticity. It is worthy of our highest respect with regard to its place as a historical document and in forming modern religious and social culture. But it is not the definitive source of wisdom and command regarding God. No book could be. To place the Bible in that position is to place it above God Himself.

THE NATURE OF CHRIST

I am a native Californian, from the city of San Diego. When I go there, I am aware that I am in the state of California. San Diego is a city in California and can be considered both California and part of it. But California is not confined to San Diego, or necessarily defined by it. In the same way, Jesus is an aspect of God we can relate to because of His humanness. But God, the Infinite Spirit and Eternal Design, cannot be limited to our concept of, as the Apostle Paul said to Timothy, "the man Christ Jesus" (1 Timothy 2:5).

When I say God is not a Christian, I am not saying that Christ is not God. I am saying that God is not Jesus. God is neither confined *to* nor defined completely *by* Christ. Though our theology teaches that Christ is sent of God, ordained and anointed by Him to be Savior and to redeem humankind, He is not a substitute for or even a duplicate *of* God. He is an aspect of God, but not God in His Infinite Essence.

I have come to the conclusion that I am not monotheistic, but pantheistic—I believe God or Divinity is everything and everywhere. This is a belief in an omnipresent God. If God is everywhere, then He is in everything and everyone—all religions, peoples, cultures, ideologies, concepts, and beliefs. And all books.

In a sense, I accept the *agnosticism* of my faith. I accept the fact that I don't and cannot entirely know God—I no longer believe that is possible or even necessary. I am happy with what I *do* perceive of God, and I enjoy the opportunity of living to know that there is infinitely more for me to know. I no longer believe so much in "a" God or "the" God. I just believe in God.

DOES IT TAKE FAITH TO BE A CHRISTIAN?

In Christian logic, there are some basic questions that should be asked: Does believing make you born again, or does being born again make you a believer? Is it more important that you accept Christ or more likely that God in Christ accepts you? What is the Good News—that we give our lives to Jesus, or that He gave His life for us? Does receiving the Gospel make a person righteous, or does the Gospel simply proclaim that we have been made righteous by the sacrifice of Jesus? To make exclusion obsolete, these questions must be pondered. Which came first: faith or redemption?

Faith is a powerful and necessary component to a well-rounded spiritual journey. However, it is more a privileged state than a requirement for obtaining eternal life. Dogmatic and/or industrial faith is simply not as important as traditional religion has made it seem. This argument continues a debate that is as old as North American settlement. Since Christians came to these shores, the debate has raged: Is faith the key to salvation, or are good works what God wants? What of the devoutly religious person who commits terrible deeds, or the atheist who helps the poor and acts with honor and integrity? Who will go to heaven? Will either? Will both?

The Apostle Paul asked, "What if some did not have faith? Will their lack of faith nullify God's faithfulness?" He answered his own question: "Not at all! Let God be true, and every man a liar" (Romans 3:3–4). God's divine plan for our lives overrules every other force on earth. Would God send His only begotten Son to buy our salvation, but then make it contingent upon whether or not some missionary would hear and obey His calling, raise enough money to purchase a ticket to Africa, India, or Asia in time to reach the so-called heathen dying of a disease or the victim of a natural disaster? A benevolent God would not leave such things to chance. If God is a redemptive God, He would both inadvertently and deliberately redeem all, not just some.

THE PROBLEM OF BLIND FAITH

Faith demands that we accept as real that which cannot be proved by science or perceived in the everyday material world. But today the concept of faith, in which what is hoped for is perceived as true, has been replaced with *blind faith,* in which faith replaces reason as the source of knowledge. Questioning is discouraged or forbidden, and is, in fact, regarded with hostility. Not only is this kind of misguided faith not part of God's plan for salvation, it actively harms Christianity in our culture.

God is in all things and the answer to all questions. He created the world and everything in it, and He created the human intellect, our most divine, godlike aspect. Do you think God is not equal to any question? Why would anyone assume that God does not want His people—all people—to question His actions or the meaning of His perceived words? The Creator is the greatest of mysteries; uncovering new truths about that mystery requires that we approach it dynamically, with questioning, curiosity, and intellect. That is what will make Christianity a living belief system and faith an adventure. When skepticism is treated as a sin, and blind, ignorant faith as a virtue, we stultify Christian thinking, and the religion becomes an artifact, dead to the modern world, like a specimen in a museum. Blind faith does not serve God's purpose. Questions do, especially since the party that fears inquiry is not the Lord, but hypocritical, power-hungry religious leaders who know that informed faith undermines their authority.

ST. OPRAH

In his best seller *The Da Vinci Code,* Dan Brown wrote:

> Theoretically, every faith in the world is based upon fabrication, which is indeed one of the definitions of faith. Faith is the acceptance of something we imagine to be true but cannot necessarily prove. Every religion describes God through metaphor, allegory, and usually some form of exaggeration. This trend can be traced back as far as the earliest civilizations of humankind.

People tend to have more confidence in their faith than in God. They have made a god out of their faith. For years I have admired

Oprah Winfrey, and I have gone so far as to say she is my favorite televangelist. I am not sure that she would be flattered by the comparison, since televangelists don't have a very good reputation these days. But if televangelists came across more like Oprah, Christians and Christianity would be much more welcomed in the world.

For years, I have thought that Oprah does what Christians should be doing. Her spirituality and compassion for others—her advocacy for women and her fund-raising for charity—is a better example of God's love than all the institutionalized evangelizing in the world. Instead we ostentatious Christians have proceeded to try to *sell* Christianity to the rest of the world, as if it were a used car that we're trying to prove to be better than the next guy's car. We tend to think that we own Jesus and that we are His primary sales force, if you will.

That is a fatuous, narrow-minded view. Evangelizing Christians who travel the world preaching that *faith* in Jesus is the only solution to the problems of so-called pagans do a disservice to Christ Consciousness. God gave us other means to solve problems: our minds, our creativity, and our ability to work together. Missionaries who claim that faith is the solution for a hungry child or for a village devastated by AIDS make all Christians targets of parody, such as in a satirical article in *The Onion* headlined, "Poverty-stricken Africans Receive Desperately Needed Bibles." For those who do not have to worry about where their next meal is coming from, faith is a luxury. For starving people it is a prayer of desperation. If Christianity wishes to rehabilitate its image, we must focus on using our compassion and love to create solutions, not shout doctrine.

Evangelism is not about trying to prove to the world that Christianity is the greatest or only legitimate religion. Evangelism is *showing* love, not talking about it. Love itself is the Gospel, and its message immediately and automatically connects people to the

Divine in the earth and reminds them of their inextricable tie to it.

Evangelism is not "getting people saved"; it is informing people that they *are* saved and inspiring them to reconsider their lives and their invaluable spirits.

YOU DON'T NEED FAITH TO BE SAVED

I have felt "saved" now for over forty-five years, but only in the last five or six years have I actually felt *safe*. I had faith to be saved, but not to feel safe from God's wrath toward those whose faith may at some point fail them.

Romans 3:1–4 deals specifically with the question of faith and the role it plays in redemption. This takes us back to the conflict between "works of faith" and "faith that works." Which is more important? James 2:14–26 asks the question "Can faith save him?" If faith in God and belief in the Scriptures is the only thing that confers salvation, then can we assume that even demons are saved, since Scriptures say they believe in the truth of the sacred writings (James 2:19)? And are righteous people of other religions damned in spite of their good works and lives of compassion and justice?

In Romans 3:3–4 Paul asserts that even those who do not believe will receive God's faithfulness. God's faithfulness to Himself, His Word, and His will is not affected by man's faith or lack thereof. It is not based upon man's works but upon God's work, or God's will. It does not originate from the actions of man, but from the mind and heart of the Creator.

In 2 Timothy 2:13, Paul says, "If we are faithless, he will remain faithful, for he cannot disown himself." The word he uses for "disown" (*deny* in the KJV) is the Greek word *arneomai*, which means "to contradict, disavow, or abnegate." Many preachers use that Scripture to suggest that Jesus will deny people who deny Him. This is what I heard all my life, warning those who don't give a public witness about Jesus as being in danger of being rejected by Him in the final judgment.

That is an incorrect interpretation, reflecting the Christian world's obsession with exclusion and with Christians' desire to feel like "the elect" of God. The word *disown,* as used in this passage, simply suggests that if you deny or disown Christ, He will disown *your denial.* Even if you are unfaithful to Him, He will be faithful to *you.* He's not like my sisters were when they were little girls, squabbling over something and saying, "If you don't play with me, I won't play with you!" The love of God is not so irresponsibly childish.

Ask yourself what you can do to offend air, or wind, or rain. Is it possible to violate either? So would be the case with God or His eternal Christ Principle. Denying Christ is ultimately an impossible feat. The finished work of the Cross (theoretically) is so definite that nothing can change its effect. If my biological children one day decided that they wanted to deny being my children, would their decision make it so? No. They would remain my children, and I their father. They are my children with or without their vote or permission. They had nothing to do with their biological makeup. Such things were decided *for* them, not *by* them.

To quote Rev. Robert Farrar Capon, ". . . the law of God condemns us all until, while we are still sinners, grace comes and liberates us from its curse without a single condition attached; no improvements demanded, no promises extorted, just the extravagant, outrageous, hilarious absurdity of free grace and dying love."

WHY BE A CHRISTIAN?

In response to Capon's stunning revelation, some people have asked the legitimate question, "If everybody is already saved, what is the purpose in being a Christian, and what value is there in being born again?" Paul presumed a similar question in Romans

3:1, when he addressed what he thought his Jewish brethren were thinking: "What advantage then, is there in being a Jew, or what value is in circumcision?" Paul answered his own question: "Much in every way! First of all, they [the Jews] have been entrusted with the very words of God."

You could replace the words *Jew* with *Christian*, and *circumcision* with *born again* or *awakening*. The Christian requirements for being saved are nothing more than the entrance rituals for the most exclusive religious club in the world. The doctrines, dogmas, and mantras that we have expected people to recite are oaths and vows of initiation, not salvation. They have little to do with spirituality.

According to Scripture, all sheep and all souls belong to God. They may be misplaced through ignorance or rebellion, but not a one is *replaced*. The term "winning souls," often used by evangelists, suggests that someone (the soul) is a loser. It sounds competitive and condescending. The term subliminally suggests aggression—even militarism. We Evangelical Christians are quite comfortable with such terminology, but it serves to alienate non-Christians.

The objective of evangelism is not to convert. The objective should not be to convert anyone, but to convince everyone that they are loved, cherished, valued, and accepted. The Good News itself, aided by the presence of the Holy Spirit, is enough. Coercing to manipulate a conversion has given Christianity a bad name in many countries and cultures, and has caused some well-meaning missionaries and their families to endure suffering, persecution, and death by locals who resented and resisted their aggression. In many ways, we have brought these horrors on our heads through our belief that Christian evangelists should suffer to get people saved. We view such sacrifices as holy and God ordained. We are taught that Christ suffered for us on the Cross, and that the least we can do to somehow repay Him is to sacrifice to win others, so His suffering won't be in vain. There is a considerable amount of guilt in the rationale.

Even Muslim terrorists assume they are doing Allah's bidding by killing and maiming innocent people, not to mention often sacrificing their own precious lives to do it. Militarism in the name of perverted religion has led to millions of deaths over the centuries, and holy murderers continue to justify their barbaric and dastardly acts by excusing them as the express will of whatever god is on the top of the charts that day.

The concept of soul winning is derived from a statement made by King Solomon in the Old Testament. It is misleading. In using terms like *winning, finding,* and *converting* souls, Christians have missed the point of the Cross. They think the efficacy of the Cross is dependent upon one's faith. But evangelism is not a numbers game; we should not be tallying how many people we converted on a certain day and writing it on a chalkboard like the salesmen in the David Mamet play *Glengarry Glen Ross.* The Gospel is a declaration of the *fact* of redemption, not a suggestion of the possibility that is contingent upon whether you hear it or accept it according to dogma.

Why be a Christian? Christians are no more or less saved than anyone else; what we are is aware of the means of that salvation and its reality. Our purpose is not to force-feed our doctrine to others but to be Christ's proxies on earth, reflecting God's love and graciousness—something that many non-Christians and people of other faiths often do much better than we do.

Evangelism is reminding people of what they already know. It is reconnecting them to their pre-incarnate consciousness. Once they remember who they are, they forget who they have become through their spiritual amnesia. They go on to live lives of peace and joy and help make the world a better place for everyone, regardless of faith. All else is ego.

That which is to give light must endure burning . . .

—*Viktor Frankl*

THE DEBT IS PAID

One of my favorite songs sung in church when I was a young boy was "Lift Him Up." The lyrics say, in part: "How to reach the masses, men of every birth, for the answer Jesus gave the key. He said, 'If I, if I be lifted up from the earth, I'll draw all men unto me.'"

We sang this song with great passion, energy, and sometimes tears. However, if, in fact, "all" means "all," then there should be no real argument here with the "allness" of Inclusion. We are not just quoting a song, we are singing Scripture from the Gospel of John 12:32. The word he uses for "draw" in this passage is the Greek word *helkuo,* which means "to drag" or "to haul." And, unless you interpret the word *all* as "only those who accept or believe," then it is an inclusive term that excludes none.

If the debt in fact has been paid, we will never receive an eternal invoice for our sin. That's the Good News! People still make errors in judgment and commit acts that we call sin, but the message of the Gospel is that all sin for all of humanity throughout the generations has been atoned for by the Lord Jesus Christ.

Some argue that even though the debt has been paid, the person needs to acknowledge and believe it (be born again) to be saved. First of all, this commonly translates as "the person must join my church, tithe, give offerings as I direct, and do what I say in order to be saved." But this claim is nonsense. Each one of us will live a spiritually debt-free life even if we never recognize or enjoy that freedom consciously. That's why preaching the Gospel is so important. Making people aware of their redemption will make them more receptive and trusting of God. They will believe that God is love, rather than law and judgment. They will live with greater joy, hope, security, and possibility.

The process is like the fisherman casting out a net, dragging the bottom of a river, and pulling up everything the net catches.

After the fish are caught, the fisherman owns them all. God throws none of us back. If those caught in the net are murderers and addicts, abusive or psychotic, they're all redeemed and restored to their original purpose in God. We call this "cleaning fish." We can't clean them before we catch them.

In my conversations with people about Inclusion, this is one of the principles that many find so troubling and offensive—they *need* to have punishment and eternal damnation for murderers, rapists, drug dealers, and so forth. But punishment is why man created prisons and death chambers. We assume that death is automatic, imposed upon humanity without our consent, and that eternal life comes only by choice and election. God's plan was crafted without our participation or permission, and under His system, all are redeemed, even if the rest of us do not believe they should be. This is *amazing grace*. This is where I hope this book will bring some revision of this theology.

Who Chooses Hell?

> A free will is not the liberty to do whatever one likes, but the power of doing whatever one sees ought to be done, even in the very face of otherwise overwhelming impulse. This is freedom indeed.
>
> —George MacDonald

One of the most prevalent fallacies among Christians is that we humans are "free moral agents" entirely in charge of our lives, with the authority to choose our destiny. This is the popular concept of free will that we possess when it comes to making decisions about how we will live. God did not create us as puppets. But we also tend to believe that *we* have control over where we will spend eternity—and based on our interpretations of Scripture, where other people will, too. But in reality, we are only moral free agents in the most basic areas of life. In others, critical decisions were made by God without Him asking us our opinion.

You did not choose to be born. You did not choose your parents, your gender, your race, your ethnicity, or in what nation or culture you would be born. You did not choose your complexion, the texture of your hair, your eye color, or any of your other physical features. You didn't choose your social security number, birth date, or astrological sign. There are many aspects of your life that are matters of choice, but most of the essential facts about your being, as far as we know, you cannot and did not choose. You just deal with these random, predetermined realities as best you can.

Jesus said in John 15:16, "You did not choose me, but I chose you . . ." Many people protest Inclusion by insisting that God would not force salvation upon a person. Yet these same people declare that God will force death upon you and then torture you forever if you don't choose or accept His will. Excuse me? These Christians are talking out of both sides of their mouths. They say God loves everybody and that Jesus died for all, but then they insist that redemption is contingent upon whether or not a person agrees with our interpretation of what we call His word. That's contradictory and nonsensical.

Some Christians insist that God doesn't send people to hell; they choose it on their own. Who in their right mind would do that? We are taught that God's mercy endures forever. Yet this merciful God will sentence billions to His customized torture chamber forever?

This is Orwellian doublethink, the ability to believe two preposterously contradictory ideas at the same time. It demeans Christianity and Christians to think this way, and supports those who claim that we care more about condemning those who do not believe than we do about inspiring others to live like Christ in spirit.

FEAR OR FAITH

In the end, Christians who don't understand Inclusion must accept that belief based on fear of eternal hellfire is worthless. If you believe something only out of fear, you will never know what it means to believe it out of love. If you are convinced that your only alternative to faith in God is hell, does it make you faithful or just intimidated?

Following a principle primarily out of fear does not constitute New Testament faith. It is superstition. I submit that most religious people go to church, mosque, or synagogue primarily out of superstitious motivations. They fear what will happen if they do not go. They fear what may happen in this life if they don't go to church, mosque, or synagogue as much as what may happen in the next. I know—I was one of them for fifty years.

Hebrews 10:31 says, "It is a dreadful thing to fall into the hands of the living God." Christians who quote this Scripture in a foreboding light are the same ones who, while evangelizing, encourage someone to put his life in the hands of a loving God who will love him, care for him, and never leave him. How can it be both a dream and a dread to fall into the hands of the living God? This is where doctrine and Scripture become a hindrance, not an aid.

Let's look at the preceding verses in Hebrews 10. Verse 26–27 says: "If we deliberately keep on sinning after we have received the knowledge of the truth, no sacrifice for sins is left, but only a fearful expectation of judgment and of raging fire that will consume the enemies of God." Notice the phrase "after we have received." The word used there for "received" is the Greek *lambano,* meaning to "take or get hold of." Most Christians interpret the word *receive* to mean the same as "hearing" and "accepting." However, simply being in the presence of a message does not guarantee that you will understand or accept it.

Receiving Jesus or the Gospel of truth will affect one's life here on earth. However, failing to receive (or "get hold of") it probably won't bring eternal consequences. You can hear the sound of a freight train coming, but if you are not familiar with the sound, you don't know to get off the tracks. You can hear a rattlesnake rattle, but if you don't know what it is, you don't know to step away. You can be thirsty and hear the sound of a brook running fresh, cool water and not recognize its sound and ignore it.

The point is, just because a person hears the Gospel does not mean that he has understood and received it. But he is no more guilty of the sin of unbelief than a person who views art in Paris's the Louvre and sees only naked people and marble. Lack of understanding does not constitute sin. Christianity's mission is to *promote understanding*—a tougher, greater mission than promoting fear.

Faith is being convinced of a thing even if you cannot hear or see it. Faith has a point of reference. It doesn't just appear, it is evolutionary and gradual. It is wonderful and powerful if we receive Christ, but it is not pivotal to our eternal salvation. The Good News is that the bad news was wrong! In Christian theology the way it should be, it is not that a person accepts Christ in order to be saved, but that God accepts the person through Christ. That is Good News.

FINDING SHELTER, BUT NOT COMFORT

I was struck by a headline in *USA Today* about the survivors of three successive hurricanes that devastated Florida. The headline read, "Finding Shelter, but Not Comfort." A photo caption read, "Hundreds of people remain in shelters after having been driven from their homes by hurricane Ivan. The waiting and the uncertainty causes nerves to fray."

It's hard to find a phrase that so embodies religion today. Religion offers a temporary shelter against natural disasters that come into a person's life, but not much real comfort. The wars and tension we experience result in part from our feeling that religion is only a temporary shelter. You're not the owner in religion, only the lessee, and you can be evicted without notice by the restless, temperamental landlord.

Religion suggests that God was incomplete and feeble in His attempts to redeem humankind. In fact, if you reduce it to its essentials, all religion (including Christianity) is a subtle admission that the Creator, whatever His name is, is a blunderer who needs our help to achieve His ends. He's a loser. He cannot rule earth and is in fact a failure without our man-made religions to bail Him out.

Mark 7:37 says that Jesus does all things well. I wonder how many believers truly believe in this statement, or that with God all things are possible? The reference was to Jesus having healed a man who was a deaf-mute. The man was not actually mute, he was simply deaf and therefore did not know what spoken words sounded like, so he could not repeat the sounds accurately enough to be understood. In some ways, that was a prophetic illustration of the state of Israel at the time, and perhaps the state of the church and the religious world today. We haven't heard truth accurately and therefore cannot speak it accurately.

CORRECTING OUR HEARING

If "faith comes by hearing," as recorded in Romans 10:17, then our faith will never be sound until our hearing is corrected. It is not that people of religious convictions cannot speak. Our communication is stifled because we lack command of the language to which the world can relate. To the world, the church is often a "deaf-mute," unable to hear or understand what it says in its heart. That is why we are perceived as out of touch and out of sync with the real issues people face. We are more interested in ideology (what we believe *should* be) than reality (what *is*).

In early African-American history, many slaves and slave children were labeled as "deaf and dumb," yet they were some of the brightest people in their families. They were labeled as retarded simply because they were deaf and could not pronounce most words well or communicate easily. Yet there was nothing wrong with their minds. Dr. Andrew Foster, who established many schools for the deaf in Africa, brought attention to this fact.

Christianity is not disabled, but because many Christians have not heard accurately over the centuries, they have never developed the ability to accurately communicate the Gospel. Instead our message comes out garbled, so it is misunderstood. Once our hearing problem is healed, we will regain our ability to speak the truth. The message will come across not only clearly but more correct. The world may then see and say, "Jesus Christ has done all things well!"

However, this will continue to be impossible as long as we see God as angry, unforgiving, and so vengeful as to have created a customized torture chamber called hell. There are a number of scriptural interpretations supporting such a perception; however, there are far more to support the reality of a loving and merciful God. We must blend scriptural analysis with our God-given logic to discover the true nature of God, rather than what centuries of poisonous, ego-inflated doctrine has tried to embed in our minds.

When we thus open our minds and see beyond religion, we will see clearly that to have created a world destined to end in such disaster is a spectacularly futile exercise. Why would God bother? Why waste the time and effort? Most Christians are afraid to admit it, but we find it difficult to fully trust a God who is preached as the ultimate example of bipolar disorder—eternally loving yet sadistic and pitiless toward anyone who falls short of His capricious standards. It seems much more plausible that He has done all things well, and that the final result will be triumphant victory, or as the fairy tales say, end "happily ever after."

FAITH DOESN'T EQUAL RIGHTEOUSNESS

In most Evangelical preaching, we have presented God as angry, belligerent, judgmental, and jealous, and yet we are surprised when those to whom we preach want nothing to do with this God.

Believing in such a God inevitably leads to a person manifesting those same characteristics, even though the person may attempt to justify them through some kind of twist on his or her religious perspective. This is the source of such travesties of faith as Fred Phelps and his vile "God Hates Fags" movement, which, for example, demonstrates at the funerals of U.S. soldiers, thanking God that He has struck down another representative of a nation that has a "don't ask, don't tell" policy. (In Phelps's mind, this policy promotes homosexuality.) It would be better to be an atheist and believe in no God than to believe in a sick God who would countenance such vicious, delusional hatred. As a follower of Christ, I'm always embarrassed when Phelps and his motley crew show up anywhere, and millions of other Christians are as well.

In many Christian circles, faith and righteousness are considered inseparable. When people are described as "good Christians" or "good churchgoing people," that is shorthand for two things: they are people of faith, and they are decent, moral, and biblically *righteous* people. "God fearing" has the same meaning. But faith and righteousness are not the same; believing Christ's Good News does not by itself make anyone morally superior, *and not believing it does not make a person morally inferior.*

Who knows what anybody's personal agenda is? Some people would argue that faith without works is dead; I would also say in response that works without faith are crippled. To be effective, religion must have both: good works to show (rather than tell) how faith can make a positive difference in this world, and faith to elevate good works from simple acts of altruism to inspiring examples of the love of God. Too much of today's religion is faith without works or works without faith. Faith does not require religion.

Faith at its truest is the recognition of God's faith in humanity, more than humanity's faith in God. Righteousness does not mean perfect adherence to religious dogmas. It is literally a "right" or accurate perception of the Divine in us and of its influence on the soul. It is this influence, more than our deeds or behavior, that makes us righteous. Logic, light, language, and love are what produce benevolent deeds and moral integrity. There are many who adhere to no religious creed who are righteous, and many who are utterly devoted to doctrine who have no authentic righteousness in them.

THOUGHTS FIXED ON GOD

If eternal salvation is really necessary, it would have to be God's idea, not ours. Despite that, we have concocted all kinds of formulas for salvation—some that get close to a more inclusive view. For example, Erwin W. Lutzer, the pastor of Moody Church in Chicago, says, "Christ's death on the Cross included a sacrifice for all our sins, past, present, and future. Every sin that you will ever commit has already been paid for. All of our sins were future when Christ died two thousand years ago. There is no sin that you will ever commit that has not already been included in Christ's death."

Believing in this concept will enhance your life immensely. Try to imagine a world where no one fears hell but everyone recognizes the responsibility to love and live in oneness with God and humankind. This was the plan of Christ and the ultimate reality in God: a peaceful universe and a joyful existence. This is not a new thought or position. It goes as far back as the first century and before.

Notice the words of the Roman emperor Marcus Aurelius Antoninus: "A wrongdoer is often a man who has left something undone, not always one who has done something." By understanding the truth of faith, we can shape this world instead of spending so much time in apprehension of the next one.

> Fix your thought more on the God you desire than on the sin you abhor.
>
> —*Walter Hilton (1340–1396)*

CHAPTER TEN

THE GOSPEL OF GRACE

Abounding sin is the terror of the world, but abounding grace is the hope of mankind.

—A. W. Tozer

A cross the street from the country house I lived in as a child stood the Morning Star Baptist Church, pastored by the Rev. Shaw, who lived twenty-five miles away in the city of San Diego, California. Rev. Shaw was a tall, light-skinned gentleman with thin, wavy hair, hazel eyes, and high cheekbones, indicating that he was mixed with Native American blood.

He was a great preacher who could also sing quite well—always an added benefit for preachers in our community. He was loved and respected, but I was always suspicious of him because he smoked, as did many of the members of the church—openly and with no apparent shame. I often would see several of those old Baptist deacons standing out in front of their church during the service, smoking and fellowshipping together.

I thought this was atrocious; something that you would never see in front of our much smaller Pentecostal church farther up the gravel road, on the edge of our small, nearly all-black neighborhood. Our church had been founded by my great-uncle and grand-aunt before I was born. They had their first Sunday school classes for children in a renovated chicken coop. My family and I were so proud of our little church.

From time to time, the two churches would get together for combined services in which one of the two pastors would speak. I loved those services, as they were filled with energetic singing and powerful preaching in the tradition of our shared African-American cultures.

I was always astounded at how those Baptists could rear back and sing their long, drawn-out rendition of "Amazing Grace." The Baptists rarely sang up-tempo songs in those days. They tended to keep to the long, slow, often sad, somber Negro spirituals, and "Amazing Grace" was the most stirring one. Rev. Shaw would often lead it, and the crowd would join en masse, and the house would immediately fill up with some of the most passionate singing I'd ever experienced.

We Pentecostals knew that the Baptists' singing and worship was anointed, but we wouldn't dare admit it. These were Baptist people, and Baptist people—especially those who smoked and drank, as we knew many of them did—were not supposed to be anointed or even know what anointing was. I used to think, even as a child of six or seven, that the only reason these Baptist people sang "Amazing Grace" with such passion was that they knew they needed grace more than most others. After all, they had just finished smoking, and they were surely going to do it again immediately after the service was over—and probably add a can of beer for good measure.

WHAT IS GRACE?

I laugh about those times now. I think back to my entrenched mind-set even at such an early age and how bigoted and prejudiced it was. I associated grace with those who really needed God's unmerited favor—unlike us. The favor we received from God was, of course, earned by our righteous living.

What is grace? Christians talk about it constantly, but what is it? Where does it fit into our firmament of sin, faith, and salvation? Is it another matter that is more doctrine than God, or is grace something that is beyond man to taint?

John 1:29 says, ". . . Look, the Lamb of God who takes away the sin of the world!" Evangelical Christians subconsciously replace the word *world* with *church*. They assume that Jesus is the lamb who takes away the sins of the Christian, while the rest of the world ultimately dies and goes to hell. Most religions of the world are designed in an effort to mediate man's assumed conflict with God.

LIFTING THE BURDEN OF COSMIC SIN

What is "cosmic sin"? *Cosmos* is the Greek word for "world," as used in John 1:29. According to *Vines Greek Lexicon, cosmos* translates as "order, arrangement, ornament, or adornment." It reflects the order the Greeks observed in the universe. Cosmic sin is not individual sin, though its effect is felt on a personal level. It is not intrinsic sin but *inherited* sin. It is sin that underlies the entire world of man, just as electrons and protons underlie the entire universe of matter.

In Romans 5:12–14 original sin is portrayed as comprehensive and inclusive, rather than individualistic:

Therefore, just as sin entered the world through one man, and death through sin, and in this way death came to all men, because all sinned—for before the law was given, sin was in the world. But sin is not taken into account when there is no law. Nevertheless, death reigned from the time of Adam to the time of Moses, even over those who did not sin by breaking a command, as did Adam, who was a pattern of the one to come.

In other words, we all carry a freight of original sin from the moment we are born, no matter what we have done or how well we have lived. Thanks a lot, Adam.

These three verses describe the universality of Adamic, cosmic sin and its fatal consequences for all of humankind. All races, cultures, and creeds die, with no exemptions. This death is presumed to be the result of original sin. No one has to confess to Adam, believe in him, or obey some canon of laws that he set down. Death is universal, passed down from the first Adam.

According to Scripture, Jesus is a pattern of Adam. He is the second Adam, the dawn of a new human era. In a real sense, Jesus is Adam's heir: the latest in the line of iconic men. So, logically, if death reigned automatically over all of mankind as a result of the transgression of the first Adam (even over those who did not sin), is it not both scriptural and logical to assume that through Jesus, the last Adam, life will reign over those who sin, whether righteous believers or not? If the effect of the first Adam was universal and indiscriminate, it follows that the effect of the second Adam would be so as well.

GRACE IS GREATER THAN YOUR SIN

The law was added so that the trespass might increase. But where sin increased, grace increased all the more, so that, just as sin reigned [past tense] in death, so also grace might reign through righteousness to bring eternal life through Jesus Christ our Lord.

—*Romans 5:20–21*

One of the primary definitions of grace is "unmerited favor." It suggests God's favor that we do not deserve, because we are flawed and sinful. But we receive it anyway, in exactly the same manner that a parent will continue to be consumed with love for a child who does drugs or commits crimes. It is important to note here that according to the words of the Apostle Paul, it is impossible to "out sin" grace (Romans 5:20). The Scripture suggests that grace is greater than any and all sin, known or unknown, intentional or unintentional.

Hebrews 9:26 further emphasizes the weakness of sin when faced with God's grace: ". . . [Christ] has appeared once for all at the end of the ages to do away with sin by the sacrifice of himself." The Greek phrase, "do away with" or "put away" sin is *athetesis,* which means "cancel or disannul." We get our English word *antithesis* from it. It comes from another Greek word, *atheteo,* which translates "to set aside, disesteem, or neutralize." Christ's death canceled sin, making it impotent.

AMERICAN IDOLATRY

One of the most unfortunate effects of the characterization of ourselves as irredeemably sinful and God as ruthless is that we turn to other things in God's place. Humans need *something* to believe in. Even many atheists will admit that they wish they could believe in a God, because it would make the prospect of death and chaos less frightening. But with so much of our culture focused on an angry, exclusionary God, it is no wonder that so many of us put work, possessions, alcohol, or drugs in His stead. All of them seem more appealing than Him.

Idolatry means that anything other than God becomes the center of our lives. Human beings, made in the image and likeness of God, have created our own ways to find what we think will give us peace, satisfaction, or happiness—none of which is working. The ways we have devised to attain heaven are turning our world into hell, causing wars, terrorism, poverty, greed, and the rape of the earth.

To perceive God correctly, we must first understand grace. God sees the best in the worst of us, knows the worst about the best of us, and loves us all without condition or exception. Unhealed emotional wounds and unresolved childhood pain affect our perception of God and thus our relationship to and with Him. Low self-esteem has become a cliché, but it is truly a terrible thing that breeds much of the world's problems. It is born of sin consciousness, the feeling that one is inherently unclean and unworthy of love. This feeling often causes us to impersonate someone we are not. But if we understood grace, we would understand that no matter how we feel about ourselves, *we are all worthy of love*. God loves each of us no matter what we do, and that will never change. I realize this sounds almost trite, but it bears repeating nonetheless. It is the crux of the message or Gospel of Inclusion. Robert Farrar Capon said, "Grace works without requiring anything on our part. It's not expensive. It's not even cheap. It is free."

Putting an End to the Score Keeping

Unfortunately, many Christians do not know the true nature of grace or its implications. As a result, Christianity, like other monotheistic faiths such as Islam and Judaism, has what can be defined as a "self-save" policy. This doctrine is made up of several Scripture-based requirements—rules we are told we must follow if we are to avoid hell. That's how it is usually put: avoid or miss hell. We're full circle back to the guilt-and-fear-based religious mistakes that afflict our world.

These formulas, as I call them, are nothing more than pious substitutes for what Paul refers to as "works." I am guilty of similar mistakes in my years as an Evangelical Pentecostal preacher—of believing the falsehood that one needed to "earn" one's way into God's good graces by completing what amounts to a cosmic to-do list. I understand the mind-set behind such well-meaning, misguided piety. But the truth of the matter is different: the things Christians insist one must do to be saved (believe, accept, and confess Christ) are what one must do to become a *Christian*. They have *nothing* to do with actually being redeemed to God by Christ, or loved.

Thomas Merton, the great monk and poet, said that you must "quit keeping the score altogether and surrender yourself with all your sinfulness to God, who sees neither the score nor the score-keeper but only his child redeemed by Christ." He also said, "Grace is difficult to believe and difficult to accept. We want so desperately to believe that God loves unconditionally, yet we keep adding conditions. 'Okay, fine,' we say reluctantly, 'but once we accept God's grace, we'd better get our act together. We had better be successful or we won't be worthy of his grace.' We just cannot believe God can grace even our 'failures.' "

I respect Christianity and am proud of my involvement with it. However, redemption has nothing to do with becoming a Christian. Redemption took place before there ever was such a religion. There were followers of Christ two thousand years ago in Israel; at least five thousand in a single gathering, according to John 6:10–60. However, they were possibly some of the same people who betrayed and abandoned Him and ultimately voted to have Him crucified. He even referred to one of His twelve disciples as "a devil" (John 6:70). In many ways, religion in general (and Christianity in particular) has become the number one proponent of bigotry.

Grace—The Empowering Presence

Religion takes on this role because we as a people cannot accept the simple truth of grace. Grace is more than "unmerited favor." It also represents the miraculous empowerment to be and do all we are purposed to be and do. Grace is the gift of empowerment and evolving into our highest selves. St. Augustine of Hippo, one of the great Christian church fathers and theologians (354–430), declared, ". . . Grace is given not because we have done good works, but in order that we may do them." I would add that "doing" the works is both in and through Christ Consciousness. It is God who works in us both to will and to do of his good pleasure (Philippians 2:13). In his book *By Grace through Faith,* Charles Spurgeon discusses a relevant passage of Scripture, Ephesians 2:11:

> I think it well to turn a little to one side that I may ask my reader to observe adoringly the fountain-head of our salvation, which is the grace of God. "By grace are ye saved." . . . Remember this, or you may fall into error by fixing your minds so much upon the faith which is the channel of salvation as to forget the grace which is the fountain and source even of faith itself. Faith is the work of God's grace in us. No man can say that Jesus is the Christ but by the Holy Ghost. "No man cometh unto me," saith Jesus, "except the Father which hath sent me draw him." So that faith, which is coming to Christ, is the result of divine drawing. Grace is the first and last moving cause of salvation; and faith, essential as it is, is only an important part of the machinery which grace employs. We are saved "through faith," but salvation itself is "by grace," Sound forth those words as with the archangel's trumpet: "By grace are ye saved." What glad tidings for the undeserving!

Notice Romans 5:20–21, which says, "The law was added so that the trespass might increase. But where sin increased, grace increased all the more, so that, just as sin reigned in death, so also grace might reign through righteousness to bring eternal life through Jesus Christ our Lord." Grace always overrules sin.

Part of our problem in accepting grace is our obsession with payment. No one works for gifts; we work for remuneration. We expect to have to pay for something of value; if we receive something for nothing, it is probably worth exactly what we have paid for it. However, grace is given to us freely and without obligation. This makes us uncomfortable, yet it is God's greatest gift to us, aside from our very existence. Hebrews 4:16 says, "Let us then approach the throne of grace with confidence, so that we may receive mercy and find grace to help us in our time of need." Grace, the gift of salvation, is initiated and sustained by the will and heart of God. Grace is a gift that we cannot return to the giver. We receive it as we receive the light of the sun.

All men who live with any degree of serenity live by some assurance of grace.

—*Reinhold Niebuhr*

DOES GRACE EXTEND BEYOND THE GRAVE?

First Corinthians 15:29 speaks of Christian baptism for the dead: "Now if there is no resurrection, what will those do who are baptized for the dead? If the dead are not raised at all, why are people baptized for them?" I have never heard a sermon, teaching, or pulpit commentary on that passage of Scripture. We have assumed in Evangelical Protestantism that the grace of God ends with death. However, the Old Testament says over forty times that "God's mercy endures forever." If mercy endures forever, then is it not reasonable to assume that it lasts beyond the grave?

Evangelical Christianity has concluded that God saves only a living, breathing soul, but no grace or mercy remains available to the soul after the body has returned to dust. We are taught that God desires to regenerate a spirit while infleshed in a body, but He has no desire to save that same spirit after it has left the body. Are

God's love, mercy, and grace limited to the temporary function of human organs? Or is it true that nothing shall separate us from the love of God—not even death, as declared in Romans 8:38–39? The same passage continues: "For I am convinced that neither death nor life, neither angels nor demons, neither the present nor the future, nor any powers, neither height nor depth, nor anything else in all creation, will be able to separate us from the love of God that is in Christ Jesus our Lord." As Christians, our calling should be to convince all men of the richness of that grace.

Since neither demons nor death, the present nor the future, nor any powers will be able to separate humankind from the love of God, is it not reasonable to include hell in the things that cannot separate us from the love of God? Or is God's mercy limited to everywhere *but* hell? How can an omnipotent, omnipresent being be limited by anything at all?

Grace is a New Testament concept. The concept of grace does not appear under the old, pre-Christ covenant. John 1:17 says, ". . . the law was given through Moses; grace and truth came through Jesus Christ." Jesus introduced a new form of dealing with man's issues that transcended the law. It was clear that the law could not resolve man's predicament.

JESUS: COUNSEL FOR THE DEFENSE

Though I believe in the scriptural basis of a corrective judgment, in an attempt to inspire my own congregation to an evangelism based on love and faith rather than fear, I have encouraged them to put a greater emphasis on the admonition in James 2:13 (NKJV), "Mercy triumphs over judgment," rather than a hellfire-and-brimstone mentality. We cannot avoid the presumed Final Judgment, but the Good News is that through Jesus Christ, we all get to survive it. As implied in Scripture, the only accuser of humankind is Satan, the plaintiff who seeks to condemn humanity through the law, which has already been overridden by grace. The accuser of the brethren is the law. The accuser and the law together equal *Satan!*

In Christian theology, Jesus is our advocate with the Father. He is our defense attorney. We have nothing to worry about, for "Judgment Day" is the day when the universe will recognize the grace of God for all, not the condemnation of the law for all, or any! My emphasis on mercy over judgment is not an attempt to deny the Final Judgment (whatever, however, or whenever it may be, probably nothing like we've been taught) but a proclamation that through the work of the Cross, humanity is destined to survive it. In a sense, the Cross in Christian theology *is* the Final Judgment. Even if you do not subscribe to Christian theology or any theology, the concept that we are all loved carries positive weight.

EVANGELISM: THE MESSAGE OF LOVE

In his book *Soul Tsunami,* Leonard Sweet makes a brilliant observation when he says, "Our problem in evangelism is not a lack of training. The problem in evangelism is that we don't love enough." Do you need training to talk about your children or grandchildren? Of course not. You love them so much that you cannot *stop* talking about them. Sweet writes, ". . . Evangelism doesn't require training; evangelism requires love. Lack of evangelism means lack of love." Christians today are great at preaching Christianity but poor at preaching Christ. The Apostle Paul never preached Christianity. He spoke about the crucifixion of Christ and His Resurrection.

The average Christian layperson—and, sadly, many of our clergy—is unaware of the true meaning of the words *gospel* and *evangelism.* They are derivatives of the Greek word *euangel* ("evangel" in English), which is made up of two Greek words: *eu,* which means "good or well," and *angel,* which means "message or messenger." So a bringer of the Gospel or an evangelist is really supposed to be a "messenger of good," the teller of a wonderful story that seems almost too good to be true. This explains why so many people, especially fundamentalist Evangelicals, have difficulty accepting it without attaching denominational and dogmatic twists to it. It's too simple. It lacks the weight of judgment that humans have woven into their religious psyche.

Many people are uncomfortable with the power and simplicity of this pure Gospel message, so they decorate it with manipulations that they feel will secure their control of the gateway to heaven. We Evangelical Christians have come to assume that we operate the tollbooth on the "highway to heaven," and that to get there people must pay us a toll by subscribing to our brand of dogma.

GOD'S EDITORS

In Ecclesiastes 3:11 King Solomon hints as to why so many are given to this spirit of exclusionism. He says, "[God] has made everything beautiful in its time. He has also set eternity in the hearts of men; yet they cannot fathom what God has done from beginning to end." In all my years of service, fellowship, and ministry among Protestant, Christian, and charismatic/Pentecostal churches, I never heard of any serious disagreement in regard to how everything is believed to have begun. We were not around in the beginning, so it's not a source of concern. But there continue to be bitter disagreements on what will happen in the end. The looming question indelibly etched in the minds of most believers is what will happen on Judgment Day, and will they themselves make it to heaven?

Motivated by fear of the unknown, we enthusiastically edit the daily newspapers and nightly news to fit our religious biases. In the process, we have changed the message to the extent that the power has gone out of it, leaving multitudes hurt, hopeless, and angry. Paul refers to this in Galatians 1:6–7, when he says, "I am astonished that you are so quickly deserting the one who called you by the grace of Christ and are turning to a different gospel—which is really no gospel at all. Evidently some people are throwing you into confusion and are trying to pervert the gospel of Christ."

In his daily devotional entitled *Faith to Faith,* Kenneth Copeland writes what makes me believe that many preachers are close to believing in Inclusion, even if only inadvertently. In this direct quote from his devotional for the date of May 30, he writes:

Very few unsaved people today have ever really heard the Good News. Why? Because too many Christians are busy telling the world God is mad at them, and telling them that they're terrible and wrong. Some call that good news, but it's not, and it's not what God has commissioned us to share. He's given us the "word of reconciliation"! He's sent us to tell the news that God has restored harmony and fellowship between Himself and men. All men. Not just believers. Not just the people in your church, but everyone! That's right. The worst old reprobate sinner in the world is every bit as reconciled to God as you are.

Look at Romans 5:10 and you'll see what I mean. It says that "when we were enemies, we were reconciled to God by the death of his son." Reconciled. That word is past tense. God has already restored fellowship between Himself and the world. He did it when there was not one person except Jesus who believed in the new birth. He did it when the entire world was lying in sin. Through the death and resurrection of Jesus, God has cleansed and forgiven and restored to Himself every man, woman, and child on the face of the earth. All any of us have to do now is receive that good news. That's the good word God has given us. That's the word we need to share with those who are lost. If we'll do it, I can almost guarantee you, they won't stay lost very long.

BLACK ROBES AND CAULDRONS

Paul evidently was noticing the beginnings of the "editing process" two thousand years ago. In Galatians 4:8–11 he writes, "Formerly, when you did not know God, you were slaves to those who by nature are not God's. But now that you know God—or rather are known by God—how is it that you are turning back to those weak and miserable principles? Do you wish to be enslaved by them all over again? You are observing special days and months and seasons and years! I fear for you, that somehow I have wasted my efforts on you.' The Apostle here is protesting against the church of Galatia's declension back into rituals and religious dogmas. Were he alive today, I'm sure he would have the same complaints of Evangelical Christianity.

Holy days, ceremonial washings, sacred apparel, and liturgical observations are not inherently evil. But if we assert that the practice of these rituals is required for salvation, then we have edited the sovereign work of the Holy Spirit out of the process of redemption. We have reduced the message to dogmas, doctrines, and disciplines, which are powerless to confer salvation on anyone. How then is baptism or the celebration of Advent any different from the black robes and cauldrons we ascribe to witchcraft?

In *The Believer's Authority,* the late Kenneth E. Hagin Sr. wrote:

Did you ever stop and think about it; salvation belongs to the sinner. Jesus already has bought the salvation of the worst sinner, just as he did for us. That's the reason he told us to go tell the sinner the Good News; go tell sinners they have been reconciled to God. But we never really told them that. We've told them

God's mad at them and that He's counting up everything they've done wrong. Yet the Bible says God isn't holding anything against the sinner! God says he's canceled it out. That's what is so awful: the poor sinner, not knowing this, will have to go to hell, even though his debts have been canceled! Second Corinthians 5:19 will tell that.

Hagin goes on to say: "There is no sin problem, there is a sinner problem. Get the sinner to Jesus, and that cures the problem. Yes, that's a little different from what people have been taught, but it's what the Bible says."

With all due respect to "Dad" Hagin, I believe the advice should be, "Get Jesus to the sinner, and *that* will cure the problem." If the sinner or unconvinced person hears the accurate presentation of the Christ Principle, he will recognize his reconciliation to God through Christ. Jesus has already done His part in the forgiveness and the reconciliation of the sinner; the sinner just doesn't know it. It is our job as Christians to let him know.

COMMUNICATING THE GOOD NEWS

In Christian theology, the sanctified church has the responsibility to get the marvelous news of universal redemption to the unknowing world. If love were emphasized over judgment, wrath, and hell—if people felt inspired, not coerced—more people of all colors, cultures, and creeds would gladly come to Christ Consciousness. When talking with people of other religions, I hear the same refrain: They think Jesus is wonderful. It's His followers they can't tolerate.

Perhaps it is time that Christians try another approach. As stated earlier, it is not the responsibility of Christians to convert anybody, only to *convince everybody* of the unconditional love of God. The Gospel is not what we must do to accept Christ, but what Christ has done in order that God may accept us. It is not us giving our lives to Him. The Gospel is that Christ gave His life for us.

Somehow over the years, well-meaning Christians (and some not so well-meaning) have stripped the beauty, mysterious glory, and truth of the wonderful gift of salvation away from Christ and put them almost entirely upon the weak, flawed back of humanity. Inclusion gives it back to God.

> All this is from God, who reconciled us to himself through Christ and gave us the ministry of reconciliation: that God was reconciling the world to himself in Christ, not counting men's sins against them. And he has committed to us the message of reconciliation.
>
> —*2 Corinthians 5:18–19*

THE BEST THINGS ARE FREE

Romans 3:23–24 says, ". . . all have sinned and fall short of the glory of God, and are justified freely by his grace through the redemption that came by Christ Jesus." The term "freely justified" is where we run into a psychological wall. The Greek word for *freely, dorean,* translates as "gratuitously or literally, without cause, in effect, unearned or unmerited." A gratuity is given for services beyond expectation or requirement. Grace is gratuitous, not earned. So it is that grace and justification, though defined as "unmerited favor," wind up contingent upon the recipient meeting the doctrinal requirements of a particular religion. We are taught that "nothing in life is free," and we believe that concept so strongly that we simply cannot accept free grace. Our payment becomes the formulas by which we think we guarantee our salvation: tithing, fasting, elaborate rituals, an institutional sense of guilt and self-hatred. We tell ourselves that by paying this price we can control the outcome, because we fear to trust an invisible God whom we assume to be angry, intolerant, and wielding a sword of vindictiveness in the form of eternal judgment.

All religions stress the need to submit to rituals to meet the requirements for salvation. It is never free. Then, when a person has achieved salvation, it must be *maintained*. In other words, people are expected to go through the steps to obtain salvation and then do whatever it takes to maintain their status of being "saved." Is the element of human control not self-evident in this?

MAKING A LIST AND CHECKING IT TWICE

Oh! You better watch out, you better not cry, you better not
    pout, I'm telling you why: Santa Claus is coming to town.
He's making a list, and checking it twice, he's gonna find out
    who's naughty or nice . . .

What American child doesn't know that Christmas song? But within the innocent lines is a reflection of our refusal to grasp grace. The image is of Santa Claus at the North Pole, maintaining a huge database of every time a boy pulled his sister's pigtails or a girl made faces at a friend behind her back. That is exactly the way millions think of God.

God is not in the business of keeping score, though the church is. In 1 Corinthians 13:5, Paul says that love "keeps no record of wrongs." In 2 Corinthians 5:19 he writes, ". . . God was reconciling the world to himself in Christ, not counting men's sins against them." In both passages it is clear that God does not keep records of our sins, yet we are taught that in the Final Judgment God will call us to account for all the bad things we ever did in our lives. This feeds the sin consciousness that poisons our religious communities.

Jesus Christ was not intended to be viewed as just a person but as a *purpose,* which was to eternally render our sins null and void. Scripture clearly says that God will forget our sins and remember them no more. Both Jeremiah 31:34 and Hebrews 8:12 insist that God, of His own volition, dismisses all our past mistakes. The Greek word used in the Hebrews passage is *mnemosunon,* meaning "a reminder or memorandum"—in effect, a record or accounting. God is saying, "I will no longer keep records of sin. I will only keep records of sinners. I will keep their names on file as a trophy of freedom and grace. I will remember to love and forgive them infinitely."

Through Christ, God disregards sin. Understanding this takes away the lifelong terror most religious people have of the ultimate judgment. In Hebrews 4:16 we are told to come boldly before the throne of God in prayer. This is an intimidating thought, because we feel we are not worthy to be heard. But we are. God has made us worthy by choosing to do so. In "Father Consciousness," God is good, forgiving, and approachable. As I see it, any other portrayal is a falsehood, the motives of which should be closely questioned. My mandate from God as a man of the cloth in this, the second half of my life, is to re-present Him differently to those who have closed their eyes to the broader hope.

UNCHANGING GOD, UNSHAKABLE PURPOSE

Scripture says, "I am the LORD, I change not . . ." (Malachi 3:6, KJV). If this is true, is the God in the New Testament different from the one in the Old Testament? No. Look again at the actual words used. The Hebrew word Malachi uses for "change" is *shanah,* which roughly means "to fold over or duplicate," implying "to transmute, double back, or disguise oneself." In other words, God does not play tricks. He does not try to mess with your head or fool you with sleight of hand.

In this passage God is recorded to be stating, "I don't allow your reactions to Me to change who I am, my opinion of you, or my plans for you." He was speaking of His relationship with Israel, which at that time was strained because of Israel's rebellion and its backslidden state. God seems to be inferring that, were He to change, Israel would be annihilated because of its blatant disobedience. The result is a picture of God in His sovereign love and commitment to Himself, His plan, and His people.

Some people adjust their personalities to appear one way at work and another way at home, or one way at church and another way at social gatherings. As a parent, I treat my children differently when they are doing homework than when we are playing out in the yard. I am the same parent, but how I am perceived in various settings leaves different impressions of who I am. In reality, who I am never changes, but how I am perceived can vary according to the situation.

We are often presented an image of a bipolar God whose violent mood changes make the Incredible Hulk appear mild-mannered and the picture of emotional stability. This inaccurate image of God can be supported in Scripture based on a number of incidents in biblical history where He is interpreted as such. But there are far more examples that portray God as loving, patient, and kind.

REPAIRING GOD'S IMAGE PROBLEM

Eradicating the image of a temperamental, controlling, intolerant, punitive God from the public psyche is a major task, ingrained as it is in the thoughts of so many believing Christians (and members of other faiths). But it may also be the most vital work the missionaries of Inclusion can ever perform.

A former pastor on my staff with a master's degree in counseling, who headed up our counseling center, told me that at least 80 percent of his clients had problems that could be traced to bad theology. He said that erroneous ideas about God, Christ, and salvation were affecting people's marriages, families, and their senses of self-esteem and self-worth. They even had difficulty worshipping God and feeling that He was receptive to it. Correcting these inaccurate theologies and images of God is a calling that must not be discouraged by the vicious resistance to the idea of Inclusion.

Many religions simply interpret their fears of God as faithful reverence of Him. However, they have actually lost their ability to distinguish between faith and fear. They see them as inseparable. They are not. Fear has no place in a relationship where God's grace has already guaranteed our salvation.

PART III
A PARTNERSHIP WITH GOD

The upending of the model of Christianity that has held sway over the world for centuries leaves us with a difficult question: If Inclusion is the true nature of God's plan for mankind, where does that leave us? What is our relationship with God? Is there any reason not to sin if no one goes to hell? How should we regard people who hold non-Christian faiths? Perhaps most important for the future of human society, how do we know how to feel about ourselves if we cannot comfort ourselves with the illusion of being among the "elect," while all others are doomed to spend eternity in torment?

I do not have all the answers. My hope is to spark you and others to begin asking these difficult questions, to persist in the face of pressure from the forces of status quo Christianity, and to find the answers for yourself and the world in discussion. However, one thing is clear: the time of the angry, militant Christian cultural warrior must be brought to an end.

The dominionists and reconstructionists, who insist that God has called them to take over all aspects of American society and institute a biblically-based theocracy that would make such things as evolution science, women's rights, and homosexuality capital crimes, have no future in a world where Inclusion carries the day. The leaders of these movements are *not* Christ-like, though many carry the name; they are power hungry would-be demagogues, dangerous, divisive, and delusional. They would have their followers beat plowshares into swords and destroy everyone who does not believe as they do—and in the process, betray the very essence of what Jesus Christ came to communicate.

THE TIME FOR TRUTH IS NOW

It is time for Christians who embrace the truth of Jesus— who do not need to use the cudgel of religion to bolster their self-esteem or bully others into granting them temporal power—to speak truth and persuade their fellow believers that militant, power-mad, dictatorial Christianity is the disease, not the cure. All forms of Christianity are not created equal; the rank and file who adhere to doctrines that counsel political oppression, violence, intolerance, and hate have a responsibility to demand answers from their leaders as to what version of Christ they are actually following.

It is no longer enough to be a sheep. Everyone who claims to love Christ must make a choice between following Christ and serving Christianity. Which is more important? Or to put it another way, which holds more promise: the message that all men are already saved and that God will draw all into His embrace; or the propaganda that those people who do not fit some narrow human interpretation of what is acceptable in the eyes of God must be marginalized or exterminated? What gives the merchants of hate more right to speak for God than anyone else? Why do we listen to these multireligious lunatics? Why do we not call them what they are? In John 8:44, Jesus called them sons of Satan!

RETHINKING OUR ROLE

Most of all, it is time for us to re-imagine our relationship with the Almighty. So much of today's fear-based theology focuses on how unworthy, wretched, low, and sinful man is; a being that God barely tolerates and will send to the fires of perdition for any reason. Since God created us in His image, however, does that not mean in some way that we share His traits? Do we not possess divine potential, even if much of it remains untapped?

I submit that mankind is not on earth to receive God's wrath but to fulfill God's worth, which is infinite. We are the expression of God in this world, so does it not follow that we are the mechanism by which He shapes it? We are God's partners, in a way, working to hear His voice, to bring and be His message to one another, and to carry on the work of Christ, uniting the human family in peace, understanding, and compassion. Is that not a grander vision than a theocratic regime with its own gulag for liberal thinkers, atheists, heretics, gays, and abortion doctors?

Once Inclusion becomes the heart of Christianity and other religions, fear ceases. With fear conquered, our finest qualities surface: courage, creativity, innovation, kindness, self-sacrifice, and love. We become worthy heirs of the Christ Principle and personification, the bearers of His legacy into a new era, too busy spreading the Good News to worry about the end times or other doctrines. Life, love, and peace become our religion.

We have a long, long way to go before such a vision can become reality. In these last chapters, I will try to bridge the final issues related to Inclusion, so understanding and acceptance become possible.

CHAPTER ELEVEN

RE-IMAGINING GOD AND OTHER HERETICAL NOTIONS

To find in ourselves what makes life worth living is risky business, for it means that once we know, we must seek to know more. A few brave souls do look within and are so moved by what they find that they sacrifice whatever is necessary to bring that self into being.

—*Marsha Sinetar,* Ordinary People as Monks and Mystics

One of my former close friends, a powerful young preacher who, up until my so-called fall from grace looked to me for mentorship, asked me why I had willingly turned away from all I had accomplished in my life while I was at the top of my game.

I told him that while on the mountain of success where some presumed I was, I saw higher peaks in consciousness. I saw elements of God I wanted and needed to understand. I found myself stretching toward that higher awareness. Had it been possible for me to leap from one mountain to the other without descending into this dark valley, I would have. However, what seemed to some as my fall was to me like digging into the depths of consciousness in order to rise to an awareness of God I had not imagined.

GOD THE MOTHER?

Christianity is a monotheistic and polytheistic religion. It views God as one who finds expression in three separate but equal personalities: Father, Son, and Holy Spirit. This theology is referred to as Trinitarianism. For centuries Christians have denounced polytheism as heretical. However, if we view God as a Trinity, how can we say that we are not polytheistic? Questions are anathema to religion, yet this is precisely the reason they must be asked.

If not for the cultural chauvinism in our religions, God the Trinity would be a quartet, with God expressing Himself in four separate but equal personalities, including a female deity. "Mother God" would be a much more widely accepted concept in our theology were we to relinquish the gender bias within our religious culture.

According to the Hebrew Scriptures, mankind (Adam), or *Adamah,* was made in a pluralistic God's image and likeness ("Let *us* make man," Genesis 1:26). Throughout Genesis, the Hebrew word for God is *Elohim,* which is the plural of *El* (another word for God), and translates as "strength, might, Almighty, or powerful." Nearly every reference to God in the Hebrew Bible is plural, suggesting perhaps some sort of deific confederacy. Genesis 1:26 can be paraphrased as "The Gods, or Heavenly Parents, said, 'Let us make mankind in our image and in our likeness, and let them rule. . . . ' "

I will venture even a little further from the shores of orthodoxy to broach the idea that the Holy Spirit, referred to in the New Testament as the *Parakletos* in Greek, represents the feminine side of Deity. It has a meaning similar to the Old Testament Hebrew reference to Eve as the "help meet" to Adam (Genesis 2:18, KJV). The phrase "help meet" in Hebrew translates as *ezer,* meaning "aid," and *neged,* meaning "front, counterpart, or mate." The Holy Spirit is referred to as *Paraclete,* a Latin word meaning "comforter" or "one called alongside to help." This definition suggests advocacy, nurturing, or consoling—attributes often associated with motherhood.

RELIGION: ANTI-SEXUAL?

From the earliest records of civilization, deities have been referred to in the feminine gender, largely because of the association with a mother being the womb from which life originates. Many religions emphasizing "Mother Earth," including Wicca, may be a reaction to the male dominance of today's major religions.

The idea of life originating from human genitalia has given rise to many of the ancient religions that practiced sexual orgies as worship. In Jewish thought, this was why God pronounced judgment upon Sodom and Gomorrah. It wasn't the presumed homosexuality in the city that brought the Sodomites their destruction, it was their inhospitality and idolatry.

Lot and Abraham were Jewish (so to speak) and were not welcomed in Sodom without submitting to the sexual form of worship—considered idolatrous by Jews. This same spirit of exclusion is rampant today in institutional religions that close their doors to those who adopt lifestyles or political philosophies that do not hew to their narrow requirements. Inclusion confronts this exclusionist spirit or practice as religious bigotry and false piety.

A reference to the supremacy of Christ, the God man, is made in Colossians 1:15–17 which says: "He is the image of the invisible God, the firstborn over all creation. For by him all things were created: things in heaven and on earth, visible and invisible, whether thrones or powers or rulers or authorities; all things were created by him and for him. He is before all things, and in him all things hold together." These are powerful and revealing words, if properly understood.

In this passage, the Greek word for "image" is *eikon* (*icon* in English), and translates literally as "a likeness, a statue, or profile." Its figurative meaning is "a resemblance or representation." Christ is not presented as equal or identical to God, but as synchronous with Him in character, being, and purpose, in the same way that God expected the Church of Jesus Christ to reflect His Spirit and purpose here on earth. Note the number of times the terms "things" or "all things" are used. This suggests that everything is connected. There is not a spot where God is not. Or as the great theologian and philosopher Abraham Heschel said, "An architect of hidden worlds, every pious Jew is, partly, the messiah."

CAN GOD BE DEFINED?

> Inspired by the idea that not only is God necessary to man, but man is necessary to God, that man's actions are vital to all worlds and affect the course of transcendent events, the Kabbalistic (mystical Judaism) preachers and popular writers sought to imbue all people with the consciousness of the supreme importance of all actions.
>
> —*Matthew Fox,* The Coming of the Cosmic Christ

If I were to choose two words that define God for me today, they would be *spirit* and *love*. However, because of my Christian background and its unavoidable influence on my thinking, I am never too far from picturing God as an old, white, bearded man clutching an antiquated scepter, watching over the earth with an eagle-eyed awareness of every sin and sinner. I am unsure where love fits into this portrait, but anger certainly has its place.

The English word *define* is a derivative of the Latin word *fin,* meaning "end." Man is finite, but God is infinite, without finish or end. Therefore God is outside time. Since a part of how we define a being relates to its place in the flow of time, this means God *cannot* be defined. This calls into question the fundamental rightness of religion itself. Religions, after all, work to define, even confine, God according to a set of narrow parameters that serve a specific agenda. But if God has no end and no place in time constrictions—if He is all times, as well as beginning and end—then no religion can define Him. The finite cannot define the infinite.

To look at it another way, we could say that God is without conclusion—inconclusive. You could actually use such a description to support the idea that there is no conclusive scientific evidence to prove that God exists. And if there is no such evidence, then there is also none to prove that God does *not* exist. There is no way to prove or disprove the how or why of that indefinable existence. There is no way to truly define an infinite cosmic being in human terms. There are only our fragile, cherished illusions— which we defend with the righteous rage of those who know or suspect our beliefs to be false.

To define God as a Christian, Jew, Muslim, or any other religion is to reduce Him to something much less than pure Deity. Who can determine who or what God is or is not? For centuries religion has sought to do just that, but continually fails. Scripture says, "God is spirit, and his worshippers must worship him in spirit and in truth" (John 4:24). Christians have assumed that His worshippers are exclusively Christians and perhaps a few Jews. However, the point is that God does not belong exclusively to any particular religion or group of worshippers. Neither does salvation.

Why should I wish to see God better than this day? I see some
of God each hour of the twenty-four, and each moment

then. In the faces of men and women I see God, and in my own face in the glass. I find letters from God dropped in the street, and every one is signed by God's name.

—*Walt Whitman*

In Exodus 20:3 (KJV), God is recorded to have proclaimed, "Thou shalt have no other gods before me." The word *gods* indicates the inferiority of all gods beside the One Supreme God. The word "other" in Hebrew is *acher*, and translates as "lingering or loitering around afterward or behind." In other words, God is saying, you should not have any leftover loyalties or allegiances to the gods that you worshipped before. However, those "gods" didn't simply disappear. Often abstract and grotesque, they remained in the minds and often the consciences of the people, a problem that requires the evolution of our perceptions to this day.

THE DEVIL UNDER HOUSE ARREST

If the other gods ever existed, they will always exist. They are "permitted gods," authorized to live in the minds of the people, somewhat similar to Satan. But have you ever wondered why Satan was allowed existence in the first place, and why such an ideology seemingly maintains a significant role in the human drama? Unless Satan is a myth or metaphor, which he more than likely is, he could not exist without permission—or even *commission*—from the sovereign Lord.

According to the New Testament, the devil is effectively under "house arrest." He is like a dog on a leash. He can only go so far and do so much. In Christian theology, as a result of Calvary, the devil has been severely limited. He has a ferocious bark, but as it pertains to eternity, his bite is gone. He walks around *like* a roaring lion, seeking whom he *may* devour (1 Peter 5:8, KJV). However, he has no grounds upon which to stand, and no law by which he can accuse us. Jesus fulfilled the law (Matthew 5:17) and then abolished it on the Cross (Ephesians 2:15).

Revelation 12:7–9 says: "And there was war in heaven. Michael and his angels fought against the dragon, and the dragon and his angels fought back. But he was not strong enough, and they lost their place in heaven. The great dragon was hurled down—that ancient serpent called the devil, or Satan, who leads the whole world astray. He was hurled to the earth, and his angels with him." The word *place,* as used in the above passage of Scripture, is *topos,* in the Greek, from which the English words *topic* and *topography* are derived. Because of his ejection from the presence of God, the devil has lost his topography (grounds) for accusation. He is a deposed tyrant who has no authority.

But why would God banish the devil to the same earth where he would later place mankind, as the Christian Bible says? Why here, where we live and raise our families, and ultimately try to please God and get back to heaven? We know that God would not betray us, nor is He sadistic, so He must have had something in mind other than eternal damnation for those seduced by this powerful adversary. What if the "accuser of the brethren" is not some supernatural invisible entity with power second only to God Himself, but is instead the *law* or religious legalism itself, not a man in a red suit with a pitchfork? What if the devil is not a personality, but instead a *personification*—an idea?

No Other Gods

However we define God or Satan, God must occupy the sole place at the apex of our beliefs. Our sole devotion must be to the One Supreme God. He is the Lord most vehement, the self-existent and self-sustaining God, without our permission or vote. Anything else is categorically inferior.

He is the personal God, the Father, who created us and all

other beings. He is also the impersonal God, barely knowable on a personal level. This God is not religious. He has no name or title. We do not know His function and cannot accurately identify His purpose or meaning. He is breath, thoughts, and feelings. He is wind and rain, light and darkness. He is here, there, and everywhere. He isn't even a "He," unless He is also She and Them. He is everything and nothing, nowhere and everywhere. He is the *universe* itself.

This is uniquely described by the ancient Christian mystic Dionysius the Areopagite in his mediation entitled *The Radiance of Divine Darkness:*

> *Trinity!! Higher than any being,*
> *any divinity, any goodness!*
> *Guide of Christians, in the wisdom of heaven!*
> *Lead us up beyond unknowing and light,*
> *up to the farthest, highest peak*
> *of mystic scripture,*
> *where the mysteries of God's Word*
> *lie simple, absolute, and unchangeable*
> *in the brilliant darkness of a hidden silence.*
> *Amid the deepest shadow*
> *they pour overwhelming light*
> *on what is most manifest.*
> *Amid the wholly unsensed and unseen*
> *they completely fill our sightless minds*
> *with treasures beyond all beauty.*

And in *Teachings of the Christian Mystics,* Andrew Harvey writes:

Leave the senses and the workings of the intellect, and all that the sense and the intellect perceive, and all that is not and that is; and through unknowing reach out, so far as this is possible, toward oneness with him who is beyond all being and knowledge. In this way, through an uncompromising, absolute, and pure detachment from yourself and from all things, transcending all things and released from all, you will be led upwards towards that radiance of the divine darkness that is beyond all being.

Entering the darkness that surpasses understanding, we shall find our selves brought, not just to brevity of speech, but to perfect silence and unknowing.

Emptied of all knowledge, man is joined in the highest part of himself, not with any created thing, nor with himself, nor with another, but with the One who is altogether unknowable; and in knowing nothing, he knows in a manner that surpasses understanding.

"God-kind seeking man" means the Divine in all things seeks acknowledgment from humankind and all created things. The Creator craves earthly validation. If all things are of God and made by Him, then there is something in all things that desires what God desires: to be acknowledged, reckoned with, and noticed, and experienced on every level of consciousness.

CAN HUMAN WILL REPLACE DIVINE WILL?

One of the central truths of Inclusion is this: we are spirits having an earthly encounter. We are *spirit*. When more than three hundred million sperm chased one egg and one fertilized it, our genetic code was instantly established and stamped on every cell in our bodies. Such powerful scientific realities hint at the awesomeness of our "beingness," our common and individual "essences."

In light of our presence on earth and the obvious hints of our purpose for being alive, the questions still remain. What will be the outcome of our existence as humans? Where will this all end?

How will life, the world, and humankind finally conclude? Will it conclude at all or simply continue forever? What, if anything, will it accomplish? In other words, what is the point of life? Religious leaders will claim to have the answers, but the answers to such infinite questions cannot come from mere men. The answers must come from the Creator Himself. As author and lecturer Dr. Myles Munroe says, "If you have a problem with a product or a question concerning its purpose, don't go to the product for the answer, go to the manufacturer."

I have never been able to reconcile in my own conscience a sovereign God who, according to Scripture, willed that all humankind be saved, yet left the ultimate decision to the feeble, fickle will of man. Why not just say, "Mankind is saved, period"? Can the will of man overrule the sovereign will of God? If so, why doesn't man's will provide him with health, wealth, and happiness? Is it because God's will is different from man's will on such earthly matters? Does not God want us to have these things as well?

I think the answer is this: man is finite, while God is infinite. So while man's will might prevail during his short life, this is the merest microscopic blink of time in God's plan. God can afford to let man exercise his will, because He knows that in the long run, where it counts, His will shall prevail. Isaiah 46:10 (NASB) clearly says, ". . . I will accomplish all my good pleasure." What is his good pleasure? That none be lost, but that all come to repentance (2 Peter 3:9).

Again, if man's immediate will presupposes God's ultimate will, then God is inferior to man, and man is the superior influence. But what if God's will is already in place, and man's seeming pursuit of his own will is merely God's already established design playing itself out? Remember, God is not bound by time. He transcends time.

Therefore, we cannot look at the events of this world from His perspective. I believe that what appear to be the random actions of a willful, self-sovereign human species going in its own direction is actually the embellishment of a predetermined outcome. Humankind is employing its passions, hatreds, creative powers, and family embraces to slowly and exquisitely spin out the weave of God's hand on the cosmic loom. We are creating God's will each day, by our own perception. We are its agents.

The word *autopsy* means "looking for oneself; seeing personally." Since the death of much of my traditional religious consciousness, I have been undergoing a kind of spiritual autopsy to determine for myself what actually caused my death. Where am I spiritually? Am I in heaven or hell? That depends whom you ask. But in some ways, you can be in heaven and hell at the same time. It is a matter of *consciousness*. The more you abandon your Christ Consciousness to the torments of fear-based religion, the more you will experience hell—the feelings of separation, want, and alienation. Hell is being alone and stagnant.

JESUS IN A BOX

Do we need Jesus to protect us from God? Or did Jesus come to reconnect us *to* God in consciousness? When you make your religion your God, you lose the God—and the good—of your religion. Most cultures use their religion as the basis of their societal esteem. This usually begins as reverence for the Deity. This slowly deteriorates into control and manipulation, using the so-called will of the Deity to control and manipulate the people, holding them hostage to their fear of the God. God becomes a tool of intimidation for earthly purposes.

Religion wants to control both the worshipped and the worshipper. It seeks to manipulate the faith and the faithful in order to secure significance and control. Man knows that he cannot control God, but he *can* control religion, because he invented it, and he knows that by doing so he can influence the emotions and minds of those who either believe or dare not admit their disbelief.

If you put Christ in the middle of a religion, you have placed Him exactly where He was once crucified. It was the religious spirit that despised Christ, not the people. Christ was a threat to earthly power. Therefore, to force Christ to be a religious "icon," we deny ourselves the very freedoms He came to give us. We confine Him to the very walls He died to release the world from. To confine Jesus to and define him by an exclusive religious box is to betray Him all over again. His purpose was bigger than that of any religion.

Religion has never treated Jesus as it should. It has never understood or appreciated Christology for what it is—for what the Logos of Christ is and what it has achieved. Religion seeks to replace the complex Jesus with a tailor-made Christ that reflects each denomination's bigotries: rejection of science, domination of secular government by mean-spirited theocracies, hatred of homosexuals and other perceived deviants, promoting war with the intent of bringing about the Second Coming, and other misappropriations.

Jesus came to save us from religion and inspire in us relationship instead. He is not competitive and has no need to compete with anyone or anything.

CHAPTER TWELVE

WHAT SECOND COMING?

A thing is not necessarily against reason because it happens
to be above it.

—*Charles Caleb Colton (1780–1832)*

Fear of the unknown is perhaps the most profound human fear. But fear of being known and misunderstood is the most consistent concern. Even our concept of God sees Him as interested in being known and recognized for what He is.

To be known, appreciated, and validated are the essential desires in being human, and they reflects God's desire for the love and recognition of us, His offspring.

One of the accusations against my message of Inclusion is that it is a new heresy influenced by the end times or last days "doctrines of demons" mentioned by the Apostle Paul in 1 Timothy 4:1–5:

The Spirit clearly says that in later times some will abandon the faith and follow deceiving spirits and things taught by demons. Such teachings come through hypocritical liars, whose consciences have been seared as with a hot iron. They forbid people to marry and order them to abstain from certain foods, which God created to be received with thanksgiving by those who believe and who know the truth. For everything God created is good, and nothing is to be rejected if it is received with thanksgiving, because it is consecrated by the word of God and prayer.

If the message of love and salvation for all is divisive and heretical, then let us have a look at another dragon of power-hungry modern religion: the Second Coming. Through their lack of understanding and willful ignorance of complex truths in favor of simplistic notions of good and evil, the master manipulators of today's Christianity have concocted a new theology. In it, the above passage is one of many used to bolster the end times culture that now afflicts so many believers. The idea is that Christ is about to return and usher in centuries of mayhem, blood, death, and judgment. What redemptive purpose or value do we see in such chaos? And why is it such a sacred icon?

Nothing is that simple. The subtleties of God's mind and plan far exceed anything that we can conceive—and it looks nothing like the childish imaginings of a series of novels that, while well written and popular, are nothing more than fiction, based on fear and paranoia.

MYSTERY—ANOTHER WORD FOR IGNORANCE

Any study of Christian history will reveal that the theological position I am espousing is as old as the Christian religion itself. Anyone who really experiences God will know unconditional love and redemption. This is the deepest desire of the Creator and the created. The early Church accepted this view as authentic and universal. In fact, as established earlier, the idea of the ultimate salvation was the dominant theological position of the first four hundred to five hundred years of Christian history, for as long as Greek (the language of the New Testament) was the predominant language of Christendom.

However, today's Christian culture has become in large part a synonym for ignorance. I'm shocked by it: Christian parents pulling their children out of schools in favor of a Bible-based curriculum, and even some forms of home-schooling reflect this growing paranoia. Wonderful as the Bible is, it remains a two-thousand-year-old sacred document that fails in innumerable ways to apply to today's world. Will children sequestered in private Christian schools be raised ignorant of science in a world that depends on it? To treat women as chattel? To despise those who do not believe as they do? Will they be so sanitized that when confronted with the culture outside their world of religious segregation, they will become catatonic?

In my quiet moments, I wonder if the culture of ignorance and arrogance that has blossomed in much of the conservative American Christian community is not the ultimate self-sabotage. Are we preparing the next generation to be irrelevant in our culture? Are we breeding a generation of ignorant, superstitious bigots? Why is knowledge the enemy of Christianity? Why are so many Christians (and Muslims and Jews) so terrified of being exposed to any information that contradicts their beliefs? Are those beliefs so weak?

As a university-trained minister who majored in biblical literature and the English Bible, I am embarrassed at how little I actually knew about the history of the religion for which I have acted as a leader for more than thirty-five years. Tyron Edwards, the nineteenth-century theologian, said, "Mystery is but another name for our ignorance; if we were omniscient, all would be perfectly plain." Since we are not, we should be open to the possibility that there is far more than we can ever know about God, love, and redemption. But that does not mean we should not ask. In admitting that one does not know, the next step is obvious: one must seek!

WHAT IS THE SECOND COMING?

Christianity has been described in the *Encyclopædia Britannica* as the "salvation religion," the primary premise of which is that the incarnation and sacrificial death of Jesus Christ formed the climax of a divine plan for mankind's salvation. According to Scripture, this plan was conceived by God in response to the fall of Adam—the progenitor of the human race and a kind of first Christ—and it would be completed at the Last Judgment, when the Second Coming of Christ would mark the catastrophic end of the world.

As forceful and important a doctrine as the Second Coming is within the Christian faith today, in reality it was much less important in the earliest apostolic days. In those times, the Resurrection was the premier theme preached—until early Roman persecutions began to intensify. Persecution forced first-century Christian leadership to find a theology that would make it possible for followers to remain faithful to the religion in the face of torture and torment. *In reality, the emphasis on the Second Coming is a human invention based on fear, confusion, despair, and a spirit of escapism.*

The hope of the Second Coming did the trick for those who otherwise might have abandoned the faith in the face of unimaginable persecution. It also balanced reality with the ideology of "peace on earth and good will toward all men." The Second Coming implied world peace, making the horrors of persecution tolerable. But set aside the appealing idea. Is there anything to support the physical return of Christ to earth, beyond the bloodthirsty wishes of a few televangelists?

Please indulge the Christian reformist preacher in me and allow me to pontificate: In light of the long anticipated, literal return of Christ to earth, which of course is possible, I believe it is more reasonable to begin to see the Second Coming of Christ as *consciousness,* by which I mean higher awareness or higher revelation of self—Christ in you.

I see the Second Coming as a heightened awareness of Christ, a mystical and spiritual recognition of the Christ Principle. I can hear Jesus asking again, "Who do people say the son of man is? Who do you as a people say that Christ is today?"

A Course in Miracles says: "Healing involves an understanding of what the illusion of sickness is for. Healing is impossible without this. Healing is accomplished the moment the sufferer no longer sees any value in the pain. . . ."

Our present religious sickness is a decision we've made, indeed, a choice of spiritual weakness and lack. Our sickness is placing our religious institutions ahead of the true Spirit of Christ, thus making us victims to doctrines, dogmas, and disciplines that separate us from the broader consciousness of pure Spirit. The new Second Coming heals us.

FROM ONE ADAM TO ANOTHER

If, in fact, Christ was the last Adam, as recorded in Romans 5:12–14, then is it not reasonable to assume that Adam was a kind of first Christ? If so, could that not also mean that the birth of Jesus was a kind of Second Coming of Christ? And would not His coming as Christ mark the end of the age as it was prior to His arrival? The world prior to the coming of Christ was dominated by Adam's sin and the subsequent "death sentence" of all succeeding humans. Through the coming of Jesus—the last Adam—we gained a new world and were presented a new consciousness.

Notice this passage of Scripture in 1 Corinthians 15:22: "For as in Adam all die, so in Christ all will be made alive." The Greek word for "made" is *zoopoieo* and translates as "to revitalize" or "make alive again." The first Adam brought us death, but the last Adam (or second Christ) has resurrected us. We are all "born again."

Again, in a more technical and spiritual way, the Second Coming of Christ is consciousness. It is becoming aware of the ultimate defeat of death and the restoration of life through the coming of Christ. This is the Second Coming of Christ in your consciousness. A literal, physical return of Christ to earth has never made as much sense, because I was always taught that whether He comes or not, we all ultimately go back through Him to God anyway.

To assert that God is waiting patiently for the last human being to get saved and then send Christ back to earth to gather the saved people and dismiss the remainder to eternal torment is absurd and profane.

YOUR THEOLOGICAL VIEW AFFECTS YOUR WORLDVIEW

In many ways, the spiritual awakening to this truth is the Second Coming of Christ. Recognition of this profound reality debunks the theory that one day the earth will be destroyed by God through fire, which many translate as a nuclear holocaust. Unfortunately, millions cling desperately to the concept of the fiery end times as a kind of cosmic "told you so." But this dismal appraisal of the future often sparks delusional belief and behavior such as the propagation of war (in order to fulfill what some Christians see as biblical end times prophecy) or abuse of the environment. If God's going to destroy the world next Thursday, why bother with clean air?

The same insanity has led to murders of children by delusional parents. Conservative Christianity's infatuation with the end times is making right-wing churches and their leaders more and more irrelevant and desperate at the same time. These large, powerful organizations, which could be forces for progress in many global problems, instead sit idly pondering biblical verse or actively work to undermine serious issues like the study of evolution and climate change or stem cell research.

If you believe that God plans ultimately to destroy the planet, you will not reverence the environment in the way that you would if you believed the planet was here to stay. This fatalistic philosophy also hinders you from working for and expecting a better, brighter future. Why bother, when there isn't going to be a future? In their messianic zeal to see apocalyptic horrors of war and bloodshed (from which *they* will, of course, be spared), right-wing fundamentalist Christians turn this world into an artifact as disposable as the men, women, and children who do not share their beliefs. And what man cares nothing about, he ultimately destroys.

Growing up in the ghetto as I did, you could tell by the upkeep of the homes (or lack of it) whether the dwellers owned them or rented. Owners tended to care about upkeep; renters neglected and all but destroyed the houses they lived in. The same principle applies to people who expect God to ultimately destroy the planet and those who do not.

According to Genesis, God's instruction to man was to take care of the earth. Saying that God plans to destroy His creation in some future cataclysm gives some people a false sense of hope and anticipation that exceeds anything this earth can provide. However, there is nothing healthy about hope predicated on an apocalyptic war that makes the valleys run red with the blood of the unfaithful. The hope that stems from millennial end times beliefs almost always manifests as a kind of "since God is bringing all this down anyway, I may as well help Him out" mind-set.

With this kind of nihilism as a touchstone, it is easier to justify cultural destruction and human death, assuming that destruction is God's ultimate intent. Since it has always been easier to destroy than create, and since religious fanatics often seek to purify through destruction, such beliefs give rise to Hitlers, Osama bin Ladens, white supremacists, gay bashers, and suicide bombers. Those obsessed with end times place personal theological and philosophical views above human life. Coupled with the concept of an angry, intolerant, vengeful God, this belief generates global terrorism, homicide, and genocide.

UNIVERSALISM AND THE EARLY CHURCH FATHERS

In *Universalism: The Prevailing Doctrine,* Dr. J. W. Hanson says that the first comparatively complete statement of Christian doctrine ever given to the world was by Clement of Alexandria in 180. Universal salvation was one of the tenets. Clement declared that all punishment, however severe, was purificatory; even the "torments of the damned" were curative. Origen, another of the early church fathers, explained that even Gehenna (*hell* in the King James Version) represents limited and curative punishment. Like all other ancient Universalists, both declared everlasting punishment to be inconsistent with universal salvation.

Universalism was the general belief during the first three or four centuries of Christianity, when Christians were known for their simplicity, goodness, and missionary zeal. With the exception of the arguments of Augustine (AD 420), all ecclesiastical historians, biblical critics, and scholars agree on the prevalence of Universalism in the earlier centuries. From the days of Clement of Alexandria to those of Gregory of Nyssa and Theodore of Mopsuestia (350–428), the majority of the great theologians and teachers were Universalists.

The first theological school in Christendom, located in Alexandria, taught Universalism for more than two hundred years. According to Clement, its founder:

> We can set no limits to the agency of the Redeemer; to redeem, to rescue, to discipline, in his work, and so will he continue to operate after this life. All men are his . . . for either the Lord does not care for all men . . . or He does care for all. For He is savior; not of some and for others not . . . and how is He savior

and Lord, if not the savior and Lord of all? For all things are arranged with a view to the salvation of the universe by the Lord of the universe both generally and particularly.

The early church fathers were advocates not only of universal reconciliation but of ultimate reconciliation. Gregory of Nyssa said, "All punishments are means of purification, ordained by Divine Love, to purge rational beings from moral evil and to restore them back to communion with God." Or as Robert Capon said many centuries later ". . . God would not have permitted the experience of hell unless He had foreseen through redemption that all rational beings would, in the end, attain to the same blessed fellowship with Himself."

Capon says that all rational beings would "in the end" attain the same blessed fellowship with God. In the final analysis, the thinking of fear-based theologies paralyzes their adherents with horror and debilitating insecurity. If you doubt the *outcome,* you inevitably doubt the *out-from.* If you cannot trust the results of the faith, you will not trust the author of that faith. If you do not trust the end, you never really trusted the beginning. Revelation 22:13 declares Christ ". . . the Alpha and the Omega, the First and the Last, the Beginning and the End."

HOW WILL THINGS END?

The ultimate question is "How will this all end?" According to Christianity, God, who is omniscient, knew from the day that He created man in His image and likeness what man was capable of doing and what he would actually do. An omniscient God would already know how the story ends.

In Luke 10:17–20, Jesus tells His disciples to rejoice, not because demons are subject to them in His name, but because their names are written in heaven. Since this conversation took place before the Cross and Resurrection, how were their names written? If you view this scenario as literal, then who could have written them but God Himself, perhaps in creation or before it? The suggestion is that this entire issue of the redemption of humankind was decided before the foundation of the world.

> In God the end is fully present in the beginning; the beginning is fully realized in the end. He didn't have to change his mind, drop a stitch, pull out a row, reverse engines, or slam on his brakes.
>
> —Robert Farrar Capon

When my children first disobeyed, it didn't throw our household into chaos. As all parents do, we knew what our babies were capable of and expected it. We had a plan in place: discipline, rules, and forgiveness. The sins of Adam and Eve in the garden did not shock heaven and throw it into chaos. The master plan was already in place, and there was a natural response ordained by God's power and grace. The last words of the Bible: "The grace of the Lord Jesus be with God's people. Amen" (Revelation 22:21).

Also, in the book of Revelation the finality of all things involves masses of humanity cast into "the lake which burns with fire and brimstone, which is the second death" (Revelation 21:8, NKJV). Even before John is purported to have received his revelation, Paul writes the ultimate response to the question of death, the first or second. He says in 1 Corinthians 15:26 that the last enemy to be destroyed is death. Could not that statement include the ultimate victory of Christ's blood even over the lake of fire, whatever that represents metaphorically?

It is also reasonable to note that John was well into his nineties, grief stricken, angry, and understandably alarmed when he wrote his gothic, gore-soaked revelation. In giving weight to his words, we should consider the emotional state of the source. Jesus his Lord had been brutally crucified nearly seventy years earlier, and most of his fellow apostles (including Paul) had also been brutally executed, along with countless believers throughout the Roman Empire. Considering all this, it is not a stretch to presume that John was distressed and emotionally unstable. Much of his revelation had to have been based on or influenced by his reality. His world was literally disintegrating.

SO WHY CREATE THE WORLD AT ALL?

This is the ultimate heresy: to question the mind of God. But why back down now? If the entire enterprise, from creation to redemption, is preordained by God, why bother with the whole tortuous exercise? Why create man, mold the world, place the flawed creation on earth to suffer and fear, kill and be killed? If the ultimate outcome is that all people—even those tormented in hell for a time—will ultimately be purged of their sin and come home to God, why not save a step and just create a race of children who begin their existence in heaven? What could possibly be the purpose of God's great science project?

I believe the answer lies in God's desire to experience or develop a part of Himself in the aspect of the terrestrial. With humanity, Deity could experience free will as opposed to sovereign will, evolution, change, and growth in a way no Supreme Being could otherwise. I think of the beings that God could have created, the heavenly humans, as rich children who grow up with a sense of entitlement, devoid of wisdom and perspective and the ability to learn from their flaws. But if part of what makes God God is the wisdom to see and create a future in time and to know what course is best to take, then where did that wisdom come from? What was its purpose if not ultimately redemptive?

We have no way of knowing, but is it not possible that God Himself had to pass through trials and difficulties in distant aeons past, before creation? You can't teach what you don't know, and you can't lead where you don't go. If it is true that God knows experientially, then would not His ultimate act of love be to create flawed beings with the potential to learn and grow to gain some sense of divine wisdom through trial and error, sin, and relative consequences? As we know, we learn only from facing our failures and fears.

PUNISHMENT: AN AGENT OF PERFECTION

Scripture teaches that God chastises those He loves (Hebrews 12:6–7, KJV). If some kind of hell exists, could not it be part of that loving chastisement rather than some vengeful act of divine wrath and torture? The word *chasteneth* (KJV) means "to train or educate using corporal punishment as an ultimate discipline."

Jeremiah 31:3 says, ". . . I have loved you with an everlasting love . . ." The Hebrew word for *everlasting* is *olam* and is the same word for "sky" or "heaven." It means "concealed," "time out of mind," or "time whose end cannot be determined." The same word is used for "mercy that endures forever," a term repeated throughout the Psalms of David.

It is difficult to reconcile enduring mercy and everlasting love with eternal damnation issuing from the same source. Theologians explain eternal damnation as God's just side in competition with His merciful side. First, justice cannot tolerate sin, so it is punitive. Second, mercy finds a way to justify the sinner through the substitutionary death of Christ. This is Christian doctrine. But the sticking point comes when traditional thinkers view judgment and punishment as automatic for all but see justification as limited to those who acknowledge Jesus. This is not logical.

Supposedly, if a person does not give himself to Christ, he diminishes God's grace and devalues the mercy that Scripture clearly says is infinite. Nonsense. You cannot diminish the eternal. To the contrary, except for some form of corrective purgation as implied by some of the early church fathers, hell as an eternal prison will have no significance in God's plan. If anything, it will be a place of temporary, corrective pain where even the most hardened souls will have their crimes purged away and their spirits renewed through toil, lesson, error, and repetition. Eventually, like those in an earthly prison, they will earn parole and take their place in God's Kingdom in the ultimate light of Christ.

So What Do We Have to Look Forward To?

Theologians have arrived at three theories of eschatology: annihilation, eternal punishment, and ultimate reconciliation. The point I wish to emphasize is the ultimate restitution of all things and people. This is our ultimate hope as Christians who espouse the doctrine of Universal Reconciliation. Even if we all have it wrong, the idea of a positive conclusion to existence is healthier than the gloom and doom of the traditional fear-based theologies.

According to Romans 8:24–25, it is our hope that saves us and preserves the earth for and around us: "For in this hope we were saved. But hope that is seen is no hope at all. Who hopes for what he already has? But if we hope for what we do not yet have, we wait for it patiently." My paraphrase of a statement made by Gordon W. Allport in his introduction to Viktor Frankl's seminal book *Man's Search for Meaning* makes a similar point: "A person who faces fully the ubiquity of suffering and the forces of evil takes a surprisingly hopeful view of man's capacity to transcend his predicament and discover an adequate guiding truth."

Most world religions have a perspective regarding the afterlife. They all have a theory regarding heaven and hell, good and evil, right and wrong, winning and losing. In general, Christians believe that in Adam all humanity was damaged by original sin. Islam, on the other hand, believes that Adam sinned alone as an individual, and that he, like anyone on earth, could turn back to God through "submission," which is the meaning of the word *Islam*.

In some non-Abrahamic religions, such as Buddhism and Hinduism, there is no emphasis on a fall of man, but sacred writings explain why the planet endures suffering and disharmony in contrast to a purer original state. Either way, a sense of right and wrong prevails in the global conscience. To most religions, their sense of right and wrong ultimately determines where and how the human race will end, in bliss or torment. Abrahamic faiths also purport to know how the world will end. Even so, knowing how and where life will end does not necessarily explain the purpose for living in the first place.

Guilt is the index of a broken relationship with God. Shame, on the other hand, is the index of human fear. A good psychologist can set you free from shame, but only God can set you free from guilt and spiritual delinquency. Counseling can help you get through the emotions associated with guilt, but only God can free you from the guilt itself. Drugs and alcohol, a good sermon, great sex—any of these can make you feel good, but only God can make you *be* good as an inherent state of being. Only God can imbue you with a spark of the Divine.

CAN WE NEGOTIATE SALVATION?

It takes faith to recognize and appreciate the spiritual transformation from sinner to saved, but faith does not cause the transaction to take place. I was taught all my life that no one but Jesus could take away my sin and guilt. I believed He could, but I was never sure He would or had. It was conditioned always upon my belief and adherence to a set of doctrines. In other words, salvation was the carrot held out in front of us to make us obey. We were taught that faith was the only answer or cure to the problem of sin, not the act of atonement itself. This always worried me as a young Christian, and this worry was an emotional nuisance well into my adult life.

As a (hopefully) wiser man, I see clearly that faith has less to do with answering the problem of sin than with understanding the truth of atonement. The hope of the human race in Christ is the Good News we need to get across to all who will listen. It is the knowledge of this truth that makes the difference in our consciousness, and thus our behavior. The Greek expression for man is *anthropos* and suggests the "upward looking one." Humankind seems always to be looking up to a higher source from which it hopes to gain validation, putting it back in harmony with its higher purpose.

The consciousness of our redemption settles the issue of purpose in a way that religion cannot. When we realize we are saved, we can stop obsessing on doctrinal adherence and instead work on realizing our higher selves in this world, the only world God has gifted to us. Once we recognize that destiny is realized in consciousness only, we can grasp hold of the deeper reality of our spirit and work together to bring this world closer to what we perceive heaven to be.

THE GOD WITHIN

After they had offered Him food, Jesus said to His disciples with regard to His purpose, "My meat is to do the will of him who sent me and to finish His work" (John 4:34, KJV). This was a hint to us, unveiling the higher purpose of the life Jesus was conscious of, the purpose any one of us can recognize and fulfill. His suggestion was that the real sustenance of His life was the fulfillment of original intent, the will of God.

My friend Dr. Michael Beckwith says in his book *40 Day Mind Fast Soul Feast* that there is only one power, one presence, one life, and it is the very essence of your life. In effect, you are what you are looking for. As the cosmic anthropologists we all are, we should look not only upward to a God in the sky but inward where God dwells in us. Dr. Beckwith says, "Ascend to the holy ground of your own being where the true Second Coming of Christ Consciousness takes place." We are God's manifestation on earth, sent here to do His will and bring forth His design. That is the purpose of life: to shape God's intent while shaping our characters and spirits, becoming more divine.

CHAPTER THIRTEEN

LOVE: THE NEW RELIGION

An obstinate man does not hold opinions, but they hold him.

—Alexander Pope (1688–1744)

Do not think of knocking out another person's brains because he differs in opinion from you. It would be as rational to knock yourself on the head because you differ from yourself ten years ago.

—Horace Mann (1796–1859)

Where there is much desire to learn, there of necessity will be much arguing, much writing, many opinions; for opinion in good men is but knowledge in the making.

—John Milton (1608–1674)

Whoever fears to submit any question to the test of free discussion, loves his own opinion more than the truth.

—Thomas Watson (c. 1557–1592)

Coming full circle, I see the enormity of the task God has placed before me. We are dealing with at least 1,500 years of entrenched religious tradition, fear-based control, organizational power, and human habit. We are seeking to disenfranchise the religious franchise. This is no easy task. But it must be done. William Faulkner said, "The man who removes a mountain begins by carrying away small stones." Jesus said that if you have the faith of a mustard seed you can say to this mountain "move" (Matthew 17:20). I have mustard seed faith; I am speaking to the mountain.

I am a fourth-generation traditional Pentecostal preacher raised in the tradition of sin and damnation, and I have come to my turning in the road. This has caused me to reconsider my presuppositions about God, the universe, and my relationship to both. This journey has radically transformed my belief about heaven, hell, the purpose of mankind, the church and the role of the evangelist in this world. I have received a revelation, and as must be the case, nothing will ever be the same.

Over the last thirty-five years, I have preached in churches and conferences to hundreds of thousands of people, and I have preached to millions throughout the world by way of television and radio. I have encouraged people to both accept and confess Christ as their Savior. I have fasted and prayed, as little as a half day in primary school to as many as forty days as an adult. I have passionately sought a special anointing to reach lost souls and bring people to a saving knowledge of the Lord. I have ordained deacons and elders, installed pastors, consecrated bishops, sponsored and/or supported church plants, recorded several successful gospel albums and CDs, written books, and hosted some of the largest conferences and religious gatherings in this country.

However, in the midst of all this good work, I have come to a liberating and encouraging realization. As I write this book, I have entered the second half of my life. Everything I spent the first half of my life building has been jeopardized by my passion for trumpeting Inclusion from the highest mountains. I cannot think of a healthier or holier cause.

LIVING IN EXILE: THE PRICE OF PROCLAIMING TRUTH

I am in the midst of the most dramatic, significant challenge of my life and reputation as a Christian leader and clergyman. This is either my second chance to have a positive impact on the world in which I live, or my Waterloo as a figure of influence on the world of faith.

After reading some of the negative media attention I received as a result of coming out with this message of Inclusion, one of my nephews wrote me a note that said, "No one is listening until you make a perceived mistake." He added, "A conclusion is a place people go when they get tired of thinking." In *Why Christianity Must Change or Die,* Bishop John Shelby Spong refers to himself as being in exile, which is very much the place in which I, and many others who embrace Inclusion or a newer perspective on long-held religious traditions, reside.

"While still asserting my deeply held commitment to Jesus Christ, I also recognize that I live in a state of exile from the presuppositions of my own religious past. The only thing I know to do in this moment in history is to enter this exile, to feel its anxiety and discomfort, but continue to be a believer. I am a believer who increasingly lives in exile from traditional Christianity. Believer-in-exile is a new status in religious circles, but I am convinced that my state will resonate with countless people who find themselves entrenched in unsatisfying religious traditions or at sea spiritually, unwilling to submit to the fear and control that make up so much of today's religious culture."

Here's a comparison that will get me—pardon the pun—crucified: in a way, I and those like me are very much like Christ.

He spoke uncomfortable truths about God and faith to the religious powers of the day. He upset the applecart of stratified religious tradition and preached a new hope. That is why He was a threat; one of the reasons He was executed on the Cross. I hope to avoid that fate; I have not the courage of the Son, and I would like to spend many years with my family and friends doing God's works in this fine world. But this awareness adds to my sense that my mission is right and in the best tradition of Jesus' mission.

A BRAVE NEW WORLD OF CHRISTIANITY

I have a new vocation: to legitimize the questions for which we seek answers and the spiritual probing that sends many of us into exile. My goal is to shatter the culture of ignorance that fears questions and condemns the questioners. I believe that a conversation must be opened with those who can no longer tolerate the narrow-minded, irrelevant theological concepts that govern our ecclesiastical institutions. This world demands that we cease referring all questions back to "God said it, I believe it, and that settles it." That is no longer a satisfactory answer. God is equal to all questions, and He did not create our sense of reason and inquiry to, as Hamlet said, "fust in us unused." We must start asking questions of and about God. The answers will profoundly affect the future and any hope of peace in this world.

The time has come for the church to invite its people on a journey into the mystery of God and to stop proclaiming that the truth of God is still bound by either our literal interpretation of Scriptures or our man-made creeds. Our hunger for God is bone deep. Old, unproven religious concepts will not serve us. It's time for a courageous new formula for faith.

I never expected to go through such a radical change of opinion at my age. How could I? But how could I not? Tyron Edwards said, "He who never changes his opinions, never corrects his mistakes, will never be wiser tomorrow than he is today."

That is something I hope to see happen to modern Christianity and to religion in general. We need to rethink ourselves and our souls in life and faith. We need to know and renew what we believe and why we believe it. Myths and fairy tales have controlled our theology for centuries; the time has come for a confrontation with newer realities and a healthier awareness of the needs of this complex, frightening, astonishing world.

HAS CHRISTIANITY BECOME A CULT?

In a word, yes. The way I see it, my cherished religion (and that of my family as far back as we can recollect) has become a major cult with all the trappings of deviant values, virtues, and vice. The franchise of religion has diluted and destroyed the mystery and the power of Christ and His cause. I am both shocked and ashamed of how we have allowed ourselves to deteriorate. We have become as clannish and cliquish as any so-called false religion. Our pursuit of political power, persecution of those who do not live according to our rules, and insistence on controlling every aspect of the lives of those who belong to our denominations have made us irrelevant and insolent.

Religions have personalities. Conservative Christianity has decided that God hates and punishes people who violate His dictates. Some of this stems from the belief that God is unforgiving and judgmental; some comes from our awareness that promoting such a God is a wonderful way to control the mindless. At their worst, religious institutions claim that if God decides who goes to heaven and hell, they can do the same in His name. This is religion at its ugliest.

In the book *Life after Death*, Alan Segal, a professor of religion at Barnard College, writes:

Nineteen extremist Muslims, indoctrinated with a caricature of Muslim martyrdom, perpetrated one of the most callous slaughters of innocent civilians in American history, not in spite of divine retribution, but convinced that their deed would ensure their resurrection and bring them additional eternal rewards before the Day of Judgment. The horrible waste of more than 2,800 innocent lives was directly driven by notions of sexual felicity after death: A group of virgin, dark-eyed beauties awaited each of the suicidal murderers.

This is a classic example of the personality of a religion: wanton, lustful, self-centered, and self-serving.

Americans have retaliated with the same zeal—killing, wounding, and pillaging villages of innocent Afghans and Iraqis. We feel justified by our "righteous indignation" and hyperpatriotism for our country, a nation we believe was raised up by God. The collateral damage is justified by our notion that God is pleased with our retaliatory violence in response to the aggression of our attackers.

OUR NEW GOSPEL MUST BE LOVE

Conceptually, being born again happened once for the entire world—through the Resurrection of the Lord Jesus Christ. However, *getting* born again is something we need to do daily as we discover more of our own souls with each new life encounter. For the true Christian, evangelizing should begin with oneself, being born again with each new day, conveying the message of hope, and re-creating this world as a place of love, compassion, preservation of beauty, respect for nature, and peace—peace and love above all else.

We owe it to God and ourselves to enter a covenant of love with every experience and encounter. The word *neighbor* consists of two English words that mean "near by." Loving your neighbor means loving everyone and everything you encounter without condition. Everything you experience has love in it somewhere. Each encounter exposes part of the self you must love, because each encounter reveals more of the essence of who you really are. Life is good. Life is God. He does not reside in a church, a Bible, a doctrine, or a sermon. He resides in you and me and every one of us. We are each a church. Christ resides in each of us, if we can find the wisdom to see Him.

AFTERWORD

EXILE—A PRICE WORTH PAYING

I don't remember the exact moment I opened my mouth at what I felt was God's behest and began talking about Inclusion, but, as with most life-changing events, I had no idea of its significance at the time.

It was the year 2000. My ministry was thriving, with more than six thousand members, thousands of whom packed a 2,200-seat auditorium twice on Sundays. But we were not really growing; only getting fat. We were "swapping sheep and recycling saints," as we say in the charismatic community. I wanted more than that. My mission was not to build a megachurch that would make me look good and possibly rich; it was to reach the unchurched and those spiritually unresolved. With that goal in mind, knowing that the "hell and damnation" rhetoric of many of my colleagues was potentially driving nonbelievers away in droves, I chose to unveil my heartfelt truth that everyone on the planet was already saved by the sacrifice of Christ but just didn't know it.

I may as well have shaken a hornet's nest. Here in Tulsa, home of Oral Roberts University (ORU), and a hub of influence in the charismatic/Pentecostal community, defying time-honored doctrine is just not done. But I did it anyway. I knew the response to this would be explosive, but I was unprepared for the venom and hatred that flowed my way from the community of which I had been a part. Threaten the money and temporal power of Christianity Inc., and you set off nuclear warheads, as I was to discover.

THE EMPEROR HAS NO CLOTHES

My congregation loved the message initially. It took away the burden of recruiting and expecting conversions. I was telling them they didn't have to go around doing the odious work of converting people, a practice that in many ways is deeply offensive ("Hey, let me tell you why what you believe is completely wrong, and why if you don't change you're going to hell!"). This has become, to many, a shame and a sham. It simply doesn't work and often does more harm than good.

The word started to spread. People from around town and then around the country bought tapes of the sermons and started telling Christian leaders, "Listen to what Bishop Pearson is saying!" Terrified of anyone breaking their stranglehold of fear, control, and religious tyranny, angry church leaders ran with the ball. When word finally reached ORU, where I sat on the Board of Regents, the issue blew up.

However, things really took off when I ran for mayor of Tulsa in 2001. I was one of the few black Pentecostals supporting George W. Bush for president, and I saw that distinction as an opportunity to get my message out through the guise of politics. I proposed a "One Tulsa" campaign, the idea of Inclusion for my troubled city, which, for all its supposed piety, has some of the highest rates of divorce, teen pregnancy, and drug use in the nation, as well as having had the nation's worst race riot some eighty years ago. So the media camped out, waiting to see if the city would elect its first black Republican mayor.

The people loved and respected me. Celebrities like Deion

Sanders and Kathie Lee Gifford did TV ads for me. I had a real chance of winning—until in the middle of the race, the Evangelical Christian community turned against me for sharing this gospel I preached. They said things like: "We can't support this man who's going to lead the world to hell." Seemingly overnight, my conservative Christian support evaporated. I started hemorrhaging my own church members immediately. But ultimately it was the best thing they could have done. Just like the panic-ridden protestors who bring more attention to a film like *The Da Vinci Code* by calling for a boycott, clueless Christian leaders only brought more interest to the Gospel of Inclusion. People and the news media started asking questions about why my own people had rejected me, and you know how deeply the institutional church fears questions.

BETRAYAL BY AN INSIDER

I discovered that what I had thought was a close, genuine family of brothers and sisters in Christ was really a power-mad cabal that would not tolerate any deviation from the intellectually, spiritually bankrupt mantra that has brought them so much money and power over the decades and centuries. I was refused access to the ORU students who had been eagerly attending our Sunday services. The university "suggested" that no one should have anything to do with me. I resigned from the board, and in mid-2001 I got a letter from Oral Roberts, the one man in the movement whom I will always respect, pleading with me not to follow the path I was on. He was concerned that I was going to start some sort of New Age cult and lead millions into hell. Oral gave me a doctrine 101 course and begged me to come back to the fold. It was a masterpiece of what we in our Evangelical Christian and charismatic/Pentecostal community believe and have believed for centuries. It broke my heart that I could not accept it—and may have broken Oral's when I didn't, although we remain close friends in heart and spirit.

I could no longer hide my personal theological crisis in the success of my ministry. I felt what I was hearing was important and from God; disruptive and insurrectionist, to be sure, but necessary, right, and irresistible. Sometimes you have to create tension to get attention. And Lord Almighty, tension was flowing like lava from a volcano. My denominational leaders—including the man I called my pastor and who officiated at my wedding, as well as at my consecration to the bishopric; and another prominent leader, whom I had helped introduce to the larger world of charismatic Pentecostals by airing his preaching on my popular weekly telecast; and most of the biggest names in the charismatic movement—along with the influential *Charisma* magazine and dozens of other national religious leaders outside the Pentecostal movement, denounced me as a false teacher, a heretic, unsubmitted to church leadership and unaccountable to church authority.

A local pastor of arguably the largest charismatic church in town publicly denounced me from his pulpit. The president of ORU and its Board of Regents turned their backs on me outright, which hurt deeply. What hurt most was that my own church members, people I had served faithfully and lovingly for over two decades, along with some members of my family, left by the thousands. Some would see me around town and refuse to make eye contact. Many of them still loved me but could not risk showing it publicly. Nearly all the businesspeople in my congregation eventually left, as you can't do business in Tulsa—at least among Christians—if you are associated with a known heretic.

TRAPPED IN THE UPPER ROOM

After my resignation, only one member of the Board of Regents bothered—or perhaps I should say dared—to check on me to see if I needed anything. Unlike what often happens among secular celebrities in Hollywood, I was dropped by the so-called *brethren* and left for dead, like the man in Jesus's parable of the Good Samaritan. There was plenty of support from other Christians, but it was covert. It was like the disciples hiding in the upper room after Jesus was crucified; they were terrified. A few came to me by night to ask questions and even offer support, much like Nicodemus came to Jesus in the New Testament. But that was all. They made an example of me. Other churches were scared stiff that the same thing would happen to them if they showed kindness toward us. The implied message was: This is a cult, and you don't just turn away from it, you turn against it; rebuking, binding, and casting it away and out like a demon. I learned quickly that if you break the rules, you will not have to wait until the afterlife to experience hell. I'm sure I am only reaping some of what I sowed somewhere along the line. I had to accept the fact that I had probably done this to someone else.

Of course, the reason the response was so vitriolic was not my message; we had heard the same thing from other people and scholars over the years. The difference was that they were secular and white. The brilliant religious scholars Karen Armstrong, John Shelby Spong, Donald Neale Walsch, even Deepak Chopra, and dozens more have been writing books questioning assumptions about God and faith for centuries. We dismissed them as unspiritual, overly intellectual, hell-bound atheists or confused agnostics. It is that easy to condemn when you allow yourself to be willfully ignorant.

But me? I was one of them, an Evangelical, with influence that reached far—particularly but not exclusively into the African-

American, charismatic/Pentecostal hierarchy—a leader of my own successful church and ministry, a respected child of the Oral Roberts tradition. I was an insider whose words carried a hundred times the weight of all the secular Ph.D.s out there. No one could believe that I was contradicting the accepted myths about Christianity. The community was shocked. Then it became enraged. It was very much like the whistle-blowers who finally came out of the woodwork to begin shedding light on President Bush's lies about the Iraq war. They exposed the agreed-upon deception by having the temerity to tell the truth and were excoriated as liars and traitors for doing so. Secretary of State Colin Powell appears to have felt such heat and coercion.

THE SCARLET LETTER

So began the campaign to destroy Carlton Pearson. I knew it would be vociferous and violent (literally; I have already arranged increased personal security for the publication of this book), but I did not expect it to be as vicious as it became. Some people just turned away from me. But the most brutal, poisonous treatment came from charismatic Christians, black and white alike, who outright turned on and against me. In attempting to stop me and in predicting my journey to hell, they revealed themselves for who they truly are. Some of these dear people truly cared for my soul and hoped desperately to rescue me from my peril. Others simply dressed as sheep were actually wolves hiding in religious robes. They were not acting as men and women of God. They acted more like men and women addicted to temporal power and influence—wealth junkies who love their megachurches, big names, big cars, and big bank accounts more than they can begin to love Christ or truth or one another. Threaten what some of these have built, and may God help you.

The denunciations began in pulpits and in the pages of magazines like *Charisma*. Have you lost your mind listening to Carlton? He's crazy. He's of the devil. He's the Antichrist. He's a heretic. He'll lead you into hell. The paranoia and panic was staggering. I had the scarlet letter on me. I was slandered and libeled every day—and still am by some of these paranoid religious zealots who think they actually serve God by attacking people like me. Some suggested I should have sued ORU and *Charisma* magazine, but that would serve no redemptive purpose; besides, I would never consider something like that anyway. I bring this up only because I would like to see that hateful and hurtful spirit purged from all of us who claim to be carrying on Christ's legacy. I have been greatly embarrassed by it as I've tried to explain it to the many non-Christian friends my message and ministry now attracts.

The relentless pressure started to have an effect. All of my non-black staff ministers left at the same time in a coordinated walk-out, which triggered the spontaneous departure of hundreds of other nonblack families, soon followed by hundreds of the rest. African-Americans tend to be far less inclined to abandon their churches and spiritual leaders than most other ethnic groups. But when written public statements regarding me and the message were issued by large and influential African-American charismatic clergy and leaders, it became open season on Carlton Pearson.

Sunday morning crowds dropped to a few hundred loyal stalwarts. Five or six thousand people walked away from the community we had built. I basically lost my ministry. I lost everything. Offerings dropped by as much as $50,000 a week. We lost millions in property, and our church headed into foreclosure. We were nearly forced to declare bankruptcy, when at the last minute a company came in and bought our debt, and we were able to walk away. But we lost $3 million in equity, business property, and even some intellectual property. My marriage suffered severely as my personal income was cut to a third of what it was, and my wife lost interest and respect for much of what I had introduced to her as the Body of Christ. My children were taunted at school, and lost many of their friends whose parents would no longer allow them to associate with the children of a heretic. Even Christian businesses in our town avoided us. Our last service at the 8621 South Memorial Drive location was New Year's Eve 2005. After that, we were basically on the street.

JUSTICE ACCORDING TO TULSA

How did my charitable, Christ-like brothers and sisters react to my downfall? They weren't showing up at my door with casseroles. They reacted with both sadness and glee, assuming my misfortune to be the judgment of God on me for my deviance from the accepted traditions. My financial fall was seen as inevitable and just. Some in the mainstream Christian world have a cruel and vengeful nature. To them, my loss was like AIDS for gay people, or like the South Asian tsunami for Hindus, Buddhists, and Muslims: the righteous wrath of an angry God against the people of whom "they" don't approve. Violence is endemic in Christianity. This is why millions of so-called Christians tacitly approved or at least looked the other way as Hitler tortured and decimated over six million presumed or perceived "Christ murdering" Jews. Pat Robertson is lauded for talking about assassinating Hugo Chávez. We kill gays and bomb abortion clinics and insist we're doing the work of Jesus. Nothing is further from the truth!

That is *precisely* the same gale of hate, intolerance, and blind ignorance that blew down the Twin Towers; just replace Allah with Jehovah or Jesus. I had been the victim of institutionalized terrorism in the name of a bigoted, power-crazed version of Christ.

My wife's "spirit-filled" cosmetologist refused to continue doing her hair. The Christian-owned cleaners who offered to clean our clothes free as a seed into our ministry called to tell me that my wife and I were no longer good soil to sow into. The Twin

Towers that were my ministry and family simply had to come down, and the Pentecostals and Evangelicals of Tulsa and the rest of the country did everything in their power to see that they fell. The people who embraced us and loved us through our ordeal were the very people we had been taught were not saved and were on their way to hell.

Progressives, gays, and churches like the Unitarians, Unity, United Church of Christ, and the Episcopalians embraced us, along with Muslims, Jews, and a host of other non-Christians, including atheists and agnostics. They became our friends and remain so to this day. We found out that sometimes the people who are most Christ-like are not members of the religion that bears His name. Thus the title of my next book: "God Is Not a Christian."

THE ROAD BACK

The good thing about hitting bottom is there is nowhere else to go but up. On the first Sunday in January 2006, we were in the Trinity Episcopal Church downtown. They are open-minded people of God, and their vestry gave us 100 percent approval. This is an open and affirming church, the kind of church that reflects the spirit of Inclusion and of Christ. Tulsa needs that kind of religious leadership and influence, because religion has sickened and impeded this town for decades. Tulsa has one of the highest gay populations per capita in the United States, but it's a community that's forced underground by institutionalized hate. Why do we have the second highest divorce rate in the country? In part, it's because of the pressure of the religious community, often unreasonable expectations, and the idea that prayer alone, not a good marriage counselor, is what couples need to address their problems.

But things started to turn around when I began writing this book in 2001 and began doing more and more interviews, especially with *This American Life* on National Public Radio. I wrote the book to answer questions, because I discovered that out-side the condemning, enraged aegis of my former charismatic community—in the "reality based" world—people were genuinely interested in Inclusion. More to the point, they *thanked* me for offering an alternative to the fire-and-damnation model of religion and for questioning the power structure of Christianity Inc. Today a lot of the negative media attention has dried up; 90 percent of the communication I receive is positive. The only negative attention comes from the Christian media, which continues to brand me a heretic. They think I'm an arrogant, unaccountable jerk. "He's going to lose his ministry, family, and his soul. He's going to hell, and he's going to take millions with him," they say. They think they are obligated to stop me. Some actually perceive it as their God ordained duty! I understand their angst; I used to live at the same address.

On the other hand, the secular world has embraced me. Television shows like *Dateline* have interviewed me. There is a movie in the works about my life and journey. Newspapers in Los Angeles, Atlanta, Philadelphia, and other cities have run great stories about Inclusion. The secular world is at least sensible, built on intellect and intelligent questioning, and is often more spiritual. Much of my old world is paranoid and illogical, schizophrenic, and fear based. The logic of our doctrines is anti-Christ in spirit. To the charismatic leaders who still hold their congregations in a grip of ignorance and terror, Christ is imaged as a wimp still stuck on the cross asking for a glass of water, instead of the triumphant Savior who took out the devil and sin. This is the image we project of Christ. They actually think Carlton Pearson can victimize Jesus and take captive His redeemed souls.

With this book, though, people are starting to say, "That son of a gun might be right." There is such disillusionment and anger in the nonchurch community. Non-Christians think we're intolerant jerks. They despise us not for our faith (which is what we tell our congregants to make them feel persecuted) but for our big-otry, our hatred of those unlike us, our willful ignorance, and our arrogance in trying to change the beliefs of others to make them more acceptable to us and to God. Too many evangelical leaders simply don't care. They are intoxicated with self-serving self-centeredness, and they are paid well for sowing discord and self-righteous hate.

CREATING A MOVEMENT

But here's the ironic thing: If I recanted, my old world would wel-come me back with open arms. If I made a public apology and said that I was vexed and tormented by demons or influenced by evil people, if I said, "I want to warn you against this danger to the Body of Christ," I could make a quarter million dollars in hours. People would welcome me back, kill the fatted calf, and the entire religious world I used to be part of would come back to me and accept me back to them. I could call Pat Robertson and the Trinity Broadcasting Network, say, "I want to make the statement on your show tomorrow," and I'd be there tomorrow, live. The people would weep and rejoice that the prodigal son had come home. It would start a revival.

However, I wouldn't be able to live with my conscience or look at myself in the mirror. I would feel as if I had denied my own Christ Consciousness and my strong convictions of God's uncon-ditional love for all of humankind. And the fact that I would be welcomed back so easily reveals the truth about today's Evangelical Christian community:

It does not care about belief. What it wants is conformity.

I will no longer conform to a doctrine that holds so many in blind, unreasoning fear of social and cultural reprisal. That is totalitarianism. Do I miss my old life? You bet I do! No one wants to be an exile on an island of his own making. I have regrets every day. Every day I hurt and wonder if it was all worth it. I miss so much of what I had: material comfort, respect, and a loving community of faith. I feel the loss, the pain, the grief. I loved these same people who have distanced themselves from me, and I still love them. I love all we did and had together. I miss the great Azusa conferences and all my dear running buddies, some of whom I've referred to here. But as Jesus once asked, "What does it profit a man to gain the whole world and forfeit his own soul?" Yes, I love and miss the brethren, and sweet little saints who don't have a clue of what actually happened, some who don't even realize anything has.

But I would not go back. Because much of what I had was built on half-truths and deception—the lies that millions of Christians tell themselves every day. They believe this perversion of the teachings of Christ—which tells us to exclude, doom, condemn, oppress, kill, and subjugate—is the way Christ would conduct His ministry were He here on earth today. It is not! And despite all I had and all I have lost, I could not hold my head up before my fellow man or before God had I not been willing to walk away from all I had built, to accept exile, to experience and share what I believe and know to be the truth.

And, of course, what comforts me is that I am not alone. A movement is beginning around Inclusion consciousness, and it is beginning with Christian and non-Christian people—intelligent, educated, and responsibly inquisitive people asking hard questions about religion, God, and belief, along with less educated people who just love God and love others and desire the unprejudiced freedom to do so. There is nothing wrong with questioning God; He is equal to all questions. What is wrong is suppressing the need for knowledge that God placed in us. Tens of thousands write to me in letters and e-mails; some are angry and convinced I am hell-bound, but most thank me for asking questions they didn't know how to ask, and for lending my credibility to an issue that might have been dismissed if it came from someone else.

There have been many men (people) speaking this truth. One day there will be a monument. But now, there is a movement. It has already begun. I didn't start it, I joined it. There are probably more disenchanted Christians in the world than there are faithful ones, not to mention millions of other weary religionists looking for a way out of the rut. Churches and religions have abused people for centuries, and they have much to answer for. This movement will sweep the world; it will not wipe out religion as the fear preachers like to cry, but it could and might end religion as a device to control, steal, and oppress. Christ Consciousness—the understanding that we don't have to convert, just convince people they are loved by loving them—will grow. People will learn that we can cohabitate—that we don't have to go along to get along. I think a significant amount of that will be accomplished in my lifetime.

We will get the charismatic Evangelical community to the table eventually. They will be significant in making this movement go forward; and they will have to come to the table if Christianity is going to survive. They are disenchanted, but they are hiding because they are afraid to give up the things they have and face their fears. They will repent and rethink. Many of them are sincere and honest God-loving people who do care, but have forgotten not only their first love but to love first.

They can have so much more—indeed, we all can, and we will. We can have a world stripped of a threatening, bullying brand of faith, one where the message of universal love and salvation brings peace, contentment, cooperation, tolerance, and even celebration. This is not my will. It's not "*my* will be done." It's God's will. Exile is a small, worthwhile price to pay for serving such a loving and lofty purpose, to bring God's glorious world and His children together.

The journey continues, with the best yet to come.

NOTES

Scripture Index

Index by Chapter

Introduction

Chapter 1: What Is Inclusion?

CHAPTER 7: THE GOSPEL OF HATE
Page

CHAPTER 8: THE GOSPEL OF HELL
Page

CHAPTER 11: RE-IMAGINING GOD AND OTHER HERETICAL NOTIONS

SCRIPTURE INDEX—ALPHABETICAL LISTING

ACKNOWLEDGMENTS

This book is the result of both a private and public journey I've been on since the beginning of this new century. And during these last seven years, as the song says, "I lost it all to find everything," especially me!

I could not have made it through the most dramatic transition of my life without the few people who somehow either remained loyal to me personally or who entered my life during this critical and pivotal time of transition and transcendence, with strength, vision, and incredible encouragement. I mention here only some of them, though there are many more who prayed and sent warm and positive energy toward us. I thank and bless you all.

I want to thank my wife, Gina, and my children, Julian and Majesté, for allowing this fifth and at times unwelcomed member of our family to consume so much of my time and attention in a way with which all of you competed and at times complained about. Thanks for loving me enough to miss me and for your support and understanding. Can't wait to turn more attention toward you all!

Thanks Mom and Daddy for watching your son traverse through what I'm sure was pitiably painful for you and, I suppose, at times embarrassing. Your unmitigated love, support, and prayers are priceless. You too, Godmother and God-brother Rodney; we are family!

Thanks to the remnant of only a few hundred out of thousands of "HigherD-ers," now "New Dimensionites," who weathered the storm with me, lovingly refusing to abandon ship as it rode the tempestuous waves of rejection, denigration, and persecution, but has now arrived at the harbor of our still evolving consciousness. You have allowed me to lead when and where none of us was sure we were going. I love you as I love my own soul and am honored to serve you. Our best is always yet to come!

Thanks, Benjamin, I could not have made it without you and your team. You put it all together—there's no one like you! Thanks Gwen, Toneille, Pastor Jessé, Pastor David, and Nilsa—could not have made it without you. Thanks, Dr. John, my ever-trusted and trusting friend and confidant; Dr. Harold Lovelace, a God-sent messenger; Mike Williams, a brilliant teacher; and Bishop Kirby Clements, my apostle and friend.

TJ, you came just in time. Mark Thompson, my favorite photographer; Doug and Rebecca, you know who you are to me. Thanks, Russ Bennett, for your warm and gracious guidance, and you too, Yvette Flunder, my sister and friend, along with all my new UCC family, Robin Meyers and the Mayflower Church, Oklahoma City, and Leslie Penrose and the Community of Hope, and Paul Ashby and Fellowship Congregational Church here in Tulsa. Thanks, Dr. Hansen, for your warm and faithful spirit.

Thanks, Rich and Bryce, you guys are awesome. Russell Cobb and NPR, you started an avalanche of blessing. Father McKee and Trinity Episcopal Church, in downtown Tulsa: you are true followers and examples of the Christ Principle and Person—thanks for taking us in! New Dimensions Worship Center will be part of your rich history forever.

Thank you, Oral and Evelyn Roberts, for refusing to love me less. I am your "sun burned" son forever.

Bibliography

The American Heritage Dictionary of the English Language, 4th ed. Boston: Houghton Mifflin, 2006.

Babinski, Edward T. *The Abominable Fancy.* October 22, 2005. www .edwardtbabinski.us/history/abominable_fancy.html.

Beckwith, Michael A. *40 Day Mind Fast Soul Feast.* Camarillo, Calif.: DeVorss & Company, 2000.

Berdyaev, Nicolas. *The Destiny of Man.* New York: Harper, 1960.

Bonda, Jan. *The One Purpose of God: An Answer to the Doctrine of Eternal Punishment.* Grand Rapids, Mich.: Eerdmans, 2003.

Brown, Dan. *The Da Vinci Code.* New York: Random House Inc., 2003.

Capon, Robert Farrar. *Kingdom, Grace, Judgment: Paradox, Outrage, and Vindication in the Parables of Jesus.* Grand Rapids, Mich.: Eerdmans, 2002.

———. *The Mystery of Christ . . . and Why We Don't Get It.* Grand Rapids, Mich.: Eerdmans, 1993.

———. *The Romance of the Word: One Man's Love Affair with Theology.* Grand Rapids, Mich.: Eerdmans, 1995.

Chambers, Oswald. *The Complete Works of Oswald Chambers.* Grand Rapids, Mich.: Discovery House Publishers, 2000.

Douglass, Frederick. *In Organizing for Social Change: A Mandate for Activity in the 1990s.* Edited by K. Bobo, J. Kendall, and S. Max. Washington, D.C.: Seven Locks Press, [1849] 1991.

Draper, Edythe. *Draper's Book of Quotations for the Christian World.* Carol Stream, Ill.: Tyndale House Publishers, 1992.

Dyer, Wayne W. *The Power of Intention.* Carlsbad, Calif.: Hay House, 2004.

Edwards, Jonathan. *Sinners in the Hands of an Angry God.* Enfield, Conn.: July 8, 1741.

Field, Henry. *The Field Museum-Oxford University Expedition to Kish, Mesopotamia, 1923–1929.* Chicago: Field Museum of Natural History, 1929.

Foundation for Inner Peace. *A Course in Miracles,* 2nd ed. New York: Viking Press, 1996.

Fox, Mathew. *The Coming of the Cosmic Christ.* New York: HarperCollins Publishers, 1988.

Frankl, Viktor E. *Man's Search for Meaning: An Introduction to Logotherapy.* Trans. Ilse Lasch. Pref. Gordon W. Allport. New York: Washington Square Press, 1969.

Fudge, Edward W. *The Fire That Consumes: A Biblical and Historical Study of the Doctrine of Final Punishment.* New York: BackInPrint.com, 2000.

Gore, Al narr. *An Inconvenient Truth.* Dir. Davis Guggenheim. Paramount Classics, 2006.

Halley, Henry H. *Halley's Bible Handbook with the New International Version.* Grand Rapids, Mich.: Zondervan, 2000.

Harvey, Andrew. *Teachings of the Christians Mystics.* Boston: Shambhala, 1997.

Heinlein, Robert. *Time Enough for Love.* New York: The Berkeley Publishing Group, 1973.

Johnson, Samuel. *The Rambler* (three volumes). London: Thomas Tegg, 1826.

Jones, Rufus M. *The Spiritual Reformers in the 16th and 17th Centuries.* Boston: Beacon Press, 1959.

Jukes, Andrew. *Letters of Andrew Jukes.* London: Longmans, Green, & Co., 1903.

Lewis, C. S. *A Grief Observed.* New York: HarperCollins, 2001.

Malik, Dr. Charles Habib. *The Two Tasks.* Wheaton, Ill.: Crossway Books, 1980.

Manning, Brennan. *Abba's Child: The Cry of the Heart for Intimate Belong-

ing. Colorado Springs: Navpress, 2002. Camarillo, Calif.: DeVorss & Company, 1966.

Nouwen, Henri. *The Return of the Prodigal Son*. New York: Image, 1994.

Schaff-Herzog. *The Encyclopedia of Religious Knowledge,* Vol. 12. Grand Rapids, Mich.: Baker Books, 1984.

Schmidt, Wilhelm. *The Origin and Growth of Religion*. New York: Cooper Square Publishers, 1971.

Segal, Alan F. *Life after Death: A History of the Afterlife in Western Religion.* New York: Doubleday, 2004.

Sinetar, Marsha. *Ordinary People as Monks and Mystics: Lifestyles for Self-Discovery.* Mahwah, N.J.: Paulist Press, 1986.

Spong, John Shelby. *Why Christianity Must Change or Die: A Bishop Speaks to Believers in Exile.* San Francisco: HarperSanFrancisco, 1999.

Stein, Leo. *Journey into the Self: Being the Letters, Papers & Journals of Leo Stein.* New York: Crown Publishers, 1950.

Strong, James. *The New Strong's Exhaustive Concordance of the Bible: Classic Edition.* Nashville, Tenn.: T. Nelson, 1991.

Trine, Ralph Waldo. *In Tune with the Infinite*. San Diego: Book Tree, 2003.

Walsch, Neale Donald. *Friendship with God: An Uncommon Dialogue.* New York: Putnam, 1999.

Yaconelli, Michael. *Dangerous Wonder*. Colorado Springs: Navpress, 1998.

For more information about the message of Inclusion, register to receive Bishop Pearson's eNewsletter at: www.GospelofInclusion.com.

Printed in the United States
By Bookmasters